Before the Dawn

An Autobiography

Gerry Adams is the author of *Falls Memories* (1982), a local history of the Falls Road area of Belfast, *The Politics of Irish Freedom* (1986), a statement of his political beliefs revised and expanded as *Free Ireland: Towards A Lasting Peace* (1995), *A Pathway to Peace* (1988), *Cage Eleven* (1990), an often-humorous and semi-fictional account of life in Long Kesh internment camp, and *The Street and other stories* (1992). President of Sinn Fein since 1983, he served as MP for West Belfast from 1983 to 1992. In line with the republican policy of not recognising the authority of British parliament, he did not attend at the House of Commons in Westminster.

GERRY ADAMS

BEFORE
THE DAWN

An Autobiography

Mandarin

The lines from Denis Ireland's poem are reproduced
by kind permission of M M Ireland.

The lines from F O'Donovan's *On the One Road* are
reproduced by kind permission of Waltons Music, Dublin.

Photographs 7, 8, 9, 10, 11 and 12 were first published in
Patriot Graves by P Michael O'Sullivan (Chicago 1972).

Photograph 20 is reproduced by kind permission of
Pacemaker, Belfast.

A Mandarin Paperback
BEFORE THE DAWN

First published in Great Britain 1996
by William Heinemann in association
with Brandon Book Publishers Ltd
This edition published 1997
by Mandarin Paperbacks
an imprint of Reed International Books Ltd
Michelin House, 81 Fulham Road, London SW3 6RB
and Auckland, Melbourne, Singapore and Toronto

Copyright © Gerry Adams 1996
The author has asserted his moral rights

A CIP catalogue record for this title
is available from the British Library
ISBN 0 7493 2317 5

Typeset in Ehrhardt and Rockwell
Printed and bound in Great Britain
by Cox & Wyman Ltd, Reading, Berkshire

Night is darkest just before the dawn
From dissensions Ireland is reborn

On the One Road

To the smoke clouds of Edwardian Belfast
Where in front of the new Portland-stone City Hall
The voluminous statue of Victoria
Sat pendulous-cheeked
Amongst municipal geraniums
And stone-frockcoated Victorian Economic Men
Waiting for new technological Fenians
With gelignite and petrol-bomb conflagrations
To shatter the thousand-windowed warehouses Thackeray noted
Or thin the forests of factory chimneys
Up in red-brick jungles labelled Shankill and Falls
Where to a sound of blast-bombs and Thompson machine-guns
The last red of imperial sunset
Flared behind the Black Mountain.

from *Scenery Since Bloomsday* by Denis Ireland

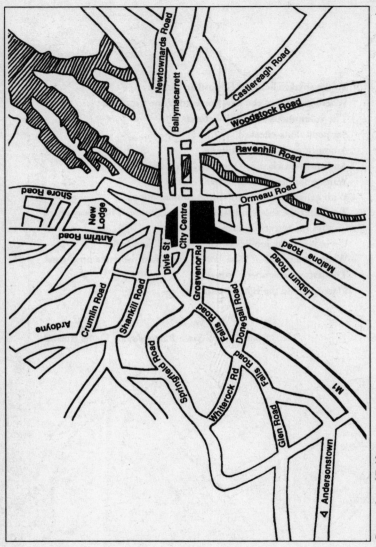

Street plan of Belfast

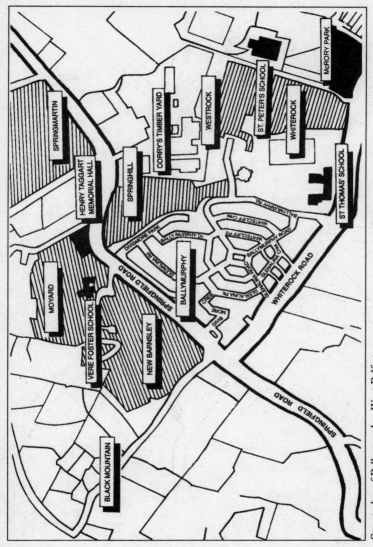

Street plan of Ballymurphy, West Belfast

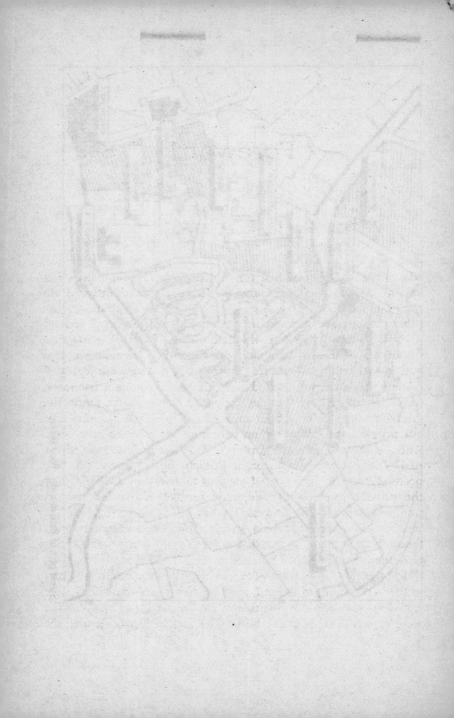

Foreword

My overwhelming personal political priority for some years has been to advance the peace strategy of Sinn Féin, the party I am proud to represent. Despite obstructions and frustrations, the peace process will remain my priority. The people of Ireland deserve a peace settlement which allows all of us to live together on a basis of mutual tolerance and equality. The attainment of such a settlement will require that we set to one side our legacy of conflict and suffering, hatred and mistrust. This does not mean forgetting everything that has happened, for who can forget the grief and pain that have been suffered and inflicted? No section of our people has a monopoly on suffering. We have all been hurt. And we have all inflicted hurt. We must learn the lessons of the past – not to recriminate, for, as William Butler Yeats said, 'We need not feel the bitterness of the past to discover its meaning for the present and future.' We must forgive each other as part of a necessary healing process; we have to agree to set aside the insidious allegiances of pain which constrain us from moving forward and create a foundation of justice which makes this movement possible.

In offering this account of my experience of some thirty years of life in the north of Ireland, most of them years of conflict, I am conscious that the conditions and circumstances of this conflict were created before I was born. The statelet set up under the

British 'Government of Ireland Act' was established by force of arms against the will of all but a small, privileged section of the population of Ireland, its area determined on a sectarian head-count. Violence, exclusion, and the denial of democratic and civil rights were the indelible hallmarks of this statelet for a generation before my arrival on the scene. There has never been peace. In every decade of the statelet's existence, political opposition to its sectarian structures has been met with measures of suppression.

I am also conscious that the elements of conflict remain today and retain their potency. For this reason I must write nothing which would place in jeopardy the liberties or the lives of others, so I am necessarily constrained. It is probably an invariable rule that the participants in any conflict cannot tell the entire story until some time after that conflict is fully resolved. Neither have I any intention of writing anything which might risk undermining the search for peace; the prospect of a peaceful settlement is simply too great a prize.

Any account of this kind is bound to be selective. Others might be inclined to concentrate on different events, incidents, individuals or organisations, and some may question my selection. That would be entirely valid. I offer here nothing more nor less than my account, from my perspective, of the extraordinary events that I have lived through.

This book would not have been written without the persistence, advice and input of Steve MacDonogh. I thank him for his patience and his help. I want to acknowledge the assistance of everyone at Brandon, especially Peter Malone and Bríd Leahy. I want also to thank Colette, our Paddy, my father, brothers and sisters, especially Liam, Uncle Alfie Hannaway, Gerry Begley, Father Alex Reid, who all helped to jog my memory. Thanks also to Clann Mac Thomáis, Eamonn McCaughley, Richard McAuley, Rita O'Hare, Micheál Mac Donnacha and the staff of *An Phoblacht*, John Gray and the staff of the Linen Hall Library, and Barra Mac Ruairí for their assistance.

Gerry Adams
Belfast, February 1996

One

I was born in the Royal Victoria Hospital in Belfast on 6 October 1948. My father Gerry Adams, aged twenty-two, a building labourer, and my mother Annie Hannaway, a doffing mistress in a linen mill who was a year or two older than he, had been married early that same year, and they were living with my Granny Adams at 15 Abercorn Street North in the Falls area of West Belfast. Although it was only a small house, with two bedrooms upstairs, two rooms downstairs and a scullery in the back, I was joining quite a large family: in addition to my granny, and my mother and father, my uncles, Davy, Seán and Frank, also lived in the house at the time. Conditions were cramped – even more so when my sister Margaret was born, a little over a year after me.

Both sides of my family had strong backgrounds in republican and working class politics. The year before I was born my father, a republican activist like his father before him, had been released after serving five years in jail. My mother, a tall, very attractive woman with black hair, was a staunch republican in her views, and her father had been a prominent trade union organiser.

The year I entered the world was a time of change internationally and in Ireland, but for the ruling powers in Belfast, it was a time of resistance to change. Belfast was the former centre of a thriving linen industry and home to the shipbuilders who had

3

built the *Titanic*. The city's economy had benefited from World War II: Harland & Wolff had been busy building warships, and 250,000 US troops stationed in the north during the war had contributed much additional income. However, large numbers of people had lost their homes in the bombing of Belfast, leaving a continuing housing crisis, with many still housed in temporary dwellings.

The British-controlled statelet created in the six north-eastern counties of Ireland was less than thirty years old, and the family and the community into which I was born opposed the very existence of 'Northern Ireland' as a separate entity under the British crown. South of the border Eamon de Valera lost a general election in 1948 after sixteen years as Taoiseach. In India, Gandhi died, just as British rule drew to a close; Britain departed, too, from Palestine as the state of Israel was proclaimed. If the times possessed a particular theme it was undoubtedly the post-war decline of the British Empire, a decline spelt out in India and Palestine, apparent in Africa, and palely reflected in the Republic of Ireland Act, whereby the twenty-six counties of Ireland left the British Commonwealth.

In 1950, when Margaret was still a babe in arms, we moved from Granny Adams's to a single large room in a gloomy, decaying house at 726 Shore Road in Greencastle, on the side of Belfast Lough. The house belonged to an order of nuns, who had given it over to a housing agent to collect the rent, and our room on the ground floor was partitioned off into areas. Upstairs was a tap for water and a toilet, which were shared with many other families. Here my mother, an articulate and gentle woman, struggled heroically to rear a growing family on next to nothing, and here we stayed for four and a half years, during which time two more children, Paddy and Anne, were born. My father did his best as a building labourer to provide for his young family, but these were difficult times, and although he was a hard worker, work itself was hard to come by, especially as a former political prisoner. Whenever he was sent looking for a job by the employment exchange they informed his prospective employers of his record and status. For a time he and an old prison friend Jimmy Bannon travelled from door to door selling fruit and vegetables from a horse-drawn cart. It was the horse, Paddy Joe, who profited most from their partnership, for both my da and Jimmy found it difficult to refuse credit to friends and neighbours, and after some time the business folded.

My mother was never overly robust, yet in her struggle to rear us and care for us she was the pillar of the family, and she plotted escape from our miserable slum room into a real house. In addition to the conditions in which we were living, the social isolation of being in Greencastle was a constant problem, given the cost of bus fares to get to Leeson Street and Abercorn Street where there were family and friends. My Uncle Seán and his girlfriend Rita used to come by bicycle to visit, but because it was so far off the beaten track they and my Granny Adams were the only regular visitors.

There was an enormous demand for housing in Belfast: overcrowding was high in the city as a whole, but nearly twice as high in the Falls, the main centre of Catholic population. Of all the houses in the city, almost three-quarters required some form of repair; at least 200,000 new dwellings were estimated to be needed to meet even basic needs. Now Ballymurphy estate, planned in 1948 to meet part of the housing emergency, had started to be built, and my mother was trying her best to get us a house there.

I recall almost nothing of my life in Greencastle beyond a sense of the dark and gloomy house, and I remember nothing at all about my first school, Star of the Sea. But one of my earliest memories is of going with my mother to the house of Seamus McKearney, a local representative on Belfast Corporation whom she was lobbying in pursuit of a house. He lived close to Inkerman Street, home of the Hannaway family, and I accompanied my mother on a number of occasions when she went from Granny Hannaway's to Mr McKearney's. Even though I was very young, I recall the day when we eventually got word that there was a possibility of our being housed. I was standing on the pavement outside McKearney's front door, while he and my mother were engrossed in conversation, he in the hall, she at the doorway.

Some time later she and my Granny Adams, my sister Margaret and I went up the Springfield Road on a journey which took us as far as the bus could go, right up on to the slopes of the Black and Divis Mountains. There we came to a huge building site in an area of green fields. We ploughed our way through the muck past heavy construction vehicles, cement mixers and lorries trundling back and forth.

My mother had a letter in her hand which she showed to one of the workmen.

'That's Divismore Park,' he told her, and I could see that she was delighted, even though what he was pointing to was only a row of foundations.

My granny and my mammy counted down along the row until we got to number 11, which was little more than a big pile of sand; but we could see where pipes were going in, and the base had been laid.

'That's our house,' my ma told us, her voice full of wonder. 'That's where we are going to live.'

Right through that summer she made her way up to Ballymurphy to watch number 11 grow slowly from the ground upwards, until eventually the day came when we were able to leave Greencastle and its dank tenement behind us. Almost twenty years later, in the wake of internment in 1971, my family was evicted by the British army from our home in 'the Murph', as we called it. Although she was in good houses after that, some in better condition, until she died in 1992 my mother never really settled. Number 11 Divismore Park was her home.

Ours was a gable house and had what appeared in my child vision to be a huge garden. It was the last house to be finished, its completion delayed when the gable wall collapsed three times during construction. There were three bedrooms: my mother and father were in the smallest, box room, Paddy and I were in the back and Margaret and Anne were in the front. We had a sheet over each mattress and a blanket on top; in the winter we pulled coats over us. We had escaped from Shore Road, and now enjoyed the untold luxury of a bathroom, but life at Divismore Park was hard enough as more children were born, more mouths to feed: Frances, Liam, Maura, Sean, Deirdre, Dominic. Soon myself, Paddy, Liam and Sean were all in the one bed sleeping two up, two down.

Ballymurphy was a place apart, a unique place to grow up in. As a new housing estate it lacked the roots that characterised the Falls, where people had lived in the same streets all their lives and everybody knew everybody else, where there were networks of families, cousins living in adjacent streets or down the same street. Neither did it possess the security of its own school, church, library and shops. It was badly built, badly planned and badly lacking in facilities, but it nonetheless possessed a wonderful sense of openness, there on the slopes of the mountain.

We were poor, but it didn't matter, at least not to us children. We didn't know any different, and we were too busy to notice. Besides, everyone else we knew was poor as well. The streets and the surrounding fields, the river, the brickyard and the mountain – especially the mountain – were our playground. All the families in Divismore Park had clutches of young children and we quickly made friends, girls and boys in separate peer groups, and throughout the summer months in particular our lives were lived outdoors. Everyone played skips and hopscotch and rally-oh and marleys (marbles) out in the street. Paddy and I were great ones for playing marleys out by the green box, as we called the electricity generator at the end of the street; we said it was our green box and tried to fight other kids off it.

At around the same time as we arrived in Ballymurphy, so too did the Magees, who came from the country, from Glenavy; they were two doors below us, and Joe Magee and I quickly became close friends. Joe and I, our Paddy, Jimmy Gillen, Frank and Harry Curran, the McManuses, the Irelands, the McKees, Dominic Grogan and Desi Carabine all knocked around together.

My life really began on the slopes of Divis Mountain, roaming with our gang. But first we had to get past our mothers . . .

'Don't dare go out into the street with that piece in your hand.'

My mother looked at us from across the kitchen table. Paddy was halfway out the door already, but he stopped, turned and looked at me. I still had my hand in the wrapping of the loaf.

'Finish your tea here!' she commanded us.

'Ah, Ma!' we chorused.

'No "Ah, Ma!" about it. Eat in the house, not out in the street.'

Our Liam shuffled up behind us, wiped his mouth with the back of his hand and looked up at me with his large eyes.

'I want the heel,' he said.

'Paddy's got the heel,' I told him. Paddy said nothing but bolted the bread and margarine into his mouth.

'Stop squabbling,' our mother shouted.

In the next room Margaret and Anne finished their tea. Margaret said something to my mother, and when she turned to reply, we three boys sneaked out the back door and across the fence into Glenalina Road.

Paddy gave Liam a bit of the heel of bread which he had clasped in his paw.

'I want the straight side,' demanded Liam.

'You'll get nothing,' Paddy said, throwing a lump of bread to Rory who bounded along behind us. 'Let's go down to Joe Magee's.'

'He's coming up,' I said, and so he was, and Joe also had a large piece of bread and jam.

'Let's go to the river.'

We cut across Divismore Park, through an entry between the houses, and down beyond the back gardens through the river. It wasn't a big river. It flowed off the mountain, meandered its way down through the back of Ballymurphy, on down and across the Whiterock Road, through the city cemetery and, as we discovered much later, through the Falls Park and then to the bog meadows.

But it was our river. We could jump it. We could put up a swing, a rope, and, Tarzan-like, launch ourselves from bank to bank. We could go up towards a large bridge where it flowed below the Springfield Road, and paddle our way into the darkness, sending echoes of our passage reverberating below the road. Once we followed the river up as far as the rock dam on the lower slopes of the mountain. There were two dams, relics of a linen industry, the smaller one presumably where the flax was retted. Some people said the bigger one was bottomless, but once we went swimming there. The dams and the yellow house had been built by a mill owner from Barnsley in Yorkshire, who called his estate New Barnsley, and when houses were built up there they inherited that name.

Today we were going to catch rats up at the bridge, or so Frank Curran told us. I wasn't too keen on the idea.

Frank and his brother Harry were waiting for us. So was Packy McKee, who had a hatchet, with which he had cut a number of shafts of fresh green branches about four foot long. He handed them out to us. Then, posting the spear carriers on the riverbank, he instructed me and our Paddy to follow him under the bridge to where there was a large drain.

'We'll throw stones at the drain,' Packy said. 'Then we'll get out of the way, and when the rats run out, you spear them.'

'I'm not going under there to throw stones,' I objected. 'The rats can kill you.'

'The rats can kill you?' Packy queried. 'How could a rat kill you?'

'Because it's poisonous,' I told him. 'Rats have poison in their tails.'

'So don't touch their tails,' said Packy.

'I'm not going,' I insisted.

'Somebody's gonna have to go,' said Packy.

'I'll go,' said our Liam.

'You're not allowed to go.'

'Well, I don't know,' said Packy. 'Yous wanted to catch rats and now when we have the chance, yous won't go. You're an old Jenny-Anne.'

'Who's an old Jenny-Anne?' our Paddy said.

'Yous 'uns.'

'I didn't say I wouldn't go,' said Paddy.

'Who didn't say you wouldn't go?'

It was getting a bit confusing.

'I'm sick of this,' said Joe, bouncing his spear up and down in the air.

'Why don't you go?' I said. 'I'll take the spear.'

'You couldn't hit a rat,' said Joe.

'I couldn't hit a rat? I could hit you!'

'Ah, come on boys!' Harry Curran shouted. 'Are we doing it or are we not?'

'Well, I'm doing it,' Packy McKee said.

Packy was wearing plastic sandals. So were most of the rest of us, except our Paddy who was wearing baseball boots. We all wore short trousers and windcheaters or sloppy-joes. All of us were scrawny, browned by the sun, freckle-faced, muddy-kneed.

Packy McKee jumped into the river. It was only eight or nine inches deep, and the water squashed back on the rest of us. Our Paddy followed him. The rest fanned out, spears in hand, waiting for the rats, except for me and our Liam. We stood empty-handed.

The bridge wasn't really very deep, and we could hear the two warriors splashing their way towards the rats' drain, their voices bouncing back.

'Oooiih!' Packy shouted. We heard the stones bouncing off the drain and falling into the water. Seconds later Packy and Paddy came flying out, water splashing around them.

'Get them! Get them! Get them!' they shouted. We all whooped and yelled and hollered, but there were no rats.

'Who do yous think yous are kiddin',' Frank Curran said. 'Yous didn't go near the drain.'

'Oh, didn't we? We went nearer to it than you,' our Paddy said.

He was soaked from head to foot, his left knee was grazed and there was a cut on the back of his hand.

'I saw one rat coming out behind me.'

'You saw nothin',' I said.

'I saw two,' our Liam said.

'There was no rats,' said Frank Curran.

'None at all,' said Joe and Harry Curran. 'Not one.'

Packy McKee pulled himself up on the bank. 'I saw a rat. He came out and ran up that hill.'

'There wasn't a rat! Yous didn't go near the drain. You went up a wee bit, threw your stones and ran back again. Yous are cowardly custard Jenny-Annes. Yous are yellow.'

'Who's yellow?'

'You're yellow.'

Just then, as our hunting expedition threatened to disintegrate, our Liam squealed.

'What's that?' he shouted. We all turned to where he stood in slightly longer grass.

'Look,' he pointed again.

It was a frog. A large green frog. I caught hold of it, feeling it cold and clammy between my palms, its heartbeat against my fingers. Its legs squirmed as it struggled to be free.

'Give it to me,' said Frank Curran.

'What for?' I asked.

'You can blow them up.'

'What do you mean blow them up?' I asked.

'You can put a straw up its arse and blow it up,' Frank said.

'You're not doing that,' I said. 'It's not your frog, it's mine!'

'It's not your frog,' our Liam interrupted. 'I saw it first.'

'But I got it!'

'I want to blow it up,' said Frank. 'You wouldn't go under the bridge and you get the frog? That's not fair. Give it over!'

'It's Gerry's frog,' said Joe Magee. 'He got it. Finders is keepers.'

'I wouldn't mind seeing it getting blown up,' said our Paddy.

'You can make it so big it's like the bladder of a football

sometimes. You blow and blow and blow. And then the frog goes pop!'

They all looked at me and at the frog. The spear carriers were especially interested.

'Look!' I shouted. 'There's a rat!' For a second they turned around and away I ran from my erstwhile comrades.

One balmy summer day we were hunkered in against the shoulder of the Black Mountain.

Our Paddy was below us, hidden in a crease in the hillside, upwind and invisible in the dense green bracken. There were five of us, including Rory. He lay between my legs, his head cocked to one side, alert to a pesky halo of flies which surrounded his head. Occasionally he would snap at them before settling back resignedly, tail barely twitching against my thigh.

Beyond us the city of Belfast stretched out in one direction towards the lough and towards other more distant hills opposite us. The city was busy. Smoke curled lazily from factory chimneys, and small and bigger boats ploughed their ways up and down the lough. Directly below us on the slopes of the mountain, streets of homes were being shaped within a great ants' hill of activity. The sounds of construction, the noise and clamour of the workmen drifted up to our vantage point, and we could see where the building site ate into green fields.

The entire vista basked in warm sunshine. It was cool where we lay half in the shade, luxuriating in the slight dampness of the peaty soil. We were waiting for our Paddy. Eventually he emerged from his hidden place. His voice rose easily and cheerfully to where we were.

> In days of old
> When knights were bold
> And toilets weren't invented,
> They did a load
> In the middle of the road
> And went away contented.

His trousers were down around his ankles. He was cleaning his backside with a handful of grass and bracken.

'G'wan, yi dirty baste!' we screamed in unison. 'You're stinking.'

He turned and tried to run as we swooped towards him, whooping and hollering. His trousers cut off his escape and as we descended upon him he tripped. We all collapsed in a tangle of skinny green-stained legs and scrawny bodies, rolling and tumbling through the cool stalks of bracken which flattened under us.

'Awh!' our Paddy screamed. 'You are killing me!' He punched out blindly.

Our Liam caught a fist in the face. 'Awhhhh,' he wailed. Our Liam was the youngest.

Paddy continued to punch and kick wildly. His trousers sailed overhead as our scrum dissolved before his onslaught. He faced us defiantly, trouserless and with tears dripping down his face. Liam lay at our feet blubbering and sobbing and clutching his head. Rory danced around us, barking excitedly.

'You're too rough,' Liam shouted.

'And you're like an oul' doll. We should never have brought you.'

Someone tossed our Paddy his pants. He caught them with great dignity. Liam meanwhile clambered to his feet. Our Paddy ignored him. He addressed the rest of us.

'You shouldn't 've jumped me like that.'

Joe threw a clod of earth at him.

'Your pants are torn,' he said, and then all together we chanted, as Paddy gazed downwards in alarm.

> I made you look,
> I made you stare,
> I made the barber
> Cut your hair;
> He cut it long,
> He cut it short,
> He cut it with
> A knife and fork.

Our Paddy hitched his trousers up.

'Let's go,' he said.

'Head 'em up, move 'em out,' Joe hollered.

We climbed astride imaginary steeds and then, strung out in single file, we cantered across the flank of the mountain, Rory running ahead of us as we made our way towards the waterfall, the mountain loney and home.

At home my father was scraping muck off his boots.

'Da,' I said, 'can I go down to Kennedy's Bakery in the morning and get a pillow-slip of mixed-ups?'

My da was concentrating on his boots, which were caked with muck. Thick, red muck. There were even little stones embedded between the heel and the sole. He was scraping them with an old bread-knife and flicking or wiping the knife on a piece of paper which he had spread before him in front of the fire.

'What?' he said eventually.

'Me and Joe Magee. We're going to go down in the morning to the bakery. For about threepence you get a pillowslip of mixed-ups.'

'What do you mean mixed-ups?'

'Diamonds and snowballs and Paris buns and jam rolls. All the stuff that's made early in the morning.'

'What about bread?'

'You can get bread as well, but that costs more. You can get baps, and you can get bannocks and you can get farls; you can get sliced bread and you can get plain bread.'

'How do you know all this?' my da said.

''Cause Packy McKee and them always go down, and Jimmy Gillen, he said he was going to go.'

'I don't know, son. What time is it at?'

'About six o'clock in the morning.'

'See your mother,' my da said.

'But Daddy!'

'Am I talking to the wall?' my da said. 'Go and see your mammy.'

'You are not under any circumstances going down to Kennedy's

14

Bakery,' my mother told me. 'The whole street will be talking about us.'

'Ah, Ma,' I said. 'Everybody goes down. Everybody. I should be able to go down. Packy McKee is only seven.'

'You're not Packy McKee. You're not going and that's that.'

'You'd never get up at that hour of the morning, anyway,' our Margaret interjected.

'Ah, shut up!' I told her. 'Who's listening to you, wee doll,' and I stamped out of the house.

Joe Magee was waiting outside. His face was glum.

'Any luck?' he asked.

'Nawh,' I said. 'I'm working on it.'

'My ma says I'm not allowed to go,' he said.

'Well so does mine,' I said.

'What about us going down anyway? Getting up nice and early. Then, when we come back, they'll all be surprised.'

'Where would you get the money?' I said.

'We could make sticks.'

'What?'

'We could chop up sticks and sell them to get the money.'

'What?'

'Are you going deaf or something?' Joe said in exasperation. 'We could chop up sticks for firewood, for people to light their fires with, and sell them around the doors. That way we'd get a few bob.'

'I don't think I'd be allowed to sell them around the doors.'

'Who would know?' said Joe. 'We could sell them around the other streets.'

And so it was that we spent our time at the back of the river and over towards the pithead, dragging up pieces of discarded wood, lumps of timber and old doors and wooden boxes. Then for hours, we would chop and pull nails and tie together bundles of jagged-edged kindling. It took a week and then we had a sizeable pile.

'What are those for?' my da asked one night. He had one foot up on the fence as he undid his bootlace.

'Well, we were gonna sell them.'

'Good idea.' He pulled his boot off. 'Here, clean that up while you're at it. Use one of them sticks and when you're finished, if you put dubbin on it, I'll give you your pay.'

The following day Joe and I got rid of our entire forest of firewood. It was easy enough. We went around the back of Ballymurphy Road into the side streets. All of our bundles were stacked up on his guider, a homemade four-wheeled buggy, and inside about two hours and four or five journeys back and forth we were three shillings the richer.

'It will only cost about sixpence or even threepence down at the bakery,' Joe told me. 'We should go down very, very early.'

The next morning I sneaked out of bed, out of the warm crush of bodies bundled together in the double bed in our back room. Our Liam never stirred. Paddy mumbled a bit and Sean, who was the smallest, opened his eyes for a moment before going back into a deep sleep. It was chilly and I felt apprehensive as I made my way across the bare floors and downstairs in my socks. With two pillow-slips pressed under my arm, I went out through the front door and down to where Joe waited for me at the corner of Ballymurphy Drive below his house. Dawn was slowly shifting the darkness as we made our way, chattering noisily to each other, across the river, skirting around Westrock Bungalows, over the top of the pithead and down over the brickyard on to Beechmount Avenue. I was surprised when we arrived at Kennedy's Bakery to find such a large queue of people lined up in the cobbled yard. A side door was open into which everyone piled, and behind the counter there were stacks and stacks of crates of fresh bread, still warm, baps and bannocks, farls, brown bread and white bread, and acres of buns. Apple cakes, diamonds, sore heads, snowballs, Paris buns, currant squares, flies' graveyards, ice cakes, plain cakes, fruit cakes. Slowly the crowd made its way past where a cheerful assistant shoved small bread or cakes into pillow-slips. Soon it was our turn. Joe and I had two pillow-cases each – one for pastry and one for bread. For fourpence we left with a bag in each hand, our grip tight around the neck of each pillow-case in case it might slip from our grasp and spill its precious cargo. Proud as punch, we headed back slowly, up around Beechmount on the journey home. By now it was light.

'Do you fancy a diamond?' I enquired.

'Maybe a custard,' Joe said. 'Just the one.'

We stopped to sample our wares. The custard buns were still warm. We had two each. And then a diamond and then a Paris bun.

'Ah,' said Joe, 'we'd better hurry.' And so we did. Back across the river, he sneaked into his house, I sneaked into ours. I put two or three buns to one side in a hidden place for our Paddy, Liam and Sean. The rest I arranged neatly on our dining-room table. A ticket of bread, five farls, six baps, some nice crusty rolls. And then, the pile of pastry. I shook the crumbs, coconut flake and crusts out of the pillow-slip for our Rory, patted him on the head and then padded my way upstairs back into bed.

Everybody was delighted when they got up later, though my ma gave off a wee bit.

'I told you not to go down there,' she scolded. But that was all.

When he came back that night my da said everybody on the building site was jealous of him. He was the only one who had buns. Even our Margaret was impressed. She said nothing, but I knew. After that, Joe and I went down to Kennedy's every so often. But now my ma always gave me the money.

TWO

Our neighbours in Divismore Park were good people. In the late 1950s and early '60s, the Murph got the name of being a rough area, but it was an undeserved reputation. Ballymurphy was no better or no worse than any other poor working-class area anywhere in the world, though in the 1970s it was to prove itself a resilient, courageous and resourceful community. In the 1950s there was no evidence of any of this. Then Ballymurphy was yet another jerrybuilt dumping ground for the many young families who were delighted to leave slum accommodation or overcrowded parental homes for a place of their own. In my travels over the years, I have seen Ballymurphys everywhere. In Britain, across Europe, in cities throughout Ireland, in the USA and in South Africa. They all have one thing in common. Hardworking parents, even when unemployed, doing their best to give their children the best possible opportunities. Our house was one of these.

Logistically, I don't know how my mother managed to feed so many, managed to prepare meals three times a day; to clothe ten children. The pressure became all the more acute because there wasn't always much clothing for the children or there wasn't always much food to put on the table, and yet my mother probably had less than any of the rest of us. Indeed it was not unknown at that time for women to collapse from malnutrition while feeding their large families. When he could get work, my father worked hard, but it was my mother who managed and who coped, my mother who, like so many other women, fought tooth and nail to rear us, aided by Granny Adams and Granny Hannaway, and with the assistance of Lavery's pawnshop.

Paddy Lavery's stood at the corner of Panton Street and the Falls Road. Its front window seemed to have everything in it, from boots to clocks and even fishing rods, and when you went in you were faced with a high counter completely surrounded with bric-à-brac, and rows of suits, pledged between masses to feed the family or pay the rent. There was no stigma attached to going to the pawn: it was just one of the everyday realities of life. And it was a reality mediated and managed by women, by my mother, my sister Margaret, my Granny Hannaway, even in a furtive way in terms of their husbands. On occasions there would be a sudden rush and commotion: my Granny Hannaway might have taken my Grandfather Hannaway's suit and pawned it; now, on a Thursday or Friday, there might be a funeral and she'd desperately want to get it out before he realised that it was missing. As they endlessly juggled sparse household budgets, women were frequently putting shoes or other items belonging to their husbands into the pawn.

Once during a spell of changeable weather, I heard two women talking.

'The weather can't make its mind up. One minute it's teeming with rain, the next the sun is splitting the trees.'

'I know. You wouldn't know what to pawn, would you?'

My mother was never overly strong and she suffered for years with a goitre problem. She was also quite a gentle person, who never drank and didn't smoke, but she must also have been tough in her own way. In rearing the family she must have been sorely pressed: she just had kids after kids. Yet somehow she always seemed to have something for us all to eat; she always had us clothed; she even managed to get us toys. But by the time she had paid the toys off, it was Christmas time again and there was another set of toys to be bought. Christmas clubs, check men, insurance men, tick men were regular visitors to Divismore Park. As the family grew, the girls took on a lot of the housework and child minding from quite a young age. Men and boys, by comparison, were relatively pampered. My mother sang a lot around the house, songs like 'The Kerry Dances', 'The Spinning Wheel', 'After the Ball Was Over', 'The Bold Fenian Men', 'The Lonely Woods of Upton' and 'The Boys from the County Armagh'. This was the acoustic in which I was reared.

On one occasion my mother went into hospital and my father tried to do the cooking, putting tomato soup in a pot, adding sausages, then potatoes in on top of that. Margaret's attempts were not a whole lot better, and while I found that I could make porridge, for some reason nobody else would eat it. Then a home help arrived, and we were saved. She was a big woman, white-haired and cheerful, and she could cook everything.

My father wasn't working, and he went to the hospital every day. After about four days he returned with the news that we had a new baby sister, and we all went down to the hospital. We weren't allowed into the ward, so my father brought us into the grounds and then disappeared into the building, leaving me and Margaret in charge. Then he emerged again, lined us all up, and pointed. Away up high at one of the big hospital windows, we could see our mother as she held up a small baby. We couldn't see what it was, but we all waved and cheered anyway. We felt very sad. Then my father brought us all home.

I started at St Finian's De La Salle school in 1956. It was a family tradition to go to St Finian's, which was set up, along with St Vincent's girls' school, for the half-timers at the mills, who worked half a day and went to school the other half. By the time I arrived this practice had ceased – luckily enough, because it was extraordinarily difficult to get me out of bed in the morning. St Finian's was a good school. The discipline was quite severe, but the only occasion on which I remember a teacher being particularly cruel to me was when I was slapped on my first day in school – I thought very unfairly.

The school had a small catchment area, but because of the expanding population, there were a number of other schools around it, and the closeness of everything contributed to a sense of identity, like that of a small village. The Christian Brothers taught Irish history, including political history, and used the same books as were used in their schools south of the border in Cork and Tipperary and everywhere else in Ireland. They also used many Irish language books, and important in the ethos of the school were the Gaelic sports of hurling, football and handball. The Adamses always thought of themselves as great hurlers and footballers. I played both hurling and football for the school team and, like all schoolboys with an interest in sport, considered the time spent in the school jersey as the most enjoyable part of my time as a scholar.

As soon as I started attending St Finian's, I moved to live with my Granny Adams in Abercorn Street, close to the school, though I still spent weekends and the summer holidays up in the Murph. I did not go to my granny's for reasons of any lack of capability or of affection on the part of my mother; on the contrary, she doted on me, and I returned her love as best I could; every Christmas, from the first time I had any money, I always saved up and bought her a big tin of Roses chocolates.

Granny Adams's house had a tiled kitchen and a 'modern Devon grate' with a small mantelpiece. I was back in the house in which I had passed my first two years. 'Abercorn Street North, Leeson Street, the Falls Road, Belfast, Ireland, the World, the Universe,' I wrote in my schoolbooks. There were two bedrooms. I slept in the back room with my Uncle Sean and my Uncle Frank until my Uncle Frank went away to England and then to Canada, and my Uncle Davy came back from England. As the youngest in the house, I found myself at the centre of attention. My father's first cousin Gerry Begley, who lived just down the street and was six or seven years older than me, was on hand to bring me to school and to become my friend and role model. And I wasn't long becoming friends with others in the street, like Joe

MacAtamney, the O'Neills and Barbara Scott. And there was Darkie, the dog.

But the centre of my life in Abercorn Street was my Granny Adams, or Margaret (Maggie) Begley, as she was known by her maiden name. A quietly religious person, who allowed no bad language, she didn't 'lick the altar rails'; she was quite strict but she was very warm. A very small woman, robustly built and quite modern in her attire, she had been a half-timer. She had a singular influence on me, and seemed to possess a remarkable sense of balance and moderation. I remember her saying that you could never trust a man who didn't take a bottle of stout, yet at the same time she was totally opposed to drunkenness. A very tolerant person, who obviously had come through very difficult times, she spoiled me as the child among adults; as they say in Belfast, I was her blue eye.

She possessed a great regard for education, an innate sense of dignity and respect for people, and she taught me not to give cheek, to show no animosity and always to have time for people. Because between the ages of eight and twelve I was thought to lack confidence, and I had a slight stammer, which my sister Margaret used to mimic when we were fighting. I enjoyed my granny's undivided attention and the quietness of the house, where there were no girls. I don't remember her ever trying to politicise me; she may have been influenced in her attitude to me and to politics by what she had been through with my uncles, Dominic and Paddy Adams, and my father, who had been very active republicans; indeed, she may have actively discouraged me from taking an interest in politics.

My grandmother had witnessed two generations of political opposition and knew full well the hardships of struggle. Her husband had been active in the Irish Republican Brotherhood (IRB) and had died young, leaving her to rear a young family of six sons: Paddy, Dominic, Sean, Frank, Davy and Gerry, some of whom became active in the IRA. She had also had two daughters, Margaret and Elizabeth, and a son Peter, all of whom had died in infancy. My father, Gerry, had been shot and wounded by the

RUC in 1942, at the age of sixteen, in an encounter on the day after the hanging of Tom Williams, a republican who had been injured in a clash earlier in the year when an RUC man had been killed. My father, old Gerry as he has become known, was sentenced to eight years for attempted murder and was unconditionally released after five years.

My Granny Adams read a lot, frequently calling to the Falls Library, which was a stone's throw from where we lived, and to the library in Clonard Monastery, and I always went up with her when she was getting books. She read Maurice Walsh, and I read her copy of Charles Kickham's *Knocknagow* at an age when it must have gone well over my head. I didn't wear glasses at that time but later in Ballymurphy I made it a firm regular habit to read for hours in bed at night by the weak light of the streetlamp through the bedroom window, and before long became the only member of our family wearing glasses. I enjoyed a wide range of the popular books of the time: Enid Blyton, *Just William*, Jennings and Derbyshire, Biggles, Billy Bunter as well as the range of English comics, the *Beano*, the *Dandy* and the *Topper*, and I eagerly turned first of all to the adventures of Dennis the Menace and Desperate Dan. This diet of English stories was augmented by *Our Boys*, an Irish magazine produced by the Christian Brothers.

Abercorn Street North was very narrow, and all around it was a network of very busy little streets, with a secondary network of back entries, or alleys. At Getty Street, steps flanked by iron banisters or railings led down from the street into the entry. The pavements were high and were set off by large brown kerb stones. The whole Falls area, especially around Leeson Street, was riddled with yards, back entries and stables.

The gas-lamps which lit the streets weren't that high, so it was quite easy to 'speedy up' them. On the crossbar just below where the lamp itself was, we hung ropes for swings. We played handball at the huge gable at Harbison's corner and all sorts of games at the bottom of Abercorn Street, where it went into Sorella Street and Dunville Street, a small area at the bend adjacent to the Dunville Park where you weren't annoying anybody. There was a rag store and a small builders yard, and we used the gates of the yard as goalposts. Apart from racing and football, we played hurling, or cricket or rounders using hurling sticks, and 'kick the tin'.

Amongst the sparse regular traffic were the carts of the coalman and the 'reg' men. We used to hop the horses and carts, and once I fell off, marking my head. Another frequent visitor to the street collected kitchen waste for the pigs. Of an evening a man used to go around lighting the gaslights. At my Granny Hannaway's house in Inkerman Street, there was a gas-lamp attached to the wall, and I remember my mother telling me that it was by the light of this lamp that she had read at night.

The houses of Abercorn Street and its neighbourhood were old, and no one in the area had indoor toilets or bathrooms. To this day people ask, 'Are you going to the yard?' – meaning, 'Are you going to the toilet?' Tin baths, which were kept hung up in the yard, were placed in front of the fire on bath nights and filled with buckets of water. The small yards were invariably white-washed and sometimes had a one-foot base of black tar. Some people had window boxes, in which geraniums were very popular, and some kept fowl. Everybody kept their coal in the yard, along with a big mangle and the bath. My granny used to have a chicken, and one Christmas they killed it. But when this special Christmas roast was carved, the whole inside of the animal turned out to be black because it had lived picking through the coal – or that's what they told me anyway.

There was a cold box in many yards, a mesh box for keeping butter and other perishable food. Meat was a rarely encountered luxury, except that shin was used for soup, and bacon and cheap cuts made occasional appearances. Soup was a typical Saturday or Sunday meal. My granny was a very good baker, creating baked griddles, griddle bread, soda breads, wheaten breads, oven bread, and then she cooked bread pudding from all the scraps. The life of the streets was very open. I was often sent to a neighbour with soup, and vice versa.

We always had dogs, and I inherited my first one when my uncles Sean and Frank went to Canada, though I suppose he was really my granny's dog. Darkie was big, black and tan, and very sensible. If you were walking up the road and he saw a peeler, Darkie would drop away behind; that was because we didn't have a dog licence. Once when I was going to the Murph, my granny came with me on the bus and Darkie ran alongside, arriving totally exhausted when we finally alighted at Divismore Park; I don't think he ever went back to Ballymurphy after that.

And then there was Rory. He was a small dog, a mongrel terrier, and a Ballymurphy dog, born and bred. We spent all our free time on the mountain: our Paddy and Joe Magee, maybe some more of our friends, and Rory and me. We got to know every inch of the hilly terrain, from the Gully to the Hatchet Field and the Riddley Rock, to chase hares and rabbits, to pick wild berries and watercress, to take primroses and bluebells for transplanting to our garden, and to listen to birdsong. Once when some wasters set fire to the mountain, we were caught in the blaze. We tried to cut around the fire, but the smoke was choking us and in panic we plunged through the burning undergrowth. Sparks and bits of collie were flying everywhere. We credited Rory with saving our lives as he led us homewards. I remember my da saying that a dog will never forget the way home. I don't think I have ever been without a dog since then, and the enjoyment of walking dogs, especially across open fields or hills, has remained with me all my life.

Through much of my childhood I moved back and forth between Ballymurphy and Abercorn Street. Events like my Holy Communion or Confirmation took place around the axis of Abercorn Street, which was where my sponsors came from. When I was eight my granny went to Canada to visit my uncles and I moved back to Divismore Park, but when school started again I continued to go to Abercorn Street for my lunch; my newly married Uncle Davy and Aunt Sheila lived there now after returning from a time spent in England.

I had the advantage of two homes and I was also able to call in to the houses of various branches of the family, foremost amongst which was 14 Inkerman Street, home to my mother's people, the Hannaways. The Hannaways, not least because of my grandfather's background, and because he was in a job where you wore a shirt and tie, may have been just slightly farther up the social ladder, though trade union officials were by no means paid as well then as they are now. The whole family had been reared in this very small house, with a kitchen/living room and scullery downstairs and two bedrooms upstairs. It looked like a smaller version of a typical rural house, with an old-style wide fireplace and a roughly surfaced floor.

My great-grandfather, Michael Hannaway, had been a Fenian; coming to Belfast from Sligo, he had settled in Dunmore Street in Clonard and had worked as a supervisor/compositor at the *Irish News*.

William Hannaway, my grandfather, a tall man whom I am said to resemble, was very much a socialist republican, and he worked with both Jim Larkin and James Connolly. Larkin had arrived in Belfast in 1907 as organiser of the National Union of Dock Labourers and had played a notable role in the lockout and strike which had involved some 2,500 dockers and other workers, even briefly spreading to the ranks of the Royal Irish Constabulary. James Connolly had been appointed Ulster organiser and secretary of the newly formed Irish Transport and General Workers Union in 1911, and from then until early 1916 he and his family had lived in Belfast in a house at Glenalina Terrace on the Falls Road where it faced the Whiterock Road. As secretary of the barmen's branch, my grandfather had played quite a role in building up the union, and he had travelled a lot, especially in England. Billy, as he was known, was not a great churchgoer, but he was generally quiet in his manner and was never heard to curse, even when he had drink on him. He had been one of de Valera's election agents when Dev stood in 1918, though he came to detest the man later.

He had married Alice Mulholland from Castlewellan, and they had had four children before she died at a young age. Her sister,

Georgina, had also been living in Inkerman Street and she had then taken over running the family and become a mother to the children. She also soon became William's second wife, and they had first a daughter named Annie (my mother), then Ena and Seamus. Georgina, my Granny Hannaway, was quite a small, thin woman and very quiet; she had very long grey hair and a huge pigtail, and she wore a pinafore; my early memories are of her wearing a shawl, though later she graduated to a coat.

My abiding memory of my Granny Hannaway is of her helping my Uncle Seamus to get ready to go out. Seamus was a very tall man, whereas she was tiny. Having washed and ironed all his clothes and polished his shoes, she would fuss around him as he finished dressing, and then when he put on his coat she would dust him off, reaching up on her toes to wipe his shoulders with the clothes-brush.

The Hannaways were always republicans, and members of each generation found themselves crossing the tracks of the preceding one as the struggle against injustice continued. My Grand-aunt Mary was an active member of Cumann na mBan, the women's IRA. Years later, when Alfie Hannaway – her nephew and my uncle – became involved in teaching Irish classes in Twinam's Hall in Cromac Street, Mary pointed out to him that the same hall had been used in her day for Cumann na mBan meetings. Alfie's brother Liam was in D Company of the IRA, as were members of the Adams family, and he remained a very active republican right up until his death in 1981. My Granda Hannaway, his father, died in December 1962.

My two sets of grandparents lived a relatively short distance from each other, Inkerman Street lying between the Falls Road and Ross Street. We children spent lots of time with our extended families, and my sister Margaret developed with our Granny Hannaway a relationship similar to the one I enjoyed with Granny Adams. Both grandmothers continuously helped our parents to rear us, and I'm sure they did the same with all my cousins.

The intimate connections of family houses were also reflected in the patterns of West Belfast life as a whole, which had the character of a series of villages. The Falls, with its own pubs, its own shops, the library and the schools, generated a specific sense of community, and we rarely ventured into the centre of town except around Christmas. On each side of the Falls were two- or three-storey buildings, between which trolley buses trundled along slowly, almost silently on the overhead wire. There was a self-contained, enclosed feeling to the area, while from almost every street one could see the mountains, which always held a special attraction for me. Even in the midst of a tight, close-knit community you could glimpse the greenness of the place. As well as the mountains, there was the Falls Park, a walk of exactly one mile from the gate of St Finian's, and we went there once or twice a week with the school.

On one occasion a group of students from Queen's University came to Ballymurphy and brought a group of us to a party in Queen's. We were told that this was because we were deprived. As we wolfed down bowls of trifle and plates of buns in a large panelled room we congratulated ourselves. Being deprived was a new experience.

One day we had to go to the clinic in Durham Street to get our BCG injections, so at the top of the Whiterock Road we climbed aboard the number 11 trolley bus, which slowly whirred its way down Whiterock Hill, down the Falls Road, and into Divis Street. Getting off just above Townsend Street, we walked, a reluctant line of seven: Margaret, Anne, Paddy, Liam, Sean, and Frances and me; my mother and father making us nine in all. My injection felt very sore, but I didn't let on, and afterwards we all piled into my Aunt Ena's house where my cousin Sammy lent me and our Paddy his tricycle and we whizzed up and down Durham Street, our ordeal quickly forgotten.

A couple of weeks later we learned that Paddy had TB and had to go into hospital. Discussing it with Joe Magee and Harry and Frank Curran, we couldn't figure it out, because Paddy looked all right and he could run as fast as any of us. The hospital was at Crawfordsburn, on the shores of Belfast Lough, a long way from where we lived, and my mother would be all day away visiting him. Our Margaret used to mind us, or at least she thought she minded us; I missed our Paddy, though there was more room in the bed. He was in for a long time, during which the job my father was working on finished.

'Do you fancy going down to see Paddy?' he asked me one day.

'Aye, Da.'

'Can I come?' said our Liam.

'We're gonna walk,' said my da.

'You can't walk that far, Gerry,' my ma said; 'it's ten miles.'

I don't know how we ever made it, but when at last we got there, it was a big house with a large garden and swings. Paddy was wearing a big, long gown and he was very pale. He was glad to see me, and I told him what was happening and what we were doing, but I didn't want to tell him too much unless he'd think that we were just getting on without him. A man who was visiting his son in the hospital gave me a half-crown, and me and my da got a bus home again.

Paddy came back home about two weeks later, and from then on he had to have butter, while the rest of us got margarine, and cod liver oil, orange juice and yeast. Indeed, all of us got the cod liver oil, which I used to collect sometimes from a clinic in Huskey's, the big house just across the river from where we lived.

The next time I visited a hospital was to see my new sister. Joe Magee broke the news to me.

'Your mammy's going to have another baby.'

'No, she's not. Sure, we've no more room,' I said.

'But she is.'

'I don't believe you,' I said.

'Well, we'll see. I heard my mammy telling our Kathleen that Mrs Adams is gonna have another wee mouth to feed.'

I told our Paddy. He didn't believe me either.

'Where do you get babies?' he asked.

'Oh, you're too young to know that,' I replied. 'You don't find that out until later on.'

'What age do you find it out at?'

'Oh, I don't know, but not yet anyway. You're too young. My

da told me last week. Do you remember last Saturday night when we were getting our bath? He was drying me down and he said he had to tell me the facts of life. Do you know what he said? To keep my wee man clean and stay away from bad women.'

'What's bad women?' our Paddy asked.

'I don't know. How do you expect me to know?'

'Do you keep your wee man clean?'

'Of course I keep my wee man clean.'

We got a bath every Saturday night. By the time the last one got in, there was a scum mark around the side of the bath and suds floating about the top, and the bathroom was covered in steam, but I liked being last because you could stay in the longest. The dirt that lodged between your toes if you had been out playing football all day sometimes used to just rub off when you pushed your feet together, and then your fingers would get all mottled and dimpled with the water. I hated getting my hair washed; the soap would get into my eyes. Then my da would come in and wrap the big towel around me and lift me up out of the water. That's when he told me the facts of life. He said, 'You're getting too big for this. You'll soon be too big for me to lift out.'

Sometimes me and our Paddy would get into the bath together. Paddy thought he could swim, but he couldn't really, and I could hold my breath under the water for far longer than him. We used to splash, and then my da would take the needle, and that's when he ended up putting us in one at a time. It's funny about the facts of life. Joe Magee said that his mammy said that we shouldn't know about the facts of life. Sometimes it was hard to understand grown-ups.

It was a strange time for me anyway. The summer was almost over. My feet could nearly stretch out to tip the bottom of our bed. We were in the back room. We were going to get bunk beds and we got oil cloth on the floor. The wee girls got oil cloth first. I didn't fancy it; it was freezing on your feet. The floorboards had cracks between them. Sometimes if you had a penny you could stick it in a crack. Bits of fluff used to gather there. Sometimes when I couldn't sleep I used to run my finger up and down a crack and think about the facts of life.

My ma and da used to sleep in the wee room; there was very little space in it, just their bed and a built-in wardrobe. One day the nurse came along with the home help, and then a woman called the midwife. They all went into the big front room, the girls' room, with my ma. I heard shouting and a lot of noise, and then I heard a baby crying. Our Maura and our Anne were a bit frightened, and I went up the stairs to see what was going on. I was chased down again, but not before I saw the white sheets over the wee girls' bed, all covered in blood. That scared me. Then later on we were all brought in. My ma was lying in bed: she looked very, very tired, but she had a nice smile. She had our wee baby brother.

'Ma,' I said to her, 'what was all the blood?' and she blushed a wee bit.

'Now then,' the home help said, 'you'll find out all that when you find out the facts of life.'

It's funny, isn't it? My da never told me about that.

All the rest of us were born in the Royal. Our Sean was a twin, and although he was the weaker of the pair, he survived and Brendan died soon after. Two other brothers, Seamus and David, died and are buried in unmarked graves in the poor ground in Milltown cemetery.

While the greatest family burden was carried by my mother, my father was an industrious man in his own way. He was one of a generation of Irish men who were totally spoiled by their families, but he had nevertheless a very responsible attitude towards his family, and one day I discovered how the pressure of rearing a large family could also bear on him. He was working on the buildings at Queen's University, and I was sent to bring his lunch over to him. When I arrived at the building site, I saw him coming down the plank walkway; there were two men in suits and ties coming against him, and as they approached him he stepped aside into the wet mud to let them pass. When I asked him why did he step aside like that, he replied: 'If you have six or seven children to feed, you'll step into the muck, son.'

In terms of the IRA, my father had served his time, but he nevertheless took an interest in political developments at a time when the new repressive measures in the north of Ireland had not succeeded in securing the silence of republican opposition. In 1954 an IRA raid on a barracks yielded guns and ammunition. In 1955 republicans standing in Westminster elections secured the biggest anti-partition vote since 1921. Withdrawing in ignominy from Suez in 1956, the British found themselves faced with a new campaign in the north of Ireland as the IRA attacked targets across the Six Counties. The Northern Ireland government's response was to introduce internment once again and spike the border roads. Although the IRA was not active in Belfast during the border campaign, a lot of Belfast republicans were interned, and he would have known most, if not all, of them. Our house was raided, but my father was not interned. When the news came on, my parents would listen to the reports of IRA actions with special interest, and we children would be told to shush, to be quiet; I recall periodic reports of customs posts being blown up. I also remember a team of young people discovering an ammunition box of rounds of ammunition and perhaps grenades, dug into a bank of the river above the bridge.

None of this really meant a lot to me or my mates. In 1960 I went to Dublin to the great All-Ireland Gaelic football final which was won by County Down. I have been in love with Croke Park ever since and perfectly at home in Dublin. That first trip down south was a great adventure, for the adults in the party as well as myself. I went with my Uncle Paddy and other men by car – a memorable event in itself. I have very fond memories of my Uncle Paddy, who was a knowledgeable, unassuming, well-read man with a keen and enquiring mind. Robbed, like many working-class people, of the opportunity to fulfil his potential, he educated himself, becoming a competent typist on an old second-hand typewriter and moving on to shorthand. I heard that in his younger days he had been an extremely hard man, unbeatable in bare-fist fighting. As a political prisoner, he had escaped from Derry jail in 1943. A keen sportsman in his youth, he maintained great interest in all that concerned young people; an amiable, extremely tolerant man, he was, like me, fond of dogs and walking.

The match I recall only vaguely: the press of the crowd and the unique Croke Park atmosphere has replaced memories of an outstanding game. Afterwards the adults adjourned to pubs where I was fed gallons of brown lemonade and had numerous threepenny bits pressed on me. Dublin was thronged with northerners, and all the way home bonfires burned cheerfully on the roadside. The Cup was going over the border, and even though I barely comprehended what the border was, I chanted 'the cup's going over the border' along with the rest. We had won the All-Ireland, and although my home team was County Antrim, it seemed to me that all northerners shared County Down's victory. They didn't, of course. The unionists ignored Gaelic games, but I was barely conscious of their existence or of the more sectarian forces within Irish society. My main concern was to win an All-Ireland hurling or football medal with Antrim.

One night a week we used to go for our religious instruction to confraternity down in Clonard Monastery, and if we left early we could spend the bus fare on sweets. We cut down the Springfield Road and joined hundreds of other boys in the chapel. To me Clonard was a wondrous place with high, high ceilings and a huge high altar. The altar boys wore long, red soutanes and white gowns. The priest's incense spiralled upwards through the shafts of sunlight which came slanting down from stained-glass windows at the very top.

It wasn't a long service. Father McLaughlin, who was in charge of the confraternity, got up and made a joke or preached a sermon and then we sang a few hymns. I didn't mind it at all; in fact, I found parts of it good fun. As Father McLaughlin conducted the whole chapel full of young fellows, we would sing 'Tanto Mergo, make my hair grow.' Every section of boys had a prefect, and we had to be careful in case we'd be caught.

It was evening by the time we come out of 'confo', and the evening had a different feel, with shadows coming, the day having cooled off; we could sense the change, and things became quieter as we embarked on a rambling return home through territory we regarded as our own, long-extended playground.

We walked up the road, often stopping at the Flush River. Here beside the cotton mill there was a deep ravine, and often we slid down its high slopes right down to the river. Although we weren't allowed in the river, we were forever going into it. However, one of us was found out once when, having dried himself off, he went up home.

'You were in the river,' his mother said as soon as she saw him. 'No,' he lied, 'I wasn't.'

'You were,' his mother said, pointing to his head and the back of clothes, which were decorated with white patches. There had been bleach in the river that day and he was rightly caught.

Once some wee lads stoned us at the Flush and we ran like anything; somebody said they were Protestants, but I didn't know what they were stoning us for. Up above the Flush a school stood off the road behind a tall wall, and opposite it were two terraces of houses, a small street and a shop; the people there were all Protestants except for one fella we used to call to sometimes if his father wasn't in.

Carrying on towards home, it was all green fields, and as we passed the Springfield dam we stopped to watch the swans, the water herons and at different times of year the ducks.

Opposite the Monarch Laundry on the right hand side lay the Highfield estate and the West Circular Road where mostly Protestants lived; above stood an Orange hall. Away on up lay more fields: Huskey's on the left hand side of the road, Farmer Brown's and Beechie's on the right. On yellow houses here a date indicated that they had been built a hundred years or so before.

Then we arrived on home ground: the Murph. Down the slope, the steps, Divismore Park, and our house. And if we were slow coming up, having played at the Flush too long, when we reached as far as Divismore Park we might hear the long shouts of

34

our Margaret: 'Geeeerrrryyy, you're a-wanted!' and 'Paaaaddd-dyyy, you're a-wanted!' The sounds might be heard too of others out shouting for Joe or Harry or Frank. Then the lamps were lit as Divis Mountain began to fade and the stars appeared.

Sometimes we would stand, put our heads straight back and look up at all the thousands and millions of stars. One night Joe Magee's dad brought us just about half a mile above the Murph to listen to the corncrakes. That was beautiful, and from a height we had a view down over the city of Belfast; then we put our heads back and looked up at the sky, all the time hearing the corncrakes.

The priest told our class that we had to tell all our sins in confession. I wondered about that. How could you tell all your sins? Every single one? I started to try to take notes when I was committing a sin, which was fair enough because I had a week to go till my first confession, but all the sins, of my whole life? Sean Murphy, who sat in the desk beside me, said it was only mortal sins; venial sins didn't really matter. Sean said that Protestants got it easier: they didn't have to go to confession; they didn't have to tell their sins. But then, Protestants weren't going to get to heaven, he said.

The whole class went down to St Peter's; we marched down in twos, filed into the pews, with their cold, shiny seats. As one by one we genuflected in the side aisle, we moved to sit on the bench either side of the confession box, and as the line dwindled we were carried forward into the confession box.

The boy coming out smirked at me as he held the door open. I knelt down in the semi-gloom as the door slammed behind me; above me there was a small ledge and from beyond the ledge I could hear the mumble of a man's voice. A moment later I heard the slam of something being drawn closed, and then above my head an aperture opened and a friendly adult voice boomed manfully down on me.

'Good morning, my son.'

'Bless me, Father, for I have sinned. This is my first confession.' I hesitated.

35

'Go on, my son,' the voice encouraged me.

'I gave backcheek to my mother five times, Father. I gave cheek to my granny twice, Father. I wanted to kill my sister Margaret four times, Father.'

'You wanted to kill your sister Margaret?' the voice asked.

'Yes, Father.'

'And when was that?'

'Well, once last year, Father, in the summer, and then on Christmas Day when she opened up my stocking, and then on Easter when she broke my egg, and then yesterday, Father.'

'And does your sister Margaret annoy you?'

'Yes, Father.'

'Well, you know you're going to have to be more patient.'

'Yes, Father. Oh, and I said a bad word, Father, fifteen times.'

'What did you say?'

'I said "frig", Father. Father, I robbed an orchard, once. And me and my friends tied thread to oul' Ma Doran's door and we played "kick the door" all night . . .'

'Is that all, son?'

'No, Father. I hit Terence McManus. He was hitting our Paddy, Father. Our Paddy always gets me into trouble. He said that Terence McManus kicked him and my da sent me out to hit Terence and Terence is bigger than me but I bled his nose. I didn't mean to, Father . . .'

'That's all right, my son,' the voice intoned patiently. 'Go on.'

'And I beat Billy Dunne in a fair dig. He took our Paddy's kitten and my da sent me out to get it back.'

'What happened then?'

'Billy hit me with a brick in the back of the head and I smashed my teeth on the ground when I fell. I got him later with a hurley stick.'

'Is that all?'

'Our Paddy's kitten got its head caught in a tin of stewing steak and it died. I cursed at our Paddy that day. I got my teeth broke over him, Father. For nothing.'

'Is there more?'

'Well, Father . . . I've cheated at marleys sixty-seven times.'

'How did you do that?'

'Everybody does it, Father. I move my man when I'm taking a shot and . . .'

'Sixty-seven times?'

'At least sixty-seven times, Father.'

'Could it be more?'

'It could, Father.'

'Go on, my son.'

'That's all, Father.'

'Well now, I want you to say a good act of contrition and for your penance I want you to be more patient with your sister and say one Our Father and three Hail Marys.'

'Thank you, Father.'

His voice mumbled the comforting words in the dark above me as I said a good act of contrition. There was an instant of silence when I finished. Then,

'God bless you, my son.'

'God bless you, Father.'

The shutter slid closed above me with a little thud. I heard the slam of another slide being drawn open in the other confession box at the other side of the priest. I levered myself slowly up off my knees and fumbled for the door behind me. I came immediately face to face with the image of the crucified Christ which hung on a cross to one side of the shutter which separated me from the priest. For a second I felt truly sorry for all my sins. Every one of them. I pressed my lips against the crucifix and then, pushing open the confessional's door, I stepped piously out into the aisle.

Three

Joe Magee and our Paddy and I continued to tramp the mountain. Now, as we entered our teens, we graduated from walking to cycling. Joe and I went often to Glenavy and up, down and around all the countryside along that part of Lough Neagh. We made our own bicycles from frames scavenged at the pithead and second-hand wheels, with new tyres perhaps. The soles of our shoes were deeply grooved as a result of wedging our feet against the front tyres to act as a brake.

From camping in our back garden or in Joe Magee's in Joe's big brother's tent, we moved further afield. We joined An Óige, the Youth Hostel Association, and ventured along the Ards Peninsula, hitchhiking to Portaferry. John Surtees was one of our heroes, and our gang journeyed to motorbike races at Dundrod to enjoy the high-speed thrills. We also discovered a lucrative sideline in the collecting of empty, refundable lemonade bottles, which littered the racecourse when the competition was over. We went picking potatoes once, but that was hard work.

When television first came to Ballymurphy only one house on our street could afford a set, and some days we were all allowed in to see *Crackerjack* and other programmes. At nights a crowd of us would stand peering in the window to watch *Bronco Laine*, *Sunday Night at the Palladium* or *Rawhide*. Television also gave us a window into a wider world. When John F. Kennedy was elected as the first Catholic president of the United States, Irish Catholics took pride in him, then mourned his death in November 1963. Many nationalists and republicans also identified with the black civil rights struggle in the US, where hundreds of thousands marched for civil rights in Washington, and Martin Luther King declared: 'I have a dream'.

The world in 1963, as my childhood drew to a close, was on the move: by the end of the year Kenya became the thirty-fourth African country to achieve its independence; empire had faded; Roman Catholicism was taking new, reforming steps; the solitary action of a Buddhist monk in setting fire to himself in Saigon provided sombre example, while the civil rights movement in the US was faintly echoed in Ireland where in January 1964 the Campaign for Social Justice was established.

Meantime in St Mary's I was less concerned with national or international current affairs than with the affairs of academia. French and Latin, English and Irish, Mathematics, Science, History and Religion formed my daily diet. I learned it all by rote and now, decades later, I recollect little. At home my brothers and sisters studied also. By now most of us were at school, except for Margaret, who was working.

My father was in and out of work all the time. He was quite strict around the home, whereas my mother was more easygoing. During protracted periods of unemployment, my da busied himself planning and attempting improvements to number 11, and Paddy and I were invariably dragooned into helping with the work. Sometimes this involved little more than our being sent to the nearest building site for a bucket of sand or cement.

'Ask any of the workmen,' he would instruct us. 'Tell them it's for your daddy. They won't mind.'

At first we rebelled against such missions. The prospect of being refused, or even of asking for anything from complete strangers, intimidated us, but rebellion was futile. It was with a sense of mortification that we journeyed up Divismore Park with an empty bucket clanging between us, to clamber up the steps and across the Springfield Road to where the Henry Taggart Memorial Hall was being built. Minutes later we returned triumphant and weighted down with booty.

Some of my father's home improvements were repair jobs, but he also undertook bigger projects. The building of a partition and door between the living-room and the rest of the house to create a separate dining-room was a major job of work of which he was justifiably proud, and the erection of a wooden fence around the entire front and side of our garden was a mighty endeavour. The palings were produced from dozens of pallets which our Paddy and I spent hours separating. During such efforts nothing was wasted. Crooked nails were straightened, pieces of wire were carefully stored, screws were treasured. All of these bits and pieces were stored in tin cans, and my da's sparse assortment of tools was kept with other oddments in a big metal box. Pride of his possessions was a cobbler's last which he had brought with him from Belfast Prison on his release. The biggest job of all was the building of a shed, coal bunkers and steps out our back.

The Franklin Laundry on the Springfield Road lay just above Highfield, but on the opposite side close to Corry's timber yard. From it a fleet of vans delivered freshly laundered linen all over Belfast city. One day the back wall of the laundry, which flanked one side of the waste land which stretched down to the pithead, collapsed, its ramparts instantly reduced to a rubble of bricks.

My da came in one day and announced to my mother: 'Just the job for our back; the boys can bring them up while I'm at work.'

We protested. How could we carry bricks so far? It was miles away!

But we did. My da built us a wee handcart, with pram wheels at the front, a sizeable box-shaped body, two sturdy legs and a pair of long handles at the back. He compromised only once in the face of our protestations, accompanying us on our first trip to the laundry to introduce us to whoever it was had given permission for him to take the bricks away. Then for weeks, day in and day out, we ploughed up and down the Springfield Road, dragging or pushing our cart.

We got to know about bricks, about building them and stacking them, about selecting only complete ones, even if plastered with mortar, and rejecting other less perfect specimens. Then the bricks had to be washed. The inside of the wall had been painted, for all the bricks were blue or white on one side, and our Paddy and I spent the summer cleaning them. Eventually we assembled almost fifteen hundred of the bastards.

In the meantime my da had dug away the slope which brought our back garden almost to our back door. Now we were to have a good-sized back yard flanked by a shed and coal bunkers on one side with a raised flower-bed on the other. Broad steps ascended to the next level, which was topped with a canopy of clothes-lines, and above that again was the back garden. Our Liam helped, and so did Joe Magee. Our Paddy bluffed his way. When we had finished, my da said that it was a good job, well done.

Joe Magee and our Paddy and the rest of us assembled that first night in our shed, and my da came out with candles for us.

'It's great having a wee shed for our wee gang,' he said. And so it was.

Unfortunately Belfast Corporation didn't agree. A letter arrived proclaiming our extensions to be permanent on account of their brick structure. Wooden structures such as pigeon sheds were all right, but brick was out; any permanent structure had to be a certain declared distance from the road.

'No way,' my da told my mother. 'I'll see about this.' And so there was great coming and going. A man arrived from City Hall and surveyed our back. My da got a friend of his to draw up plans and declared that he was going to seek planning permission.

The outcome was that by only a few inches our shed was declared to lie the required distance from the road. It was a great victory and we were all delighted, none more so than our Paddy and me, who had begun to imagine the nightmare of having to bring all the bricks back to the Franklin Laundry.

Like most men, my father went for a drink with his friends on a Saturday. My mother meanwhile prepared the soup for Sunday's dinner, and on Saturday evening, as often as not, my da would have a bowl of the Sunday soup. If some of his friends were with him, my mother fed them also. Some of these were old jailmates, and out of their occasional reunions came the notion that they should form an association of former republican prisoners. Thus the Irish Republican Felons Association was born, with my father as its first chairperson.

This development made little impact on me, although my first stirrings of national consciousness had made me aware that all was not well in my part of Ireland. I had no special interest in current affairs, but I knew our country was partitioned, and I had a notion that I lived in the 'unfree' part. Certainly from the coded language of my elders I was aware that aspects of life in the north were felt to be threatening. The signals I received about this, whether from parents, grandparents or teachers, were always muted, sometimes merely fragments of conversations overheard or impressions formed in the wake of some political event. I knew that many of my uncles were forced to emigrate to England and then Canada to look for work. My da went to England once to work, but after a few weeks he came home; he told us all he was homesick. At one point my parents had considered emigrating to Australia, and they processed the various forms for an assisted passage, only to discover that my father's prison record barred him. I visited my Uncle Dominic's home in Dublin fairly often. He and my Aunt Maggie lived at Whitehall, and as my cousins and I visited the Phoenix Park, the Zoological Gardens, Nelson's Pillar, O'Connell Street and other parts of Baile Átha Cliath, I became aware of the different order in the capital, of the tricolour above the GPO.

At St Finian's I received a good primary school education and I found that I particularly enjoyed English. I failed my Eleven Plus, but the feeling was that if I had another go I would pass it, so we went in search of an intermediate school. My mother brought me up the Antrim Road to Barr na Gaoithe, also known as St Pat's. There we had no luck, either because they hadn't got enough places or because my standard wasn't high enough. However, I got a place in St Gabriel's, above Ardoyne, on the Crumlin Road, which I then went to for a year. On the same road was Everton, a

Protestant school, and as we went to our Catholic school we had to pass it on the way. There was no aggravation between the two sets of pupils, but we walked on different sides of the road. My social world expanded further while I was attending St Gabriel's because I went to Ardoyne for my lunch to my Aunt Kathleen, my mother's sister, and there I got to know more of my cousins, including Kevin Hannaway, whose family lived in Ardoyne at that time.

I was happy enough with my education to express to my father the ambition of becoming a Christian Brother myself.

'What use is it to be a Christian Brother,' he replied, 'and fade into oblivion?'

My father was quite religious, but a radical in terms of the Catholic church. He refused to let me join the Boy Scouts because they were attached to the church, and I once heard him arguing for an Irish Catholic instead of a Roman Catholic church. Yet he was devout in his duties.

From St Gabriel's I graduated to St Mary's, having now passed my Eleven Plus; it was seen as quite an achievement in the family that I should be going to grammar school, and there was a sense of occasion about going with my mother and my Granny Adams, who returned from Canada in 1960, to get me the school uniform. I was now one year behind most of my contemporaries of St Finian's, for the limited number who had got their scholarships had already moved ahead, while others were in building trade or other apprenticeships, or were going to England.

When my Granny Adams came back to Ireland, she was lucky to get a pensioner's bungalow in a little cul-de-sac up at Andersonstown. My father did most of the painting and decorating work on the new house, and I went to stay there with my granny in much the same way as I had stayed with her in Abercorn Street North. My Uncle Paddy created really nice gardens at the front and rear of her house, and I spent many hours tending and developing them.

At St Mary's grammar school, I met an entirely different crowd of boys from the ones I had previously associated with. Some like me were from working-class areas; others from more advantaged backgrounds were the sons of publicans, doctors and other professional people. Some came from outside Belfast, from Bangor or Carrickfergus. Theirs was a mysterious and appealing world, from which they journeyed by train to Belfast. Many of them went off on family holidays, a few even spending the summer in France or Italy – something we could not imagine. My family went to the seaside at Greencastle or to the zoo at Bellevue for an occasional day out. And yet I felt neither envious nor begrudging towards these more affluent classmates. Although I was unaware of it at the time, there was a kind of collective Catholic thinking which was conscious that, no matter what status the individual might achieve, Catholics in the north of Ireland were ghettoised, marginalised, treated as inferior. Those lucky enough to attain some advancement knew that they were only one step above the rest of us and liable to be treated exactly like us despite their qualifications or achievements.

In St Mary's we were all treated more or less equally, and our collective concern, the lot of all schoolboys, about schoolwork, homework and exams, obscured and fudged the differences in our social backgrounds. And anyway there were lots of other scholars in exactly the same position as I was, whose entrance into higher education was by dint of the sacrifices and unselfishness of our parents as much as, if not more than, our scholastic exertions.

St Mary's, like St Gabriel's and St Finian's, had a range of sporting activities, and I quickly became involved in the hurling and football teams. We played handball against gable walls in the schoolyard or in the streets behind the school, and occasionally some of us would walk across to the Antrim Road to St Malachy's College which had its own handball alley. St Mary's was an old, overcrowded school, but a fine centre of education for all that, whose ethos was to train our generation of Catholics to become citizens who could join the professions of academia or the law, and the lads from middle-class backgrounds had fairly high expectations. The whole curriculum was aimed at fulfilling that objective, so it was a narrow exam-bound course with little opportunity for diversion.

The Irish language did provide some room to manoeuvre, and Brother Beausang supplied the escape route to the Donegal Gaeltacht for weeks of great fun in Gweedore. Like their peers throughout Ireland, hundreds of Belfast schoolboys travelled there every summer. On my first visit, as our bus headed into Donegal from Derry, all of our crowd of scholars craned to see what the border looked like. To our disappointment and puzzlement, it was invisible.

That summer in the house of Eoin Ellen Boyle in Derrybeg, a dozen or so of us enjoyed ourselves immensely. In the evening we would often gather on the bridge, leaning over to watch the calm, deep waters of the river Clady as it flowed towards the salmon leaps. The Clady was a wondrous river, at times placid and clear and calm in deep pools or wide stretches, at times cascading over little waterfalls or flowing, falling in white foam over the salmon leaps. We would make our way from bank to bank, sometimes up the river itself, leaping from rock to rock, wading and falling, splashing and dashing. This evening as the sun settled slowly before us we dropped little pieces of ivy and watched as they kited down into the water. We watched for salmon.

'Ansin,' said Ciaran. ('*There.*')

'Nawh.'

'Tá ceann amháin ann,' said Colum. ('*There's one.*')

We were supposed to speak Irish all the time, and we did so to the best of our ability in the classes which took up most of our daily routine. Afterwards we spoke a sort of pidgin Irish. There were always rumours of boys being sent home for talking in English, so if we ran across an adult on our noisy way back and forth up the road from shop to café and from the river to the beach, we recited to each other prayers or songs in Gaelic.

'Sé do bheatha a Mhuire, a Phaddy.' ('*Hail Mary, Paddy.*')

'Atá lán do ghrásta, Mickey.' ('*Full of grace, Mickey.*')

'Tá an Tiarna leat.' ('*The Lord is with you.*')

If anyone heard us they merely smiled.

On the twelfth of July, the great festival of unionism, we organised our own version of an Orange march, though we had little enough knowledge of what it entailed.

> Oh, it was old but it was beautiful
> And the colours they were fine.
> It was worn at Derry, Aughrim,
> Enniskillen and the Boyne.
> Oh, my father wore it when a youth
> In those bygone days of yore,
> And it's on the Twelfth I love to wear
> The sash my father wore.

A dozen of us sang lustily as we paraded our way along the boreen towards the bonfire which we had piled high in the bog at the side of Magheragallen strand. Later as it flung sparks and handfuls of flames towards a darkening sky we huddled against a turfstack downwind of the blaze.

'It's funny, that's the first time I ever enjoyed "The Sash". I don't know whether that's right or not.' The speaker was John McAleavey. He was in our class; a quiet, studious type with fair hair and rounded features, his brown enquiring eyes peered perpetually from wire-framed spectacles.

'Ach, it's only a bit of *craic*, McAleavey.'

'There's no bigots here,' Seanie Drain slagged him.

'My Granda used to be an Orangeman,' John continued. 'Then he married a Catholic and they expelled him.'

'Oh, so you could be a wee proddie-dick, Mackers, that's what ails you!'

'That's what my Granda used to say,' John laughed. 'He was always teasing my Granny about being a papist. My Granda turned Catholic too, like. Then the Orangies came and burned him and my Granny out. That was the night after he was chased out of the shipyard. According to my da he was nearly killed. He had to swim for his life. That's when they moved out of Belfast.'

The rest of us listened intently.

'There was never any bother for years after. Then there were more troubles and there were shots fired into my Granda's house. One eleventh night. My da says July's the mad month.'

'What about where you live now?' Seanie asked him.

'Ach, it's dead-on. Only when I think of Orange marches I always think about the attacks on my Granny and Granda. There's Orange marches down our street; every twelfth they all parade up and down the street every night practising. There's only three of us Catholics in the street. Sometimes they practise outside our doors.'

John was smoking.

'I don't really mind,' he continued, 'but my mother gets very upset and my father rarely goes out during that time.'

The rest of us listened quietly to what he had to say. John lived in Carrickfergus, and unlike him we had little experience of the Orange marches. Somehow, despite our bravado, his story had a quietening effect on our festivities.

I nevertheless remained quite naive about sectarianism, partly because I didn't encounter it in my everyday life, partly because I didn't always recognise it when I did meet it. People from Catholic West Belfast shopped for bargains in the Protestant Shankill Road, and when finally one day I had saved up enough and my da gave me permission to buy a new bike, a racer, it was to a shop on the Shankill Road I went, and they didn't care what religion you were so long as you had the cash. At the same time, I knew enough not to declare in a loyalist area that I was a Catholic. If stopped, I gave my name as John rather than Gerry Adams, just as any of my contemporaries would have avoided giving names that sounded Catholic.

While still at school I went to a couple of pubs, just to try to get a job washing glasses, or to see if they were looking for part-time staff. It wasn't a problem going up the Shankill Road, where there was a good number of pubs, or at least I wasn't conscious of it being a problem, so I went up to one pub and the guy asked me my name, then asked me what school I went to. I answered St Mary's, and he said there was no job. I tried another few pubs along the Shankill Road, and each time it was the same. Puzzled, I

47

went home disappointed, thinking that there must be something wrong with St Mary's as a school. Later, however, when I happened to say it at home, somebody told me scornfully: 'Don't be so silly; you'd never get a job there.'

So I spent my years in St Mary's enjoying the *craic* and schoolboy escapades, feverishly cogging homework, cramming for exams until I passed my O levels and started my term as a senior student.

By now it was 1964. Joe Magee and I continued our excursions into the Belfast hills and, Gaeltacht days aside, I spent the summer holidays in Ballymurphy. There was a new element in our lives by this time. Sex. Or the prospect of it. Girls, for long a nuisance in their sisterly guise, were now emerging as a desirable attraction when they were someone else's sisters. They, too, showed some curiosity about us when we encountered them, at first by accident and increasingly by design in the Broadway or Clonard picture houses. Occasionally we visited the Diamond down the Falls Road, now a little geriatric for our teenage needs, or if there was a really good film showing we adventured as far as the Windsor on the Donegal Road. Here, we took our courage in both hands by leaving before 'the Queen' was played at the end. If challenged we would dash defiantly on, out of the darkened cinema, into the brightly lit foyer to emerge in a mad dash on to the main road. The Donegal Road area was traditionally a unionist one – thus the British anthem – and after such an altercation we unnerved ourselves all the way back to the Falls Road by imagining that we would be pursued by an irate mob of loyal cinema-goers.

In St Mary's our religious instructor Brother Heffernan had taken us through tomes of theology and the history of the church. I quite admired Martin Luther and his Protestant stand, and I drew no distinction between this Protestantism and that of the people of the Donegal Road. Our defiance of 'the Queen' was instinctive, our dash to safety afterwards no different from the times we robbed orchards or played 'knock the door' on our neighbours or the park attendant – the wakey – in the Falls or

48

Dunville Park. Indeed our search for female company and our attempted exploration of the mysteries of the opposite sex brought me and Joe and the rest of the street across the Springfield Road to Moyard, a newly built mishmash of maisonettes and flats. Here in the back entries and at street corners, most of Divismore Park's young turks experienced our first fumbling, clumsy sexual adventures. The young women with whom we pressed lips and limbs were, each and every one, Protestants. We didn't mind. Neither did they. And anyway their mothers had warned them only too well about boys of all denominations.

Afterwards, as we assembled at our corner to exaggerate our achievements, religion or politics were the last things we talked about. And yet as these innocent days and nights sped past, other stirrings also slowly moved towards centre stage.

Strolling to school at the age of sixteen one late-September day, in my usual somnolent state, I found my attention seized by the sight of a flag in the window of a shop in Divis Street opposite St Comgall's School. What made me notice it, and what made me and my classmates, as soon as we got to school, discuss its appearance with the kind of breathless enthusiasm usually reserved for alleged sightings of Sputniks, was that this was the Irish flag, the display of which was illegal.

That evening of 27 September, at a meeting in the Ulster Hall, a sectarian anti-Catholic demagogue named Ian Paisley threatened that if the tricolour in Divis Street were not removed within two days, he would himself lead a march to remove it. Throughout most of my childhood, although I hadn't really been aware of it at the time, the north had seen a small-scale but persistent campaign to foment anti-Catholic prejudice, spearheaded by Paisley, who founded the 'Free Presbyterian Church' in 1951. In 1956 he was associated with the kidnapping and proselytising of a fifteen-year-old Catholic girl, Maura Lyons; he heckled Rev. Donald Soper and other liberal Protestant churchmen, and at rallies bellowed forth a message of virulent religious hatred, such as that in June 1959, after which a Protestant mob attacked a Catholic-owned fish-and-chip shop on the Shankill Road. On the back of his rabble-rousing, Paisley's Ulster Protestant Association (UPA) won control of the Shankill Unionist Association and had Desmond Boal adopted as a unionist candidate in 1961. The UPA's self-professed aim was 'to keep Protestant and loyal workers in employment in times of depression, in preference to their Catholic fellow workers'.

Meanwhile, our teachers had insisted that under no circumstances were we to tarry in Divis Street, and this, of course, so aroused our curiosity that dozens of us ran as fast as our legs could carry us to peer into the window of what we were to discover was a Sinn Féin election office.

The following day District Inspector Frank Lagan of the Royal Ulster Constabulary led fifty men to break down the door of the Sinn Féin office with sledgehammers and seize the flag which had so offended Mr Paisley. People in the Falls Road were distinctly unimpressed by this piece of political violence directed against a party peacefully contesting an election, and a crowd of several thousand gathered in angry protest. By the end of the day a few buses lay smouldering, burnt by the incensed crowd.

Next day, 1 October, the protests developed into riots, the whole area simmering with a resentment which was no longer silent. Four days after Paisley's threats, Sinn Féin re-erected the flag in defiance of the police-state measures, and the RUC mustered its forces again and broke into the election offices with pick-axes to take it down. In the riots that ensued the RUC used armoured cars and water-cannon, while the rioters improvised petrol-bombs against them. Then, on the next day, 350 members of the RUC, wearing military helmets and using armoured cars, engaged in a concerted drive into the Falls to smash the resistance; as a consequence, fifty civilians and twenty-one RUC were hospitalised.

I took no part in any of this activity, but at home and on the way to and from school I could sense the tension, the charged atmosphere. Why, I wondered, did it need to be so illegal to fly a flag? Part of the answer lay in the fact that Paisley's threat came during an election in which the government didn't want to alienate loyalist voters, given the marginal status of the West Belfast seat, and so they accommodated the extreme right-wing provocation of the freelance preacher. But the deeper answer lay in the fact that, Paisley or no Paisley, the north of Ireland state was a state based upon the violent suppression of political opposition. That was why they banned the flag, and that was why they used their violence against the people of the Falls.

The impact of these events on me was to encourage me to become politically curious, and so I found myself folding election manifestos after school in the Felons Club, with some initial encouragement from my father, for the republican candidate, Liam McMillen. Although all the republican candidates lost their election deposits, my political appetite was whetted. All kinds of little things fell into place.

For example, at school I found it strange that for the exams we were only taught English history. Not that I had any problem with English history in itself, but it was difficult to understand why we should have to know all about the Wars of the Roses and nothing about our own history. My imagination was fired, however, when a man called Dick Dynan, who was an elocution teacher, came and took us for a free period and just talked us through the history of Belfast, a history which lay all around us. Our school was built on the banks of the Farset River, but we hadn't even known that, nor that Belfast took its name from the Farset River – Béal Feirste, the mouth of the Farset. So captivated was I by this revelation that immediately after the lesson I went over and looked at where the river ran underground.

When our regular history teacher returned, I asked him why it was that the history all around us was ignored. I began to question many other matters. Even in terms of elocution lessons, it appeared to me that the local dialect, and with it the sense of Belfast words or Irish words, or colloquialisms was being suppressed, and I found that I resented it a bit.

My interest in local history developed further into a conscious-ness of national history when I began to attend Sinn Féin meetings in a dingy room in the Cyprus Street GAA Club. Here I learned not about Ireland as it appeared in schoolbooks, as an occasional irritant in the course of British history, but the history of Ireland itself. Now I read eagerly many books which never featured in the school curriculum. Within a few weeks of the Divis Street riots, I joined Sinn Féin.

Prior to joining Sinn Féin I had taken no special interest in current events. Now I became increasingly aware of the causes of the discrimination that cloaked and constrained our lives; aware of consequent poverty, sectarianism and political exclusion, lack of access to decent housing and, above all, the endemic, structural unemployment. But despite my firmly republican family back-ground, I had not really formed any definite political views. Most of my friends and contemporaries had left school and many of them, despairing at the prospect of working only in dead-end jobs or else of hanging around on the dole, had left or were leaving.

I was restless but I stayed with St Mary's. One day I was filling in a form; my mother had given it to me so it was probably to do with a school grant or some related matter. We were in the living-room in Divismore Park and my ma was ironing clothes. I was seated near the fire, the document on my knee, my pen in hand; this was perhaps the first form I had ever filled in and I was being very meticulous, cross-checking everything with her.

We made our way through name, surname, parents, guardians and the rest of it. Until I came to *Nationality*.

'What does this mean, Ma? Nationality?'

She became slightly flustered.

'Why do they ask what nationality I am? Surely it's obvious. I'm Irish, amn't I?'

'Well,' she said, 'some people might put down British.'

'Why would they put down British? This is Ireland.'

'That's the way it is, Gerry. Just fill in the form,' she said a little testily.

'All right, Ma, I was only asking.'

'Well, I'm only telling you.'

I returned to the questionnaire.

'Would they expect me to put down British?' I asked again after a while.

'Would who expect you?'

'Whoever made up this form,' I replied peevishly.

'How am I supposed to know? Put down whatever you want.'

'I want to know what my nationality has to do with this silly form!'

'What you want and what you get are two completely different things.' There was a note of finality in her tone. She folded the ironing. 'Now, do you think you could fill in the rest of that without me? I'm going to put on the dinner.'

'All right,' I said.

I was beginning to get a sense of the political shape of my world. Unionists were in control and the British government seemed happy enough with the situation. It was a one-party state, 'a Protestant parliament for a Protestant people'. Attempts to change this by physical force, by publicising the injustices or by the development of a party political alternative had failed. The IRA's border campaign, which had opened in 1956, had proved a short-lived damp squib.

The prospects for anyone who became involved in republican politics were not good. Although the British Empire further afield was clearly in decline, in the north of Ireland Unionist rulers remained as determined as ever to repel the demands of any new campaign to end the partition of Ireland. When I had been only a few months old, unionist Prime Minister Brooke had declared: 'Our country is in danger, today we fight to defend our very existence and the heritage of our Ulster children ... "No Surrender, We are King's men".' In London the Westminster parliament had copper-fastened the unionist message of 'No change' by passing the Ireland Act, ruling out self-determination by the people of Ireland as a whole, thus establishing in legislation the 'loyalist veto'.

Political expression by the nationalist people, who had never accepted the partition of Ireland and the authority of the British imperial presence, was ruthlessly suppressed, as it had been since the foundation of the northern statelet. The Special Powers Act, in force since its early days, provided the minister for home affairs with extraordinary powers of arrest without warrant, the death penalty for some firearms offences, imprisonment, flogging; he could intern men without charge or trial, ban organisations, prohibit inquests, and evacuate and destroy houses. These powers, which added up to a denial of democracy in themselves, also gained specific force and effect from the fact that they were in the hands of one section of the community, the unionists, for use against the other principal section, the nationalists. Lord Craigavon, first prime minister of the statelet, had made it quite clear that 'I am an Orangeman first and a politician and a member of this parliament afterwards ... All I boast is that we have a Protestant parliament and a Protestant state.' Later, when Vorster, the prime minister of another apartheid state, introduced a new Coercion Bill into the South African parliament, he remarked that he 'would be willing to exchange all the legislation of that sort for one clause of the Northern Ireland Special Powers Act'.

St Patrick's Day parades were banned or baton-charged by police. Republicans had been interned on the occasion of a British royal visit in 1951, and in the same year the policy of suppression had gained further power from the passing of the Public Order Act, giving the government or RUC power to ban or re-route parades at will.

Elsewhere in the British Empire, Nkrumah had become the first of a generation of African anti-colonialists to be elected prime minister of newly independent states, while in Kenya British forces exacted a terrible revenge in their campaign of counter-insurgency terrorism. The coronation of Elizabeth II in 1953 had temporarily lifted the hearts of British Empire loyalists. In 1954 the Northern Ireland government at Stormont had pressed ahead with further suppression of political opposition, the Flags and Emblems Act making it illegal to interfere with the symbol of unionism, the Union Jack, while giving the police power to take down any other flag, i.e. the Irish tricolour.

Faced with the lack of democracy, with the Special Powers Act, the lack of adult suffrage, the gerrymandering of local government and the ban on republican parties, I was convinced that the injustice of the system must be challenged. Even as I developed my fledgling convictions, the long freeze between the unionists in the north and the Dublin government was starting to thaw, warmed by the heat of economic modernisation. The logic of cross-border economic co-operation had been recognised for some time, and behind the scenes business and political interests had pressed for practical action. When Taoiseach Sean Lemass travelled the 100 miles from Dublin to Belfast to meet with Captain Terence O'Neill, prime minister of the northern statelet, it was the first time in forty-five years that the two governments on the island had engaged in talks at the highest level. It seemed to many that a new era of detente was dawning and that this would be reflected in reforms which would at least moderate the sectarian discrimination of the northern state, but on our black and white television we saw Ian Paisley and a handful of his associates protesting at Stormont. Paisley threw snowballs, which I thought was funny. 'That man's a troublemaker,' the older people said.

At school Brother Heffernan probably had some notion that my thoughts were tending to veer towards political interests and away from academic pursuits. During a theology class we were having a discussion about giving to Caesar the things that are Caesar's and giving to God the things that are God's. I asked how it was that the Catholic church excommunicated IRA people. How come, I demanded, did the church make this judgement and what was the theological basis for it?

Around this time a number of people were arrested at Cloonagh House, then the residence of a senior British army officer. They refused to talk, even refusing to speak to the priest during confession, and they became celebrated in newspaper headlines as 'The Five Silent Men'. Joe McCann, an apprentice bricklayer, was a particular friend of mine, Sean Murphy was a fellow student at St Mary's – I knew them all.

I was seventeen and restless at school. Most of the people I associated with were working, and I was now politically involved, or at least interested. My father was out of work again, and as the oldest child I was conscious of the fact that I was bringing no money into the house. One day I saw in the *Irish News* that they were looking for a bar apprentice in the Ark Bar, and on an impulse I decided to go for it. It was only a quarter of a mile from St Mary's school, so it was only a moment's walk to go over there. I walked up and the man in charge said, 'Yeah, there's a job here for an apprentice'. The wages were something like £10, which was quite a lot of money then; the lads I knew who were apprentice bricklayers and the like were only earning between £4 and £7. I went back to Brother Heffernan to tell him I was leaving, and whatever he said wasn't enough to stop me.

It was a source of some considerable pleasure and pride to my family that I had succeeded in getting to grammar school, and so it came as a shock to them when I arrived home and told them I was leaving school and getting a job. But at least I was now able to present my mother with a pay packet.

Undoubtedly it was a mistake in terms of career choice because I ended up in the worst of all possible worlds. Had I decided not to go to St Mary's or had I left after O levels, I could have got a trade. While I had some notion of continuing my education after my A levels, and a vague ambition of going to university, any such ambition was soon overtaken by politics. Had I applied myself at school, I would have had reasonable career prospects. But for most people there was little prospect of a career, and for men the prospects of steady work were very limited. There was more work for women, in the stitching factories, clothing factories, and what was left of the mills; others worked as domestics. Men from working–class backgrounds could get apprenticed to a trade, if they were lucky, or they became labourers, and the labouring work could break even the strongest of them.

The Ark was one of many pubs owned by Catholics in Protestant and mixed areas of the city, but this posed no problem as far as the Protestant clientele of the Ark were concerned. Situated at the corner of Broadbent Street on the Old Lodge Road, it drew its customers from the neighbouring streets bounded by the Crumlin Road on one side and the Old Lodge Road and Shankill Road on the other. Within a very short time of being taken on, I was being left on my own to look after it. I'd walk to work from Divis Street, up Townsend Street and across the Shankill Road to the Ark, open the place up and scrub it out. On a nice morning, I'd be walking about the place, inside and out, preparing for opening, and I'd be meeting people in the street: older people and women of all ages who were going to the shops, men walking their dogs. It felt good to be working: I enjoyed the sense of responsibility, and the wages were fairly good; I had no regrets at that time about leaving school. Often I would go swimming in Peter's Hill baths during lunch breaks. During good weather I cycled to and from work along the Shankill Road and across the West Circular.

The Ark was a very small, old-style pub with a tiled floor, huge high windows, a single bar, a back room and a snug. Upstairs darts matches were held, and the only time the pub was crowded, apart from holiday time, was when there was a darts match, or perhaps a meeting of some kind. Porter was the staple drink, firkins of it being delivered weekly from Guinness's on the Grosvenor Road, and sales of spirits were minimal.

I liked the people who drank in the Ark Bar, and I think they liked me. One very entertaining old boy had been in the Battle of the Somme. I was only a kid, and he was in his sixties or seventies, but we were of the same city and I felt an absolute affinity with him. On one occasion I sang a verse of the loyalist anthem, 'The Sash', in Irish and he followed me with the republican song, 'Kevin Barry'. At the end of the night, as we barmen cleared away glasses and empty bottles, the customers stood for a collective rendition of 'God Save the Queen'. It would be wrong to give the impression that everything was grand;

sectarian polarisation became frigid around the July parade, when the Orange people became quite triumphalist. But I presented no threat to anyone; I was just a lanky teenager.

While I was working in the Ark I was participating in Sinn Féin educational classes and Wolfe Tone Society debates and discussions; I was becoming an activist. When the planners set about the destruction of the Pound Loney area – a district of densely packed tiny houses at the bottom of the Falls – in preparation for the building of a multistorey development to be called Divis Flats, I and other republicans joined local people in protesting. A slum clearance programme had been announced in December 1962; now in 1966 the Pound Loney area was formally declared a redevelopment area, and they set about the work of demolition. While we were all for the replacement of old, substandard housing, we were opposed to the plans of the government in London, which saw system-building in multi-storey units as the answer to the demands of the housing crisis, and which structured grants to local authorities to favour the new methods.

The old housing was desperately poor, but the Loney was a good area with its own sense of community, in which the same families had lived in the same streets for generations. We were convinced that high-rise flats weren't the answer. How could you live up there? How would you get the pram down? Where would the children play? On a balcony fifty feet up in the air?

We held demonstrations and protest meetings, trying to influence how the area would be rebuilt, arguing for traditional housing rather than high-rise blocks and describing the planned development as 'a multistorey carpark disguised as a block of flats'. Young, energetic and irreverent, we leafleted and we mobilised; we tried to democratise what we were at by getting a proper committee off the ground. At one of our protests, we even enlisted Joe McCann's granny's dachshund, putting a banner on it which read 'No High-Rise Flats'. We were attacked by Canon Padraig Murphy and were denounced as 'communists' and 'men of evil intent' by Bishop Philbin, but our campaign was very popularly supported locally.

When the same demolition of the old streets started in the Protestant Old Lodge Road, no one protested. I stood with the locals at the door of the Ark and watched as the bulldozers went in. Everyone was sad, and some of the women showed a little anger, but none of the men listened to them: they were only women after all. And no one listened to me; I was only a wee Catholic barman.

In 1966 the fiftieth anniversary commemoration of the 1916 Easter Rising saw a resurgence all over Ireland of republican and nationalist sentiment, and in Belfast the huge parade was resplendent with banners, flags and marching bands. The Stormont government of Terence O'Neill, which had gone to such efforts to tear down a single flag just eighteen months earlier, now reacted hysterically to the commemoration. For three days the railway line from Dublin was closed by the government and the RUC B Specials were put on standby. A *Belfast Telegraph* hoarding announced 'Full Scale Alert' and 'IRA Threat'. Yet the IRA was powerless to pose any significant threat to anyone, and despite the scare-mongering the parade, on which Kevin Hannaway and I acted as stewards, passed off without incident. It was featured on television news, and people in the Ark Bar remarked upon seeing me amongst the stewards at the tail end of the parade, but they did so in a light-hearted way.

One of the myths of the time was that the government in Dublin was particularly supportive of the republican position in the north. True, de Valera, who had participated in the Easter Rising, was still president, but the establishment possessed an ingrained antagonism towards republicanism. The taoiseach, Sean Lemass, was a pragmatist whose concern was to develop the Twenty-six-County state as a modern capitalist economy, and even though the fiftieth anniversary of the 1916 Rising saw a widespread popularisation of the writings of the 1916 leaders and an increase in nationalist sentiment, in intellectual circles an anti-nationalist historical revisionism was beginning to assert itself.

At the time of the Easter parade the unionist government engaged in extraordinary alarmism. Fifty years earlier they had been part of an all–Ireland situation with the British in charge. By the skin of their teeth they had secured a six–county state which they could control. In the bloody birth of the new statelet, there had been pogroms: in Belfast more than 10,000 Catholics had been expelled from their jobs; 23,000 had been driven from their homes, and more than 500 Catholic-owned businesses had been destroyed. Leading the pogroms had been the Special constables of the new state. As the *Manchester Guardian* had reported: 'These people have committed no offence unless it be an offence to be born a Catholic. . . . On the simple charge of being Catholics hundreds of families are being continually driven from their houses . . . In these operations the Specials provide the petrol, fire-arms and immunity from prosecution.'

The north remained under a permanent state of emergency. Republicans were imprisoned in every decade. The unionist instinct was to rise to any hint of threat and to ban parades by Catholics. They also experienced a geographical and constitutional insecurity, fearing that they would be gobbled up by nationalist Ireland.

For Catholics in Belfast the sense of exclusion was immediate. We lived for the most part in relatively small enclaves. In East Belfast the Sirrocco works was a major employer within that enclave, yet no Catholic worked in it. The Goliath crane of Harland & Wolff cast a giant shadow over Catholic homes, yet almost no Catholic worked there. In West Belfast, Mackies foundry was the main employer, yet very few Catholics got jobs there. It was so everywhere in the city. Throughout the Orange marching season, which extended from June to September, nationalists lived in fear, as whole areas were placed under effective curfew to allow sectarians to express the perceived historic triumph of Protestants over Catholics in the seventeenth century.

As Catholics began to seek their civil rights, the Campaign for Social Justice received the backing not only of the Catholic conservative Nationalist Party but also of the Northern Ireland Labour Party, which voted in 1965 for the repeal of the Special Powers Act and was moving to support the demand for 'One Man, One Vote'. But a dynamic reaction to demands for democratisation was building up within loyalism – a reaction which, if not led by Ian Paisley, was certainly incited by him.

In February 1966 Paisley launched the *Protestant Telegraph*, a weekly paper dedicated to anti-Catholic tirades. In February, March and April, the Ulster Volunteer Force (UVF), made up of a small group of Paisley supporters headed by Gusty Spence, a former activist with Ulster Protestant Action, carried out a series of petrol-bombings of Catholic homes, schools and shops. In April, Paisley set up the Ulster Constitution Defence Committee and its militant vanguard, the Ulster Protestant Volunteers (UPV). On 7 May 1966 an elderly Protestant woman was killed in a UVF attack on a Catholic pub. On 22 May the UVF declared war on 'the IRA', and on 27 May they shot John Scullion, a Catholic who had no connection with the IRA; he died on 11 June. In their ideology, indeed in their theology, there was little distinction between an IRA activist and an ordinary, uninvolved Catholic. On 6 June, Paisley led a demonstration through Cromac Square against the Presbyterian General Assembly; he led the picket through the Markets area and local people protested at the incursion. The RUC responded savagely against the local people, beating a path through this nationalist area. In so doing they succeeded in inciting fear on the one hand and encouraging a triumphalist, bully boy attitude on the other hand.

As I left mass at Clonard Monastery on 27 June, I met Liam McMillen, who told me that a barman called Peter Ward had been killed at the Malvern Arms, a Shankill Road pub, the night before. Four Catholic barmen had been drinking there, and the UVF had shot three of them as they left the pub, killing Ward. In the context of Paisley's gospel of hatred, all Catholics were regarded as 'disloyal' and as the enemy. On 23 July a large crowd of Paisleyites went on a rampage in Belfast city centre, stoning the Catholic-owned International Hotel, where Peter Ward had worked, breaking shop windows, and going to Sandy Row and trying to burn down a bookie's which employed Catholics.

I was not conscious of any affinity or support from those people in the Ark for what had happened. However, the peaceful polarisation of loyalists and nationalists was fraying at the edges. With the Twelfth approaching, I asked my boss for the union rate for working a public holiday; instead I got the sack. So it was that my Catholic employer evicted me, not the Protestant customers, to whom I bade a sad farewell.

Almost immediately I got a job in a centre-city pub, the Duke of York, where I not only enjoyed the work but also received an education. Here the issues of the day were endlessly and informatively discussed by the wide ranging clientele, which included members of the Northern Ireland Labour Party, whose head office was just around the corner. A number of the trade union offices were in very close proximity. Communist Party stalwarts like Betty Sinclair frequented 'the Duke', and people in the republican leadership such as Liam McMillen and Proinsias MacAirt also socialised there. It was a place where one could read *The Irish Times*, in those days a paper not readily obtainable in working class Belfast, and where journalists drank. Many of the customers supported the Irish rugby team and were in the habit of going quite frequently to Dublin, a city the customers of the Ark would not have dreamed of visiting. There were people here who went to Donegal for their holidays, people who had visited Moscow and the Black Sea. The first time I ever heard the bouzouki was when one of the clientele from the Duke of York went off busking somewhere and brought the instrument back.

It was a small, picturesque, low-ceilinged pub with no ventilation; it had a long bar, brass rails, swing doors, fine oak and good cartoons on the walls. Next door to the public bar was a lounge bar which we served through a hatch. Jimmy Keaveney, the owner, was a nice man and the perfect publican. Small, tubby, bespectacled, with receding hair, he habitually dressed in cardigan, waistcoat, shirt and tie. It was a family business and sold one of the best pints of porter in town, using the big old firkins. They also sold barley wine from the wood, which we were only allowed to serve a certain amount of because it was so potent. Jimmy's mother and sister lived above the bar and I have happy memories of their hospitality. When I wanted to move from cycling to a motorbike I got an advance on my wages to use as a deposit, and I bought a Honda 50 on hire purchase.

During the lunch hour a stream of people came to the pub from the businesses in the busy city streets around; they were a mixture of bankers, judges, journalists, office girls, and owners of shirt factories, spinning factories, travel agencies. On weekend evenings a crowd of about ten sang Percy French songs in the snug, including in their repertoire other, mostly Irish humorous songs, with maybe a bit of Bing Crosby thrown in for variety. 'Joe Hill' was one of the party pieces of a different crowd, who preferred the public bar and whose taste ran strongly towards politically progressive material. Amongst them were Jimmy and Edwina Stewart of the Communist Party and some of the bigger union bosses representing workers in the Belfast shipyards. This was a time of a great revival of interest in traditional music, which was well represented in impromptu sessions in the lounge. Ballads provided the staple fare here, and amongst those who played in the place on occasion were Ted Furey, father of the Fureys, and members of the Dubliners. Some people sang quite republican songs, like 'Henry Joy', but in general the ballad-singers avoided party songs as such, favouring instead good northern songs like 'Slieve Gullion Brae'. Some, like Proinsias MacAirt, sang in Irish, commanding complete silence and rapt attention from their audience.

A brilliant and immensely popular *Newsletter* columnist drank in the Duke of York. A Pickwickian figure, Ralph (Bud) Bossence had spent his childhood in Detroit and he had a habit of coming out with Damon Runyonisms. He was a remarkable character — very small, but massively fat, with very small hands and an amazing girth — like an Easter egg man. His laughter often rang through the bar, and he and his friends used to have great fun. They might plan a walk around the Hollywood Hills or a day trip to Donaghadee; at the anniversary of Wolfe Tone, they said they were going up Cave Hill, but they got no further than the Bellevue Arms public house. We relished his accounts of their hilarious experiences. In his writing he celebrated life, good food, drink and his enthusiasm for the movies, jazz and Glentoran soccer club, and always his interest was in so-called 'ordinary' people. In one column he wrote: 'the day when the peers outnumber the proletariat in my writings I'll collect my cards.' That was Bud Bossence, and the highlight of our week was when something that had happened in the Duke of York constituted even a sentence in Bud's column. A funny, in-house feature of his column was that sometimes he would write: 'as the Curate said to me the other morning'. And 'the Curate' would be one of the barmen, perhaps me or any of the others. Instinctively interested in writing, I gained from Bud a sense of how even a throwaway remark could be crafted into something that was truly entertaining for his readers.

The Duke of York was politically a very liberal establishment in which all the affairs of the day were discussed, and there were several progressive influences on me at the time. The first edition of James Connolly's writings I read was given to me by a customer called William Mullan, a trade unionist who had been involved with the Outdoor Relief riots in 1932. Some people wore CND badges; there were small anti-Vietnam war demonstrations, and I went on one of them. The crushing of Czechoslovakia in 1968 was a catastrophe which touched us all. South Africa featured strongly, too, in conversations.

Jimmy Keaveney closed the doors of the Duke's on the morning of the Twelfth of July, when only regulars were allowed in. That morning we could hear the Orange bands building up in Donegal Street, or wherever they were meeting. Occasionally a few noisy bandsmen would try to gain entry to 'the Duke' and thump loudly on the doors when they were ignored. On a number of occasions I watched the Orange marches on Royal Avenue, without feeling threatened, and once I dodged across one, which was supposedly suicidal, because I was late. One night leading unionist politician Robert Porter (Stormont Minister of Home Affairs, 1969–70) visited the Duke's. While he and his entourage relaxed inside I slipped out and with the help of the nozzle of a vacuum cleaner I rammed a potato up the exhaust of his limousine. Presuming that this would cause it to break down, I was exhilarated at my audacity. Later I felt foolish, imagining what could have happened if I had been caught. How could I explain myself? Arrested for possession of a potato?

My father lobbied me to get our Paddy a few hours' work. I was extremely reluctant to ask, but eventually during an extremely busy night I suggested to the boss that Paddy could help out washing glasses. And so he did, travelling down with me to work on the back of the Honda in the evenings.

Work days in the licensed trade generally allowed for a three-hour break for bar staff. Some days I went home for lunch but as my wages increased I took to wandering around the city centre, enjoying my sense of independence and adulthood. I quickly relaxed into the familiarity of making and finding my own space in the daily routine of small things, like buying a magazine at the newsstand at the post office in Royal Avenue or browsing for a book in Smithfield market before having bacon, egg and chips in a small local café or a long pleasant glass of stout and a sandwich in Kelly's Cellars or the Crow's Nest. These were quiet times of the day, with few people abroad, at least in cobbled backstreets or small hostelries. They and I had become part of each other's routine.

I continued to knock about with our Paddy, Frank Curran, his brother Harry, Joe Magee and one or two others. There were several venues for dances in the city, including some larger places where you might hear the likes of Joe Dolan or Dicky Rock perform, and Joe Magee and I would often go to dances and *céilí* on a Friday or Saturday night after finishing work.

Joe and I continued with our camping expeditions, and on one occasion we took an especially memorable hitch-hiking holiday. Just around the corner from the Duke of York was Easons, the newspaper wholesalers, and one of the drivers there told me that if we got down there at 5.00 a.m. he'd get us to Derry. And so early one morning we found ourselves in the van, driving through very deep mist on the way up, and we felt a great sense of adventure as we were dropped into Derry. It was 7.00 am, there were no trains and everywhere was closed.

Walking out the road to Donegal we got a lift on the back of an open lorry and we lay back, gazing at the mountains and the blue sky as we drove into Donegal. After three days and nights camping beside a graveyard in Gweedore, we made our way to Sligo and on to Galway, where we conspired in vain to make passionate love to two women in black bikinis whom we met on the beach. We stayed for a while in the city of the tribes, which was buzzing, as ever, with young people, traditional music and its own particular brand of hectic *craic*, and there by fluke we met on the main street three Belfast republicans, Proinsias MacAirt, Liam McMillen and Jim Hargey, who had just come back from the Aran Islands.

Liam McMillen and his associates were all in their mid-thirties at this time. Known as 'Billdoe' or 'the wee man', Billy (Liam) was a chubbily built, thickset and rosy-cheeked little man with a full head of black hair. He was a Gaeilgoir, a fluent Irish speaker, and an enthusiast for Irish music. He had been involved with Saor Éire, a small but energetic republican group, in the 1950s and had been interned at that time. Later he became active in more mainstream republican activities. A single man, he lived with his mother in Ton Street in the Falls. He and MacAirt and Jim Hargey, like Joe Magee and myself, were in the west of Ireland on holidays.

Joe and I travelled on down to Kerry, staying at Banna Strand before moving on to Killarney, where we took a boat out on the lakes and cycled through the Gap of Dunloe on hired bikes. One dusky evening we had an encounter with a bull after mistaking a farmer's instructions and going into the wrong field. The following night found us on the Cork/Kerry border in hilly country, but we eventually got a lift to Macroom and thence to Cork. We arrived when it was pitch black, put our tents up in the

66

dark, and went to sleep to the sound of cars drawing up in what seemed to be a lovers' lane beside us. We got up the next morning to find the whole populace of Cork driving past where we were camped, on the edge of a main thoroughfare.

We stayed in Cork for a few days, went to the Blarney Stone and kissed it. From there we made heavy weather of getting as far as Tipperary, but a couple of lifts took us right into Dublin, and to my Uncle Dominic's in Whitehall. We had spent about ten days on the road, exploring the length and breadth of the country, and now we spent another couple of days fooling around Dublin, visiting O'Donohue's and other pubs which hosted music sessions, before heading back to Belfast. Having left with £20 each in our pockets, we returned with about £4 apiece, delighted with ourselves and our big adventure.

On another excursion we camped at Bray Head south of Dublin. Here we had the seaside town with all its diversions before us, the Head and the mountains behind, and we walked the cliff-top path out to Greystones.

When I graduated from my trusty racing bike to the Honda, Joe and I headed off on frequent short trips, especially to Mrs Kearney's near Glenavy.

On one visit we parked the motorbike in her yard and sat in the street outside the long, low, stone-slated cottage where she lived alone. Mrs Kearney was a relation of Joe's, and for years he and I had been coming here. Once we had even walked, but mostly we had hitch-hiked until graduating to bikes, and we had spent many evenings cycling from the Murph up along the Glen Road. Now the Honda got us there in no time at all. Sometimes as we chugged our way up and down little hills on country roads of melting tar, oozing between white hawthorn hedgerows, Joe and I sang at the tops of our voices with the sheer exuberance of it all.

Mrs Kearney fed us scone bread, griddle cakes and strong tea. She lived in two rooms of the cottage, the unused section of which had two more rooms filled with bric-à-brac, with churns and butter pats, with old presses, harnesses, reins – all of them relics of bygone days.

When we had first come to Mrs Kearney's, we would be tired and footsore after our day's cycling or tramping, so we wouldn't stir far, ready to accept her warm hospitality with gratitude, and glad of the rest and refreshments. Now with the Honda we arrived fresh, ready for a walk, and on this day ready to hunt.

The shotgun belonged to Joe – or to his brother, but Joe had permission to use it. We had written permission from two farmers whose land adjoined Mrs Kearney's, so we could tramp across her land and theirs right down to the lough shore. At the point of the lough, which we had walked to many times before, a little river made its way into a wee bay, and there in the bay a barge was moored. Lough Neagh is an immense expanse of water; ripples of waves like a tide ebbed back and forth along the grassy shore. Often we sat on the barge eating sandwiches or white or brown bread and butter and drinking bottles of milk while the midges ate us.

This day we skirted the bay. We were making our way to another place, a piece of slightly raised ground, flanked by hedges and riddled with rabbit burrows. Mrs Kearney had asked us to take a more circuitous route.

'Don't cut through Trimble's land,' she said. 'He's my neighbour, and no harm to him, but he's very bitter. I don't want him to have any reasons to raise objections.'

Trimble, of course, was a local unionist, so we took Mrs Kearney's advice. With Joe in front and the shotgun cradled in his arms, we inched our way towards our quarry.

'It's important to keep downwind,' Joe whispered to me. 'Stay this side of the rabbits. Our Brian hunts wood pigeon more than rabbits, but he always says, "Stay downwind or you'll never get a decent shot." '

Eventually, after much delicate manoeuvring, we reached what Joe deemed to be a good vantage point.

'Look,' he said, 'we can see the entire run.'

And so we could, but perhaps the rabbits had also seen us because we sat for an hour and a half waiting and waiting and waiting.

'Let's have a shot anyway, Joe,' I said.

'No,' he said.

I'd asked him earlier as soon as we had arrived at Mrs Kearney's. Indeed, I had asked him when he had first been given permission to take the gun with him. As soon as we got out to the country, I had asked: 'Can we fire off a few shots?'

'No,' he said, and then, 'We'll see.' But as soon as we arrived at Mrs Kearney's, he was adamant. 'The rabbits aren't stupid. If they hear shotgun blasts, there'll not be one of them within miles of the place.' He needn't have worried. For all his precautions the rabbits weren't giving us a free shot anyway.

The shadows were lengthening and the evening beginning to settle when reluctantly Joe stretched himself erect in our hiding place and motioned to me. 'That's it; let's head back.'

'But can we not have a shot first?' I said.

'Let's wait,' he said, 'till we're nearer the house.'

'Well, can I carry the shotgun?' I asked. 'You've got carrying it all the time.'

'It's very dangerous,' he said.

'I'm not stupid,' I replied.

'You're not? Well, hold on a minute,' he said.

He broke the gun and placed it in my hands.

'Keep it broken, and if you see a rabbit, close it again, but stay in front of me; don't point the gun at me. And don't put your finger near the trigger.'

'All right,' I said, chastened by the seriousness of his tone.

The gun wasn't heavy; in fact it was rather light, but awkward going through hedges and over fences. By now the grass was wet with dew. We were skirting a field. Ahead of me I could see the lights of Mrs Kearney's house.

'Look,' said Joe, 'there's rabbits!'

On instinct almost I closed the gun, pulled it to my shoulder, nestled its smooth wooden butt against my chin.

'Where?'

'There,' he said.

About forty or fifty yards ahead of me, I could see the two shapes, silhouetted, dark against the ground. I pulled the trigger.

Joe shouted excitedly, 'You've hit it!'

And then I heard it squeal.

'Jesus, Mary and Joseph!' I said. The squealing sound became a plaintive, wailing scream.

Joe was running ahead of me. He reached the rabbit, which was hopping round in circles, all the time crying hysterically. He grabbed it by the back leg and then punched it behind the head. It hung lifeless for a second, then convulsed and jerked and convulsed again. Joe flung it from him to the ground.

'Well,' he said, 'that's our dinner.'

'Did you hear it crying?' I asked.

'Aye,' he said. 'You hit it wrong. But it's all right now. I put it out of its misery.'

Four

On a mild Saturday morning I went to be measured for a suit at Burtons. After walking up and down outside the shop, peering in at the besuited and sportsjacketed dummies, I ventured inside, where the terms of the HP, or hire purchase, agreement were smoothly spelt out for me by an extremely friendly salesman. I paid over my deposit and he passed me on to an older man who measured me. Then the first man arrived back with so many samples of material for me to choose from, books of them with reams of different colours, patterns and cloth, that I became flustered and picked black because it seemed a safe bet. Afterwards as I walked back to the Duke's, I was sorry that I hadn't taken my time. Maybe a lighter colour would have been better; maybe a different style, something a little Teddyboyish? Or a Beatles type?

A week later I collected the suit, at the same time making my first HP payment. Then I was off up North Street to buy a new shirt and tie. I was landed.

'You must be chasing,' my da said as I was going out that evening.

'Give my head peace,' I grunted at him as I adjusted my tie for the umpteenth time.

'Give's a wee whirl round,' he continued. 'Let's see how the new suit looks from the back.'

'Leave him alone,' my ma interjected. 'Will you be in late?' she asked me.

'I mightn't be in at all,' I snapped, 'if he doesn't wise up.'

I glowered at my da. He glowered back at me.

'What did you say? That's it, Annie: I don't know what kind of children we're rearing! There's no come or go in any of them. No respect. I don't know why we bother.'

My ma hustled me out of the room.

'You shouldn't talk to your da like that,' she admonished me.

'Ma!' I protested.

'Don't "Ma" me. Go on out: have a nice time. Your new suit is lovely. Now, tell your father goodnight.'

'Ma . . .'

We were in the hall. I could hear my da moving about in the living-room. I was all dolled up in my new gear, and the bus was due any minute down the Springfield Road. My ma looked beseechingly at me.

'Good night, Da,' I shouted, bending to kiss my ma on the cheek and dashing out the door. I didn't give my da a chance to reply.

Later, as I examined my reflection in the bus window and scrutinised my face for pimples or blackheads, I thought of that night's dance after I finished work. The rancour of my da's refusal to treat me like an adult soon faded as the bus sped citywards and I contemplated the possibility of touching for a girl. Especially the one who let me get her a coke last week. I was for the Marquee again tonight. This was a favourite venue, especially since it had moved from the Astor Ballroom to an old warehouse in Skipper Street near the Duke of York. Rory Gallagher and Taste, Sam Mahood and the Soul Foundation, The Group, High Wall and The Tigers were just some of the groups which played there.

Other nights were spent far from the music and dancing of the Marquee, as I studied, absorbed and discussed the political

72

history which had recently become of intense interest to me. In a sense I had absorbed an ethos of republicanism while growing up, even though I had taken no great interest in politics, but now I was keen to understand and get to grips with its foundations and principles.

Republicanism as an ideology based itself on the rights of self-determination, which had been denied to the Irish people by centuries of British rule. Strongly influenced by the French revolution, it had first been articulated in the late eighteenth century by Wolfe Tone and the United Irishmen, who had sought to break the connection with England; to substitute the common name of Irish person in place of Protestant, Catholic and Dissenter; and to create a secular society. Later, Fintan Lalor of the Young Ireland movement awakened a new sense of national consciousness and identity, bringing greater breadth and definition to republicanism. Lalor wrote:

> The entire ownership of Ireland, moral and material, up to the sun and down to the centre, is vested in the right of the people of Ireland. They and none but they are the landowners and law makers of this island, that all laws are null and void not made by them and all titles to land are invalid not conferred by them.

The Fenian movement, or Irish Republican Brotherhood (IRB), of the late nineteenth and early twentieth centuries had fostered a progressive nationalism which expressed a belief in culture and identity as well as in political independence. Its influence was associated with a great national revival and the foundation of national sporting and cultural organisations such as the Gaelic Athletic Association and the Gaelic League/*Conradh na Gaeilge*.

Republicanism had always been a living and developing ideology, and in the early years of this century the radical revolutionary writings of James Connolly had a profoundly significant effect on the movement. All of the elements and influences that had gone into the making of republicanism were

73

crystallised at the time of the Easter Rising of 1916 in the finest declaration of its principal elements, the Proclamation of the Republic, which stated in part:

> We declare the right of the people of Ireland to the ownership of Ireland and to the unfettered control of Irish destinies, to be sovereign and indefeasible. The long usurpation of that right by a foreign people and government has not extinguished the right, nor can it ever be extinguished except by the destruction of the Irish people. In every generation the Irish people have asserted their right to national freedom and sovereignty: six times during the past three hundred years they have asserted it in arms. Standing on that fundamental right and again asserting it in arms in the face of the world, we hereby proclaim the Irish Republic as a Sovereign Independent State, and we pledge our lives and the lives of our comrades-in-arms to the cause of its freedom, of its welfare and of its exaltation among the nations.
>
> The Irish Republic is entitled to, and hereby claims, the allegiance of every Irishman and Irishwoman. The Republic guarantees religious and civil liberty, equal rights and equal opportunities to all its citizens, and declares its resolve to pursue the happiness and prosperity of the whole nation and of all its parts, cherishing all the children of the nation equally, and oblivious of the differences, carefully fostered by an alien government, which have divided a minority from the majority in the past.

In the general election of 1918, Sinn Féin had stood for an independent republic, promising to abstain from taking their seats in the British parliament in Westminster and to establish instead an independent parliament in Ireland. Of the 105 Irish seats at Westminster, Sinn Féin won seventy-three in an overwhelming endorsement of its policy. In January 1919 the first meeting of Dáil Éireann, an independent parliament, was held in the Mansion House in Dublin, and a Declaration of Independence was adopted. The affirmations of the Proclamation were developed further in the Democratic Programme of the First Dáil in

1919, and Sinn Féin became the principal vehicle of republicanism, supporting the armed campaign of the IRA and maintaining a policy of abstentionism from the British parliament at Westminster.

The philosophers and thinkers of the 1916 Rising had not, however, survived it, and this set the stage for counter-revolution and civil war. Defeated in that traumatic struggle, many republicans abandoned politics in the context of a monopoly of politics by the establishment, and as the partitionist state grew in the Twenty-six Counties, a reliance upon repeating the Proclamation became less and less adequate as a representation of republicanism. Just as I was trying to come to grips with all this history, the republican leadership was attempting to carve out a new direction and a new relevance for Sinn Féin.

As I became increasingly involved in republican politics, I socialised more with people connected with the movement. Soon Joe Magee, like many of my contemporaries, had left Belfast far behind him. First a friend of ours had joined Marconi and Joe had suggested that he and I should both apply. I didn't bother, but he sent away a form himself. At the same time we both decided that we wanted to go off and dig ditches and build roads for people in underdeveloped countries, and so we applied to Voluntary Service Overseas. Marconi replied first, and off Joe went for courses; before long he had qualified as a radio officer. He was away for months at a time, returning laden with Senior Service cigarettes, which we used to smoke as we walked along the roads. Then he disappeared for good, travelling the world; returning briefly to get married, with me as his best man, he settled later in Australia.

The social life we enjoyed in Belfast in the late 1960s was no different from that enjoyed by our contemporaries in Dublin, Limerick or Cork – with two exceptions. One was the latent sectarianism, now becoming more obvious, and the other was the level of unemployment. For republicans our social lives were becoming increasingly politicised as fund-raising events became more frequently a part of the local scene, and as political activity intensified. Often I found myself going to ballad sessions which had been organised to raise funds. I also started going out with a series of girls and I became very friendly with Joe McCann, and with his wife-to-be, Anne. Joe was just a few years older than I was. He was a tall, bedenimed figure, very fit and strong; a bricklayer by trade, he was a natural radical. Anne, from the strongly republican McKnight family, lived in her family home in the Markets. Later, when Joe was imprisoned, a group of us used to call to Anne, in an effort to ensure that she wasn't too lonely as a 'grass widow'.

When she and Joe got married and had a child, they asked me to be godfather. At the chapel there was a row when the priest refused to christen the child with the Irish version of her name, and this row stimulated Joe's interest in critical perspectives on the church. In particular he became interested in an organisation called Grill, a left-wing religious group which was an offshoot of an English undergraduate left-wing journal called *Slant*, and which sought to make the Christian gospel a radical one. Amongst those who were associated with Grill were John Feeney, a student radical in University College Dublin, Father Austin Flannery and Reverend Terence McCaughey, a Presbyterian. My background was Catholic but not orthodox and I became interested in Grill along with Joe; in retrospect my combination of interest and scepticism owed a lot to the influence of my father.

From the age of seventeen I was playing a fairly central role in the republican activism, such as it was, along with nearly twenty other people of my age. There was little in the way of structure as far as the republican movement was concerned. In addition to the activists and the leadership, there was a wider republican family. A group of leading activists nationally was trying to regroup the republican struggle, but in Belfast republicanism was clandestine, quite factionalised, and very much a part-time occupation.

Sinn Féin was very introverted, cohering as it did around a few spinal republican families; some of these, like both sides of my family, could trace their involvement back as far as the Fenians and the Irish Republican Brotherhood in the last century. In

Belfast, as in the rest of the north-eastern six counties, republicans had been isolated by partition and traumatised by the pogroms which had heralded in the new 'Protestant parliament for a Protestant people'. Despite the undoubted weakness of Sinn Féin and the IRA in the 1930s, '40s and '50s, republicans were interned in numbers by the unionist government in every decade.

Following the failure of the IRA's 1950s campaign on the border, the republican movement was in a considerable state of demoralisation, and in 1961 the total strength of the Belfast IRA was twenty-four, their total armaments consisting of two short-arms. It wasn't that republicanism had died, but it had suffered a substantial defeat. Amongst those few who remained active, a process of reassessment was begun.

Indeed, the '60s were characterised by a turmoil of debate, the deliberate impetus for which came from the national leadership in Dublin. The emphasis had already moved decisively away from the primacy of armed struggle as a means of opposing British imperialism and towards seeking reforms through political action. At the same time, a broader debate than the internal party discussion was also going on, and a meeting point for republicans and socialists, for Irish language enthusiasts, communists and others had been established in 1963 in the form of the Wolfe Tone Societies, which held seminars in Dublin, Cork and Belfast.

Republicans had, in the preceding decades, surrendered the ground of political representation in favour of conspiratorial and military activity. Nationalist opinion in the north was represented by the conservative and ineffectual Nationalist Party, which failed to satisfy the needs of the emerging, better-educated Catholic middle class, a significant section of whom sought social and economic reforms within the Six County state. A rival, more reform-minded National Democratic Party was formed, and the Nationalist Party dropped its abstentionist policy, entering the Stormont parliament to become the official opposition.

Those who sought reform within the Six Counties took succour from Prime Minister O'Neill's apparent willingness to apply to the state a democratic veneer and to meet with the

Dublin taoiseach, Sean Lemass. But a more radical approach was sought by a wide range of anti-unionists, who were beginning to engage in agitational activity in pursuit of civil rights.

In the Wolfe Tone Societies, the question of civil rights had become a recurring theme, and top of a long list of concerns was the disenfranchisement of nationalists by means of the ward-rigging and voting qualifications, which existed to guarantee one-party unionist rule. The restriction of voting rights at local government level to ratepayers and their wives, and the allocation of up to six votes to the directors of limited companies, placed unionists in control of the entire political system. In Derry, for example, 20,000 nationalist votes elected eight city councillors, while 10,000 unionist votes elected twelve. As part of the control of votes, Catholics were denied equal access to housing, and as part of the control of population – and thus of votes – Catholics were denied equal access to employment. When, in 1945, the British parliament at Westminster had introduced universal suffrage, abolishing the restricted franchise for local government, the Stormont government had secured the exclusion of the Six-County statelet from the provisions of the legislation. They also went beyond that by introducing, in 1946, their own Representation of the People Bill, which restricted the franchise even more by taking the vote away from lodgers who were not ratepayers. The thinking behind this legislation was eloquently expressed by Major L. E. Curran, the government Chief Whip: 'The best way to prevent the overthrow of the government by people who had no stake in the country and had not the welfare of the people of Ulster at heart was to disenfranchise them.'

In 1965, republicans attempted to set up 'One man, One vote' committees (in those days our demands were not gender-conscious); the first Republican Club was also set up in Belfast in an attempt to break the ban on Sinn Féin and enable it to engage in fully legal political activity. At a very successful public meeting the veteran republican Liam Mulholland was elected to the Chair of the newly created 'Republican Club'. The state responded by declaring the meeting retrospectively illegal and, a day or two later, banning the Republican Club.

There was an existing ban, too, on our party newspaper, the *United Irishman*. I became involved in a hilarious Keystone Kops incident when it was decided that we would sell it so that we could get arrested and then make a political case out of it in court. A number of people would sell the paper openly on the street; then, as one would be arrested, another would come forward. No one was to resist arrest. I was one of those chosen to sell the newspaper; others who would replace us if we were arrested waited in the street and in a nearby pub. We hadn't been there long when a woman passerby objected. The RUC arrived and went through the legal routine, quoting the relevant law. When I was being arrested, I just sat down and was carted off. People were shouting and clapping as the RUC manhandled me into the back of their jeep. But meanwhile, Malachy, one of the people who was supposed to replace us, came out of the pub, forgot about the plan and, full of indignation, came flying into the middle of this orderly scene of arrest and hit one of the RUC men. Understandably enough, they all jumped on him then. He ended up on his back in his vest, having lost his coat and shirt in the scuffle. The RUC were trying to beat him; they were sitting on him and jumping on him, and I was tempted to beat him as well to make sure!

They dragged us off to Queen Street barracks. Some of our cohorts who had been waiting went to sell the paper again, while the others assembled at the barracks and 'spontaneously' produced their ready-made placards and began picketing the building. After a while, as the RUC men seemed to have lost interest in me, I just walked out of the barracks and joined the picket outside. Malachy was charged with assault, and for months afterwards we held a succession of events to raise the money to pay his fines. But our aim was defeated, as nobody was prosecuted for actually selling the paper.

Sinn Féin was not really an organisation – certainly not in Belfast. Malachy McGurran was the only full-time republican activist in the Six Counties, and maybe in Ulster. Everyone else was involved only in a very part-time capacity. A lot of republicans who had been involved as IRA volunteers had served long terms in prison and found it very hard to make a living. They had served their time as soldiers in the struggle and having done so, although they remained republicans, they usually retired from active involvement.

There was an intermingling of politics and social activity at what was a time of resurgence in Irish music. In Belfast traditional music was a growing phenomenon amongst young and old alike; in addition to small informal sessions, occasional *céilís* were organised in places like the International Hotel. The Ulster Hall became a regular venue for the Clancy Brothers and the Dubliners. When Luke Kelly of the Dubliners was in Belfast, he always turned up after his gig at whatever social event was on, and he was happy to play benefits for Belfast republicans. Billy McBurney ran a pioneering record company in Smithfield Market, recording the McPeakes, Eugene McIldowney, Sean Maguire and others, as well as some Orange bands and some interesting little collectors' pieces of traditional songs.

At home in West Belfast the Felons Club secured the top floor of an old three-storey, white-washed building opposite the Falls Park, which lay beside a small river and was hidden from the road by a dense belt of trees and shrubbery. This proved to be an ideal venue for *céilís* and *scóraíocht*, traditional music sessions and social evenings. My father played a central role in the club, while my mother assisted hugely in its development, and so it assumed a special place in the life of our family. In addition to the usual suspects, the Felons also attracted a younger crowd, and I started going out with a Turf Lodge girl, Theresa Smith, whom I met in the Felons. I also became involved in a film-making project when with a few others I scripted and filmed a short drama set in and around the Felons and in the nearby Milltown cemetery. A macabre mad professor/monster movie, it won great critical acclaim when premiered at a Felons Club session!

We took occasional bus-runs to Tyrella Beach in County

Down: barbecued, drunken, befuddled young republicans heading off on late-night jaunts. One night several of us were waiting in Belfast to catch the bus to Bodenstown early the next morning, sitting up talking and yarning, anticipating the trip ahead. 'Streaking' was much in the news at the time, and for something to do we went down the Falls Road at 7.00 am. Leaving our clothes in a pile at the side of the road, we ran across a pedestrian crossing, down as far as the bus stop, around the bus stop and back up again. In mid-streak we met a nurse going on the early shift. She smiled and continued on her way.

Annual commemorations at Bodenstown and Edentubber were political excursions with a big social content; Edentubber usually climaxed with a concert in Dundalk town hall. These events also reflected the republican attitude to the Twenty-six County state and particularly to the Dublin government. This was not only by way of the keynote speeches – the annual Bodenstown oration was a particularly significant one in the republican calendar – but it was clear also in the songs which we sang afterwards.

> Take it down from the mast, Irish traitors,
> It's the flag we republicans claim;
> It can never belong to Free Staters
> For they've brought on it nothing but shame.

This antagonism was not restricted to northerners; in fact, it was much more marked among many republicans in the south. We northerners may have been abandoned after partition, but we had some romantic view of Dublin; the others did not.

This was clear from one memorable republican demonstration in Dublin in 1966 which commenced at St Stephen's Green and made its way to Glasnevin cemetery. The colour party was attacked by the Gárdaí, who apparently objected to the carrying of a flag said to be that of the Dublin Brigade of the IRA. There was a battle royal for the entire route of the march, with marchers forming an advance guard around the colour party which was relieved in relays by contingents drawn from the crowd. Both the Gárdaí and the advance party arrived in the cemetery bloodied but unbroken. That night at a protest outside the GPO we were treated to fiery oratory and Garda baton charges; Garda cars were overturned. That same year republicans, in a flamboyant symbolic gesture, blew up Dublin's central landmark, Nelson's Pillar, ending the long blind-eyed perusal of the capital by Britain's naval hero.

However, an entirely new relationship between the military and the political aspects of republicanism was developing. When in June 1967, Cathal Goulding, chief-of-staff of the IRA, made a landmark speech at Bodenstown attacking the physical force tradition and favouring socialist policies, I had mixed feelings. Joe McCann and I discussed what Goulding had said, and Joe was quite taken by it. I was aware that Goulding was trying to move the situation on, and recognised that this was the responsibility of leadership. He openly presented himself as the chief-of-staff, and while he was not our hero, he was somebody that we looked up to as the leader of the republican struggle.

In March 1967 students at Queen's University organised a march to Belfast City Hall to protest against the ban on the Republican Clubs. I was on a lunch break with Jimmy McFaul, who worked with me in the Duke of York and who was also a republican activist, and we were looking to buy a tin whistle when we met this demonstration. There was a sit-down so we joined them in that. Unfortunately the Special Branch spotted the republican head and arrested Jimmy. Protesting students were probably not the RUC's favourite people, but for republicans they reserved a deep and intense hostility. As they hauled Jimmy away, I slid out of sight as fast as I could.

Sinn Féin members were active in a number of ways. At one level there were the Republican Clubs, and I became the press officer for the Andersonstown Republican Club, which covered a very large area including Ballymurphy. It met quite often and discussed whatever it was being asked by the Belfast leadership to do. I put out a few press releases on political matters of the day and carried out little letter writing campaigns, usually in the columns of the *Irish News*, in which I used five or six different names. Sometimes I even wrote a letter critical of the last one I had written, just to try to stir up interest in issues.

A core of Sinn Féin activists – Joe McCann, Sean and Francie McGuigan, Jimmy McFaul, Anthony Doran, a few others and I – set up an Unemployment Action Group in West Belfast, and a Housing Action Committee. These two campaigns were spontaneously organised and possessed lives of their own. Our activism was feeding into a general sense of political movement below the surface; we were few in number, but we were to some extent in tune with the needs and demands of the time. Our Republican Club operated quite separately from these campaigns and was much more formal in the way it worked within its area, meeting in one or another member's home once a week or once a fortnight.

People mobilised around our campaigns and activities for two main reasons – firstly in their own self-interest and secondly when caught by an idea. Republicans constituted a small group of people who had been caught by an idea, but it was not being transmitted to a lot of other people, at least not in a way which related to them. But when republicans got involved in local activity, to campaign for better housing or to organise some sort of structure within the community, it was they who almost naturally took leadership positions. While this low-key activism was being carried out by individuals, the battle for ideas was being fought out on TV screens, and people were moved by ideas then. The old men of the unionist establishment were being confronted by lively, articulate spokespersons from People's Democracy and from the Civil Rights Association.

When I was approached by the Sherlock family, who were living in Mary Street, a small street of two-bedroomed houses which were in very bad condition, we went to the Housing Trust to try to get them rehoused. Talking yielded no results, so we decided to embark on more direct action. We took over a flat in the Divis Flats complex, which was just beginning to open. In Derry and in Caledon similar squats had already taken place, but the Sherlock case was the first in Belfast. We brought press photographers and showed them that people were living in

83

absolute hovels. None of the houses had hot water, none of them had inside toilets, many didn't have proper kitchens, only water taps out in the yard, or in a small hallway into the yard. The places were damp, infested with rats and mice; there were problems with sewage. We had gone through all the arguments about how these people should be rehoused in proper homes, and when that didn't happen, we squatted them, having witnessed the success of this as a tactic used by Bridget Bond, a remarkable woman who led the housing protests in Derry. It was on the second day of the Sherlock occupation that we formed the West Belfast Housing Action Committee, which generated support and further agitation. Our experience, and our success in getting the family properly rehoused after the squat, gave us a major boost: it proved to us that direct action could work and that it could gain great popular support locally. Now we embarked on a campaign of picketing and occupations, and very soon other people were coming to us looking for help. We began to organise more coherently, with much more support, and the residents of the Loney district marched against the tower blocks and in favour of the rebuilding of their own traditional houses.

On the Springfield Road a child from New Barnsley, a neighbouring Protestant housing estate, was knocked down at the junction with the Whiterock Road. I went to see Frank Cahill of the Ballymurphy Tenants Association, who looked at me with a little twinkle in his eye because he had been working on this kind of issue for years, and here was I, a wet-behind-the-ears political activist, thinking I could sort it out, but he and I got on very well. I called to the parents in New Barnsley, and the upshot was that we in the Republican Club combined with people from New Barnsley to mount a successful series of protests, demanding and getting safety rails at the corner and a pedestrian crossing near by. We were delighted. Not only was it a gain, albeit small, but it was an example of Catholics and Protestants coming together. But when news of this joint campaign reached the unionist establishment, one of Paisley's people arrived on the scene. For the first time in my life I heard serious talk about 'papists' and 'pope-heads', 'fenians' and 'taigs'; the Protestants in New Barnsley ended their involvement with us there and then.

In January 1967 I took part in a meeting which decided to establish the Northern Ireland Civil Rights Association (NICRA). A month later at a meeting in the International Hotel the first executive of NICRA was elected; my fellow young republicans and I were frankly bored by the ponderous proceedings, but at least a balanced leadership for the parent civil rights organisation was elected. After years of patient, consistent work by a few committed individuals such as the McCloskeys of the Campaign for Social Justice, a new era yawned itself into existence, but none of us, I think, had any idea of the momentousness of what we had inaugurated that night.

I was not long involved in political activism when I had my first brush with the RUC Special Branch. Late in 1966 a group of IRA volunteers had gone into St Gabriel's school and, using hurling sticks, had broken up a British army recruiting class. A few months later somebody wrote 'Join the IRA' on a British Army recruiting sign and there were actions against British army recruiting offices, in which some small amount of damage was done. The Special Branch called to the Duke of York in the wake of one of those attacks and asked me where I had been on the night; I protested about them coming in during my working hours.

After this Special Branch visit, I was walking up Royal Avenue with Jimmy McFaul, carrying home two paper bags filled up with beef dripping from the pub, when we were stopped by Harry Taylor, the most notorious Branchman in Belfast at that time. He took one of our suspicious packages and plunged his hand in. There was an outer shell of hard lard which hadn't set properly, but the inside was all gooey. We went merrily on our way, leaving him helplessly shaking the dripping from his hands.

In 1967 I was involved in organising a summer camp south of the border in Drumshanbo, County Leitrim, for about twenty young republican lads. This was an open camp in best scouting tradition, and it was an outstanding success, a great social event in the parish, which warmed to the presence of all these young people from the north. Our campsite on the banks of Lough Allen boasted a large bell-tent and a couple of pup tents. We were blessed with good weather, and each day after doing all the camp's chores, we went off on walks, developing field craft. At the Tostal fair our lads played their part: one was a first-class Irish dancer, so he got up and did his steps, and then a couple got up and sang. On Sunday the priest invited us into the chapel to provide a guard of honour, and we felt honoured to be asked to perform in a ceremonial capacity. On our last night in Drumshanbo some sixty or seventy people came from the village to an open night we held, with races and a sing-song about the camp fire, on which we roasted large numbers of potatoes. I was disappointed when I was unable to go the following year.

For me there is a special poignancy about those Leitrim days. Of the lads who took part in that camp, Jimmy Quigley was shot at the age of eighteen by a British army sniper in the lower Falls. Jimmy was going across a roof and he was armed when the Brits shot him. Dee Delaney died at the age of twenty-six in a premature bomb explosion which also killed two civilians in January 1980. Geraldo McAuley, who took part in the camp the following year, was killed in Belfast in August 1969 at the age of fifteen, trying to defend people from loyalist attacks.

After the summer camp I went back a few times to Leitrim, where I had formed a firm friendship with John Joe McGirl, a county councillor who was twice my age or even more, and who lived in Ballinamore. I would take the bus as far as Newry or Enniskillen, and then I was away, free of the workaday world. On these trips I used a greatcoat an ex-peeler who used to come in to the Duke of York had left behind him. I rolled my sleeping bag in the coat in a fairly light backpack and then if I had to sleep out I used the coat as both a ground-sheet and an over-sheet.

On one of my visits to Leitrim, John Joe brought me to a strike meeting at Arigna mines. This was the stuff of political romanticism for me: to be witness to a strike and John Joe in the middle of all these coal miners in a room full of smoke, sitting around talking about what they were going to do.

He also brought me up Slieve Anierin, a mountain outside Drumshanbo at the banks of Lough Allen. We went up as far as the car could go and then we walked until we met a man who lived on the mountain on his own. What struck me as really remarkable was that he had lived about thirty years of his life in New York. I couldn't understand, the contrast seemed so enormous, and I asked him about it.

'I never wanted to leave here,' he said, 'all the time I was away.'

I got to know Leitrim very well, walking most of the area around Ballinamore, and found it to be a beautiful part of Ireland. I began to appreciate a little of what the man on the mountain had meant. John Joe loved his native area and, wishing to see its potential developed, he argued even then for the development of the Ballinamore–Ballyconnel canal link (a north–south waterway eventually re-opened in 1995). On this as on many other issues, he was far ahead of his time.

I started to venture to Dublin, where the music scene was very alive in pubs like Donoghue's and Slattery's, and to *fleadh cheoil*, the annual regional and national festivals of traditional music. At the All-Ireland Fleadh at Clones in '68 I met Ted Furey again, and he ended up in our tent at eight o'clock one mornin .. Sean Maguire had the number one hit in the charts with 'The Mason's Apron', and here was Ted, crouching down with a bottle of stout in his hand, saying, 'It's easy to play the fast ones, it's the slow ones that need the skill'! He turned up in Belfast quite a few times, and his duffle coat hung in our coal shed in the Murph for ages after he left it behind him.

Occasionally he played a black wooden instrument which, where a fiddle is rounded, was square. It was inlaid with pieces of white pearly material, and there was a fixture which allowed a horn to come out of it. He played a fiddle normally, but for a period he produced this strange item. Somebody once asked him where he had got it.

'This instrument,' he said, 'belonged to a friend of mine. He

87

was living with his mother and was happy working on the farm until he got this great love for music and he started to play the fiddle. The more he played the fiddle, the less time he spent on the farm. Then he fell in with women. Then he fell in with the drink. His mother fell ill and she sent for her son who was away carousing. She was dying and she made him promise that he'd never play the fiddle again, and he swore on her deathbed that he wouldn't. So when she died he went back to the farm and he straightened himself out and he got back into his old, industrious ways. But he was banjaxed, he couldn't settle. He would hear about a good session and he would be just dying to go. So he went away to the woods and, knowing that he couldn't play the fiddle because he had sworn that he wouldn't, he made this instrument. And it was from him I got it.'

In Belfast much of the campaigning I was involved in centred around Divis Flats, which were opened in May 1968. In a statement read at masses in St Peter's, Bishop Philbin declared that Catholics must recognise the new flats as representing a 'heart transplant'. 'Other people are going to judge us and our worth as people – indeed the worth of our religion – by the way we deal with these new sites.' Bishop Philbin, however, was not going to have to live in them. Nor were the architects or planners who had hailed such high-rise buildings as offering an opportunity for a new community to develop around 'a natural meeting place for both adults and children'; the new structures offered 'variety and pragmatism, freer organisation and building form'; they would facilitate the remoulding of society by providing people with 'a bird's eye view' on life, thereby sponsoring 'a new and more meaningful social relationship between communities'.

The reality was something quite different. Disillusionment and despair soon set in amongst those who did start living there. Adding to the physical problems posed by the flats was the fact that far from, in Bishop Philbin's phrase, representing a 'heart transplant', this slum clearance and redevelopment programme had ripped the heart out of the community, for the redevelopment, alienating enough as it was in itself, had occurred at a time

88

of massive economic decline in the area. The people for whom the decaying and neglected nineteenth-century housing had been home had worked in the nearby mills and factories. Now these mills and factories had already closed or would in the next few years, leaving an industrial wasteland and almost no alternative employment. Small businesses and workshops which had relied upon the large mills and factories also closed.

The situation was appalling. More than that, there had been no consultation at all with local people. Our campaign built up a head of steam and we found that we were getting a few hundred people to demonstrations, which we were holding regularly, at times even on a daily basis. Involved in squats and demonstrations, I was caught up in an intense focus of activity and most nights I didn't get home. Things had to be worked out, and I found myself involved with the others in the small essential details of community activism: shifts and rotas for cooking, for making placards, for getting a newsletter out, getting hold of a Gestetner . . .

While we were responding to the specific circumstances we encountered in West Belfast, agitation such as ours was also going on in Derry and in Dublin, and in London and further afield as well. Governments and local authorities were seeking to impose building and development plans arrived at without democratic consultation and having as their main concern the creation of the largest number of housing units at the lowest cost. The people who were to live in these high-rise buildings were treated by governments as their subjects, on whose behalf decisions would be taken, rather than as people who possessed the right to be involved in decisions which affected so fundamentally the quality of their own lives.

Squatting and other agitation over housing were common in Britain, Ireland and elsewhere in Europe, but the state's response had a particular character in the Six Counties, where sectarianism was institutionalised and given special powers. If the state was a Protestant state for a Protestant people, the RUC was also a Protestant force for a Protestant state, and the police reacted hysterically to our agitation. The few main activists involved were served with a total of about sixty summonses; at the time we laughed about it, but I began to wonder about the reasons that might lie behind such a gross over-reaction. RUC Land Rovers began patrolling the Loney area, where the Divis Flats stood.

The civil rights movement was building up, and when I attended debates I heard people give well-documented accounts of discrimination, and I began to develop and clarify my views of the political situation. Catholics were being denied houses as a means of denying us votes; in Derry gerrymandering was exercised in a most blatant fashion to maintain one-party control. I began to realise that sectarianism was not so much a matter of blind hatred of Catholics as something which was tactically essential to unionist rule.

The Northern Ireland Civil Rights Association had begun in 1967 in a low-key manner by offering citizens advice. The first time I spoke in front of a large audience was at a meeting in St Mary's Hall to set up a West Belfast Civil Rights Association. My knee was knocking off the seats, I was so nervous, and I made an appalling speech. Despite my juvenile effort I was elected to the executive, but it didn't do very much, and proposals for a Belfast civil rights march were turned down by the executive of NICRA.

Increasingly the demands of my political work were competing with my employment. While the long mid-day breaks and the free day mid-week were a great help, the demands of working in the Duke's at night and on Saturdays were frustrating. I revelled in the free time, and in all my time in the Duke's I never worked overtime. As the political pace increased I went to work only to get out again. I contemplated seeking a more independent occupation but I was cautious enough not to sign off at the Duke's until I spent a few of my days off testing the water. So I joined a trio of like-minded revolutionaries in a window-cleaning initiative, and bucket and chamois in hand, I shouldered a ladder around the Falls. However, we soon found that the established window cleaners had it all sussed out, with loyal regular customers. Our enterprise collapsed as, faced with a choice of cleaning windows for a living or changing the world, we took the easy option.

Our political campaigns in West Belfast were part of a bigger picture, and in the spring of 1968 NICRA held protest rallies in Newry and Armagh, after the banning of a parade to commemorate the 1916 Rising. NICRA's first march took place in August 1968, from Coalisland to Dungannon. The civil rights struggle had begun, and a broad-based, if uneasy and sporadic alliance had been forged between all the anti-unionist elements in the Six Counties.

The organisers of a march scheduled for Derry on 5 October sought sponsorship from NICRA who refused until, very reluctantly and belatedly, they decided to endorse it. When the Stormont government banned the demonstration, the scene was set for confrontation.

Realising that trouble was likely, the republicans decided at a meeting which I attended in South Derry that any leading nationalist politicians, visiting MPs or other dignitaries should be kept at the head of the parade, so that if the police lashed out they would connect with newsworthy skulls. The first busted head, as a result, belonged to an MP, but in the ensuing clash the RUC spared no one.

Having been unable to get yet another day off work to take part in the march myself, I watched the television coverage of the RUC's smashing into the demonstrators. The pictures exposed the fascist nature of unionist rule and drew international attention to its denial of elementary democratic rights. Although the initial march had only been a few hundred strong, a protest march against RUC brutality drew 15,000 people the following week. NICRA now stated its demands clearly: universal franchise in local elections, an end to gerrymandered boundaries, the repeal of the Special Powers Act, an end to housing discrimination, disbandment of the B Specials and the withdrawal of the Public Order Bill which the unionists were pushing through Stormont to outlaw civil rights demonstrations.

The NICRA leadership was always cautious, but the initiative lay not with it but on the streets. In Derry, Tyrone and Belfast, it was largely autonomous local civil rights committees which now set the pace, aided in no small measure by the reaction of unionist bully-boys, including the RUC. After 5 October 1968 a gradualist tendency emerged, made up of a strange alliance of some of the more middle-class nationalists, some of the old guard NICRA leadership and the republican leadership, but others – rank-and-file republicans, the very energetic student-based People's Democracy and the vast majority of civil rights supporters – formed a more combative tendency which sought to expose the contradictions of the state.

In November, Terence O'Neill announced a five-point reform programme, but it was too little too late. In early December he made a television broadcast in which he declared that 'Ulster stands at the crossroads', and he appealed for an end to civil disorder and agitation, and support for his reform package. NICRA responded by calling for a period of 'truce', without marches or demonstrations, but People's Democracy announced that they were pressing ahead with the civil rights campaign and would march from Belfast to Derry, setting out on New Year's Day 1969. I joined the start of the march at Belfast City Hall and walked with it for a short distance before going on to a busy day's work at the Duke's. On 4 January, after trekking across the north in a series of RUC reroutings, the march reached Burntollet bridge about eight miles from Derry. Now the RUC led the civil rights campaigners into an ambush where they were attacked with bricks, batons and boots by the B Specials.

The civil rights movement sought elementary rights which were taken for granted in Britain and western Europe. The movement had not demanded the abolition of the state, nor a united Ireland, but the reaction of unionism, supported by British intervention, brought the constitutional question to the fore, and the existence of the Six County state into question. At any time the state could have undermined the civil rights agitation by conceding these normal democratic demands; but movement came too late. Whatever civil rights reforms were granted were only granted after the situation had already exploded.

When our housing campaign first started, we had taken our demands directly to the Housing Trust; we did so almost always in support of families directly disadvantaged by Housing Trust policy. This had only a limited effect, so a few people had volunteered to leaflet the area, seeking help from others in a similar plight, and soon this became standard practice. We began to picket the Housing Trust or leaflet outside it. Sometimes, when we were lucky enough to get the loan of a car to tour the streets of the Falls, one of us would shout himself hoarse on a loudspeaker. Publicity work was generally limited to the *Irish News*: only occasionally did the local Sunday newspapers bother with our campaign, while the TV channels generally ignored us. The direct actions brought about by our squatting protests changed a lot of this.

As our campaigning continued into the spring and summer of 1969, events were taking on a new character, and I felt that we were entering extraordinarily dangerous territory. Our first demonstrations over Divis Flats and other housing issues had been quiet, peaceable and good humoured, but as the crowds grew bigger at demonstrations, the RUC were becoming more vicious. Now they were out on the streets before us; they knew we were coming and they were looking for us. We experienced a sense of excitement, of tweaking the lion's tail as a regular pattern of riotous confrontations developed. But the skirmishes with the RUC, whose ferocity was a revelation, were becoming more frequent, and we few republican activists had been identified by this stage as the leading local agitators. As we ran like hell from baton charges, we found ourselves looking over our shoulders and seeing our attackers passing other protesters and heading for us.

Throughout the summer the Divis Street protests became nightly riots as we were baton-charged by the RUC. We were, I was convinced, moving rapidly towards catastrophe, and I was absolutely frustrated that the leadership of the republican movement did not appear to understand what was happening. I found myself having numerous arguments with Liam McMillen. Riot situations were beginning to develop in Ardoyne and Unity Flats, but neither the Belfast nor Dublin leaderships were able to understand what was happening, let alone to give proper direction. All over the Six Counties, tensions were rising. The RUC, the B Specials and loyalist counter-demonstrators were clashing frequently with Catholic civilians. As loyalists mobilised to attack civil rights marches, and as they launched pogroms to burn Catholics out of their homes, publication of sectarian songs and stories, old and new, flourished. Songs with lyrics such as:

> If guns were made for shooting,
> Then skulls were made to crack.
> You've never seen a better Taig
> Than with a bullet in his back.

Earlier in the year, civil rights and People's Democracy candidates had registered impressive votes in Stormont elections, and in a by-election in April Bernadette Devlin caused a sensation when she was elected to the British parliament at Westminster. In the same month the RUC launched an assault on the Bogside in Derry, beating a man in his own home who died of a heart attack as a result, and a series of loyalist bombings, carried out by the UVF but blamed on the IRA, succeeded in their aim of bringing down Prime Minister Terence O'Neill. In May loyalists founded the Shankill Defence Association.

Sinn Féin's Ruairí Ó Bradaigh warned that it was the 'height of irresponsibility and madness to have the pressure continue from the civil rights movement, knowing where it was going to lead and being unable then to meet the logical consequences'. Cathal Goulding replied that it was up to the RUC and the British army to defend people, while Liam McMillen reported that the IRA only had enough arms for one operation, nothing like enough to be able to mount any kind of defence of nationalist areas. Leading members of the Belfast IRA went to Dublin to ask the army council of the IRA for a large supply of arms, but were turned down. When a defence committee was set up in Ardoyne, I and other activists from outside the area went there regularly in solidarity with local activists. In June, Frank Gogarty, chairman of NICRA, asked Goulding if the IRA could provide protection, but the general and overriding concern in republican leadership circles in Dublin was with programmatic documents, not with defence, though Goulding and perhaps other republican leaders did meet with Fianna Fáil TDs in Dublin to discuss the northern situation.

In July, an Orange parade clashed with nationalists in Derry, and in three days of renewed attacks on the Bogside by the RUC, two civilians were shot and wounded. In the course of two days of riots in Dungiven, a Catholic man was killed in an RUC baton charge, the Orange Hall was burnt down and B Specials fired shots over the head of Catholics coming out of a dance. On 26 July, a PD march in Fermanagh was banned and thirty-seven PD supporters were arrested.

I was gripped by contradictory feelings, including a sense of freedom, a youthful, mistaken conviction that the revolution was happening all around us and that the world was beginning to respond. There was a sense of naïveté, of innocence almost, a feeling that the demands we were making were so reasonable that all we had to do was kick up a row and the establishment would give in. This expectation, and the subsequent sense of outrage, was almost entirely restricted, at first anyway, to those of my generation; expectations amongst the older people were much lower, and in retrospect I can understand why this was so. The British statelet could not concede 'one man, one vote', or any principle of equality; it could only be sustained on the basis of inequality. That was what kept unionists in their positions as top dogs; they knew that if change came and inequality was ended they would no longer even have reason to be unionists. The slogans of the regime, 'Not an inch' and 'No surrender', must at all costs prevail.

The older people in nationalist areas had been through all this before, and they knew what we were going to bring down upon ourselves and upon them. As the situation began to build up once again, it must have felt to many of them that we were going for a rematch in a deadly fight which they had always lost. Even if anyone had articulated any of this, it probably would not have changed my attitude. But no one did, though one old barman said to me, 'Forget about asking them for civil rights. Take their money off them instead.' And a year or so later, with a fatalism which perplexed me, another man said, 'Forget about trying to change things: it will all be the same in a thousand years.' In many ways our ignorance, our higher expectations and our lack of experience, combined with the sheer exuberance of youth, made everything seem possible, and with the arrogance of youth I felt that a tide was flowing which would sweep away the old conditions that had constrained our lives. It wasn't just a matter of what was happening in Belfast, or even in the north, or even in Ireland. The songs that moved me were anthems of freedom, clarion calls of a new generation. When Dylan sang that 'The Times They Are A-Changin' ', it wasn't just a song, but the confirmation of a strongly felt reality, a feeling shared across countries, continents and religions.

The Duke of York was quite close to Unity Flats, and I went there frequently during lunch breaks to assist the small group of local activists. I spent less and less time in the Duke of York, more and more in Divis or other centres of activity. The core of activists with which I was associated worked day and night. As the summer sped by we became increasingly concerned and at the same time exhilarated by the developing situation. One thing was becoming clear: as the nationalists were getting up off their knees, the need to defend them from increasingly violent loyalist and RUC attacks would not be long in following. By July we were actively involved in trying to get people in Ardoyne and Unity Flats organised to defend themselves during the Orange parades. Someone had to do it. The republican leadership was in no way prepared for any sort of military defence, never mind an offensive. It was, instead, engaged in political semantics.

It was a heady and a confusing time. On one occasion I was speaking at a rally in Divis Street when a fellow activist from

Derry, who was more experienced than I was, insisted that if I didn't tone down my approach I would end up being arrested for incitement. By contrast, sometime afterwards we had an enormous crowd at a demonstration and a guy from PD was trying to persuade me that we should take the crowd into the city centre and destroy all the shops. We got up on the wall to address the crowd, and as this speaker was starting to utter his exhortations, I saw the RUC across the car park, and I gently nudged him off the wall. Some of our people sat on him until we completed our demonstration and dispersed the crowd.

At around the same time, when we went to hand in a letter of protest at Hastings Street barracks, the RUC wouldn't let us in, but after some of the people in the crowd got a telegraph pole and rammed the door of the barracks, they agreed to meet our delegation. A small victory in a way, but a big victory for us. The RUC inflicted quite vicious baton charges on us at the time, but these things weren't being reported.

In early August there were days of heavy rioting in Ardoyne and at Unity Flats. On 2 August the Shankill Defence Association, aided and abetted by the RUC, launched attacks on Unity Flats after an Orange march. Patrick Corry, a Catholic, was beaten to death in an RUC barracks. Catholic families were intimidated out of the Crumlin Road area by loyalist gangs. Loyalists rioted through several nights in the Shankill Road, and Stormont sources stated that the introduction of martial law in Belfast was 'a distinct possibility'. On three successive days in the first week of August, Catholic families were hounded from their homes by loyalist threats that they would be burnt out. Our Housing Action Committee had its hands full as we squatted the refugees in Housing Trust property.

The pressure cooker was about to blow. In Derry, a Citizens' Defence Association had been established at the end of July by republicans in preparation for expected attacks by the RUC and loyalists during the annual loyalist parade on 12 August. News of the onslaught on Unity Flats made them redouble their preparations as they stored materials ready for the building of barricades.

On 8 August, Prime Minister Chichester-Clark, his home affairs minister and James Callaghan, the British prime minister, met in London to discuss the situation. British troops were put on standby in Derry and Belfast in support of the unionist regime. The intensely provocative loyalist march was going ahead in Derry, and confrontation was inevitable.

On the eve of the march I was interviewed for the first time for television, about the squatting in Divis Flats; then I headed down to work at the Duke of York. I didn't know what the next days would bring, but I was convinced that we were headed for a disaster, and that none of those who had the power to avert it were at all likely to do so.

Five

On 12 August the Orange parade went ahead in Derry. At the edge of the Bogside, young nationalists clashed with loyalists, and the RUC launched baton charges. They found the Bogsiders well prepared with barricades and petrol bombs. Fighting side by side with the loyalists, the RUC brought up armoured cars and, for the first time in Ireland, CS gas. For forty-eight hours the mainly teenage defenders of the Bogside used stones, bottles and petrol bombs against the constant baton charges of hundreds of RUC and loyalists. Exploiting high rise flats with great effect, they lobbed petrol bombs at their attackers and succeeded in keeping them at bay. Residents placed bowls of water and vinegar at their doorsteps as an improvised remedy against the worst effects of CS gas. Local doctors and nurses and the Knights of Malta set up first aid stations; some people made sandwiches and tea, while others made petrol bombs. Bernadette Devlin, seemingly immune to CS gas, was in the thick of the fighting, an inspiration to the young people of the area.

Through the second day 700 RUC men backed by loyalist mobs tried to force their way into the Bogside as CS gas continued to be poured into the network of nationalist streets with their tightly packed rows of Victorian terraced houses. The siege continued all day and all night. A NICRA delegation met John

Taylor, junior minister for home affairs, to ask him to call off the siege; the government refused.

At the height of the battle of the Bogside, I attended an emergency meeting of NICRA in the Wellington Park Hotel in Belfast, at which Frank Gogarty, chairperson of NICRA, played a passionate tape-recorded appeal by Sean Keenan of the Derry Citizens' Defence Association for demonstrations throughout the Six Counties to stretch the RUC and relieve the pressure on Derry. Earlier the NICRA leadership and People's Democracy had called for such demonstrations, and many protests had already been held in towns throughout the north, including Strabane, Coalisland and Newry. The Wellington Park Hotel meeting debated proposals for more actions of this kind throughout the north. After brief and hurried consultations among the Belfast activists in attendance, I proposed that a Belfast demonstration be organised by the West Belfast Housing Action Committee, saying that our committee existed to try to get housing for people in this city and to help the homeless, and we saw a direct link between our own area of action and that of those made homeless in Derry by the actions of the RUC and the B Specials. The mood of the meeting was highly charged, and we left it with a sense of determination that the nationalist people of Derry needed and were going to get our help. A group of us went directly from the hotel to the Falls to mobilise for our demonstration. The area was already tense as we prepared for that evening's meeting. We were conscious that if we organised effectively in Belfast we could create a situation which would stretch the resources of the RUC sufficiently to compel them to lift the assault on the Bogside.

The Dublin government was in session all day, trying to come to terms with the developments, especially in Derry, right on the border. There had been widespread popular support in the south for the civil rights movement, and there was dismay and anger at the decision to allow the Apprentice Boys' march to go ahead. Now, with the Bogside under attack from the forces of the northern state, people were asking what the southern government would do to defend the people of the Bogside. Three cabinet ministers proposed that the Irish army cross the border and seize Derry, Newry and other areas of majority Catholic population.

That night Taoiseach Jack Lynch went on television to announce that 'the Irish government can no longer stand by and see innocent people injured and perhaps worse'. The Irish army would be moved up to the border to establish field hospitals, and he called for the introduction of a UN peacekeeping force and for negotiations, 'recognising that the re-unification of the national territory can provide the only permanent solution for the problem'.

It is difficult to encapsulate exactly what we expected from the Dublin government. Republicans were fairly sceptical, but yet there was a wider sense that the bubble was bursting and that everything was about to change. What is certain is that 5 October was a watershed. In the months since then, the sense of defiance had stiffened and deepened among Catholics in the north. Now we were demanding our rights and our demands were also being directed towards Dublin.

At around the time of Lynch's broadcast, I was chairing a protest meeting at the Divis Flats. By now these protests had a certain momentum which had been created by over a year's campaigning; the bigger events of the general civil rights campaign had so moved people, while our campaigning organisation had become so efficient, that we were able to mobilise speedily a sizeable demonstration at very short notice in support of the people of the Bogside.

As we assembled in front of Divis Flats our mood was one of anger; there was a real sense that enough was enough. The core of the marchers were young people who generally fought the RUC when there was any fighting, but the demonstration included people of all ages. The chant was of 'SS/RUC', the songs were 'We're on Our Way to Freedom' and 'We Shall Overcome'. Some people brought their own placards with handdrawn slogans reading: 'RUC Out' and 'The people of the Falls support the people of Derry'.

The marchers set off for the RUC barracks at Springfield Road and Hastings Street. The RUC attacked the march, and there was heavy rioting in the Divis Street area. After a number of baton charges, the RUC withdrew into Hastings Street barracks, and the demonstrators withdrew into the Falls area, erecting barricades in their wake. Within a square mile zone of Hastings Street barracks, the protesting crowds had the run of the district.

Similar confrontations were happening throughout the north. In Dungiven a crowd of several hundred people attacked the RUC barracks with petrol bombs and stones, and the RUC opened fire on the crowd. In the course of riots in Dungannon, an attempt was made to burn the courthouse, the RUC barracks were attacked and a man was shot and wounded. In Belfast on the Crumlin Road and at Unity Flats, Catholics came under attack by the RUC and loyalist mobs.

Demonstrators tried to draw the RUC from Hastings Street into the network of narrow streets, but they refused to oblige. Young people lit barricades on the Falls Road and in Divis Street. Piles of wood, cardboard and wooden boxes, rubbish and old furniture had been collected earlier for the traditional 15 August bonfires, and these were now used to keep the barricades blazing, and flames and clouds of smoke rose high into the sky. Large crowds, mostly of young people, roamed the front of the road, but again the RUC refused to engage. They were obviously under pressure.

So we went to protest a second time in the early hours of the morning at Springfield Road barracks, which stood in a side street and could be approached from several different directions. If the RUC would not come to us, then we would go to them. All of the street fighting was conducted by young people armed only with stones, bottles and petrol bombs. Earlier in the evening when our demonstration started, the IRA had put a number of armed volunteers out on the street, perhaps only four or five. I thought it was madness, and I said so to the guy in charge.

'If there's anybody going to attack the crowd,' he said, 'we have to defend them.'

'You're only going to get people killed,' I said. 'Because how are you going to know? I mean, where are you? How are you going to know between yourselves whether it's you firing or whether it's someone else?'

'You're going to have to see some of the Batt staff,' he said. 'I couldn't pull back without clearance.'

'Would you do me a favour?' I asked. 'I'll go and see about it, if you can pull the people off.'

He agreed, and I went down and saw Jimmy Sullivan and argued very strongly that to bring guns out was crazy. Were the volunteers experienced? They couldn't be. Nobody was experienced, certainly in these sort of circumstances.

In the event it was the RUC who opened fire first, when at least one RUC officer fired from the roof of the Springfield Road barracks. As the shots rang out the crowd scattered in all directions. Our Paddy was one of a number who sought refuge in the grounds of the Royal Hospital. Meanwhile a whole squad of young people went and opened a garage in Panton Street, took out a few gallons of petrol, then locked the garage again and sallied forth for another attack on Springfield Road barracks.

In the early hours of the morning, barricades were still blazing, as were some buildings on the front of the Falls Road. Dense smoke rose into the air. We were all exhausted. News was beginning to filter in of the disturbances elsewhere and of the continuing battle of the Bogside. As dawn broke the RUC finally emerged in armoured vehicles; we were robbed of the cover of darkness, they had the security of daylight. As the armoured cars trundled towards us, we slipped away. I went off to snatch some sleep.

I went into work on the morning of the 14th, but at 11.30 a.m. someone came into the bar for me, saying, 'You're wanted. You should pack in work. The wee man's looking for you.' The 'wee man' was Billy McMillen. I packed as many empty Guinness bottles as I could into a couple of brown paper bags. I went in to see Jimmy Keaveney and told him that I had to go.

'There's a job here for you when you're finished,' he said. And with that I bade him and the Duke of York farewell.

I went straight from work to Leeson Street, where Billy McMillen and Jimmy Sullivan were in the process of mobilising republicans from all over Belfast and attempting to put in place some defensive arrangements for nationalist areas. Sinn Féin people, IRA volunteers, older, 'retired' republicans, former prisoners and local community activists called to offer their services and their advice on what should be done. The battle of the Bogside was still raging. Everywhere there were arguments for direct action by the IRA; after all, it had been the role of the IRA in previous decades to mount an armed defence of nationalist areas when these came under attack. I disagreed, feeling that any attempt to militarise the situation, to bring the IRA into it and to engage the RUC on their own terms would take it out of the hands of the people and bring the entire situation down to a gunfight, which the RUC would surely win. Anyway the discussion was to some degree academic, since the Belfast IRA had scarcely any weapons. I learned that for the previous few days there had been attempts to assemble what armaments they had, and some people had even gone off in a vain effort to make an old explosive mix called Paxo, a hangover from the 1950s campaign.

According to local news reports and to the local newspapers, the RUC were stretched to breaking point. The situation in the Falls was certainly very tense. Jack Lynch's television and radio broadcast had received tremendous publicity. Field hospitals were being established in County Donegal, close to Derry, and the unionist prime minister, Chichester-Clark, had reacted angrily to Mr Lynch's speech. The Dublin government had also instructed its ambassador at the United Nations to inform Secretary General U Thant of its view that an international force should be brought into the north to maintain order. The government, however, had stopped short of asking the security council to deal with the proposal. All of this, and the continuing reports of fighting from Derry, contributed to a situation of the most intense crisis, which was felt by all.

During the course of that day, there were reports of increasing tension in different parts of the city bordering on loyalist areas, in particular Ardoyne. Radio news reports of the continuing battle of the Bogside were being broadcast regularly, and as the evening settled uneasily over the Falls, there were reports that the RUC were going to be withdrawn from the Bogside. Rumour had it that the Falls area itself would be invaded. By late afternoon the general mobilisation of Belfast republicans was complete. By now there was talk of the Irish army being rushed across the border into Newry and Derry, and there were also reports that hostile crowds were gathering in the Shankill area and on the Crumlin Road.

The meagre force of republican activists was dispatched to various parts of the city in the hope that despite the lack of arms they might be able to organise some kind of defence. Some were sent to Hooker Street and Ardoyne, some to Unity Flats, others to Springhill, which was close to the Ballymurphy area and to the large loyalist area of Highfield, Springmartin and West Circular. I was one of those sent here. Our Paddy and I and a few others were joined by some local men and later on by a local priest, Father Des Wilson. We actually had a very peaceful time ourselves. There was only one incident. The night sky above Divismore Park was suddenly lit up as a petrol bomb exploded on the Springfield Road.

'It's the Henry Taggart,' someone exclaimed.

From Springhill we could see the roof of the Taggart aflame for a few seconds. I dashed off towards the river to the scene of the attack. As I ran across the wee bridge, a young man of about my own age came crashing from the entry headlong into my arms. We waltzed around with each other for a dizzying instant in the middle of the bridge before separating.

'Where were you?' I challenged him.

'Get away or I'll throw this!' He held up a petrol bomb. The smell of it was everywhere.

'Put it down,' I commanded him.

'Aye,' he said, throwing it at me before dashing off again. I never did find out who he was. By now the sound of shooting could be heard clearly from down the road. When I rejoined my compatriots and we nervously patrolled Springhill Avenue, we could hear the noise of conflict and see flames rising from the Falls area. Eventually, it became too much. I left Springhill to the group of local men who had come out to assist us and I made my way down into the Falls area.

Here the situation was one of bedlam. A loyalist mob, including many members of the B Specials, armed with rifles, revolvers and sub-machine guns had gathered on the Shankill Road and moved along the streets leading to the Falls. They petrol bombed Catholic houses in the streets that lay on their route, beating up their occupants and shooting at fleeing residents. This loyalist mob invaded the Falls, and as it reached the Falls Road itself, it started to attack St Comgall's school. A lone IRA volunteer opened fire and a loyalist gunman was killed.

Now the RUC, coming in behind the loyalist civilians and B Specials, opened up with heavy calibre Browning machine-guns from Shorland armoured cars. They directed their firing into the nationalist area, into narrow streets and into Divis Flats itself, where they killed a nine-year-old boy and a young local man, home on leave from the British army. Meanwhile, snipers fired into the area from the tops of the mills.

Within a remarkably short space of time, the streets off the Falls Road, and the Falls itself, had been turned into a war zone. And in this war the Catholic residents of the area were almost entirely bereft of the means of self-defence. Throughout the night, the RUC roared up and down in their Shorlands. The RUC had also opened fire in Conway Street, where they used hand-guns at first and then Browning machine-guns. There was a rumour of trouble in Hooker Street in Ardoyne, where we were told that Catholic families were being evicted by a loyalist mob.

The IRA's armed intervention throughout Belfast was an extremely limited one. The real defence of the area was conducted by young people with petrol bombs and stones and bricks, though the IRA actions in the Falls area were crucially important in halting the loyalist mobs at decisive times. Some of this armed defence, although limited, was very courageous, and the wider defence by the young people was also undoubtedly brave, and between the two forms of defence a penetration of the Falls area itself was prevented. However, Dover Street was burned out, and Percy Street, and fighting continued all night in Conway Street.

As dawn arose on the morning of 15 August, it did so over a scene of absolute devastation. Six people were dead, five Catholics and one Protestant; about 150 had been wounded by gunfire and 150 Catholic homes had been gutted. A pall of smoke rose over the Falls. The old familiar streetscape was shattered. The environment that I grew up in was gone. For ever. The self-contained, enclosed village atmosphere of the area and its peaceful sense of security had been brutally torn apart, leaving our close-knit community battered and bleeding in mind, body and spirit. The everyday world in which we had passed our childhoods had been transformed, destroyed, and a sense of devastation entered our hearts. Flames still blazed from gutted buildings; makeshift barricades blocked street entrances; there was no traffic. Crowds of people were gathered at street corners or in behind their barricades or in other sheltered spots or vantage points. Single shots and an occasional burst of shooting fractured the uncertain air.

Early radio news reports that morning confirmed the previous night's rumours that the British army had arrived on the streets of Derry. Two people had been shot and wounded by the RUC. CS gas filled the Derry air like smog. When B Specials had been seen the previous day to move into Waterloo Place, it had been assumed that they would attack with guns, and nationalist Derry had stood poised for what was feared would be a massacre, since no one could have any doubt about the nature of the B Specials.

Then the British army had moved in, receiving an ambivalent reception from the people of the Bogside who were conscious that although the troops were being moved in to relieve the battered, exhausted and discredited RUC, they were also stepping into a breach between the nationalists and the armed B Specials.

Internment had been introduced, and twenty-four men had been lifted throughout the Six Counties. These included Billy McMillen and most of the Belfast leadership. Apart from the heavy shooting in Belfast, one man had also been shot dead in Armagh; there had been disturbances in Newry, Dungannon and elsewhere throughout the north. The situation in Ardoyne had been especially serious. RUC armoured vehicles had broken through defensive barricades at Hooker Street and penetrated the area as far as Butler Street. They were followed into Hooker Street by a loyalist mob hurling petrol bombs and stones into houses. In the shootings of that evening, two local men were killed by the RUC. The IRA defence of the area had been totally inadequate. A number of people had been sent in to back up the local republicans, who fought very bravely, but they were armed only with short-arms and a mere handful of ammunition.

In the Falls, as the dawn filtered into morning, many Catholics who had been evicted from the streets running from the Falls Road itself to the Shankill returned to see what damage had been done. Many were accompanied by friends or relatives, and those who were able started to salvage their belongings, using hand-carts, cars and vans to take away their furniture and household effects. As more and more people returned to the streets, lorries and other vehicles were hijacked, and barricades were going up everywhere.

In the early hours of the morning in a lull, as confirmation of the arrests came through, Jimmy Sullivan sent word that we should leave the area. Some of us were sent to the Grosvenor Road. From there we moved out of the shattered streetscape, and I went with a few others from the Falls to Andersonstown and a house on Finaghy Road North. Here we were joined by other republicans. Every one of us was exhausted, but as we sat there on that early Friday morning, we swapped yarns and retold the story of the night's happenings. Eventually, when we had exhausted the various versions of our stories and when we had heard all the radio news broadcasts, we slept.

When we awakened in the late afternoon, there was an air of

unreality about our situation. We were under strict instructions not to leave the house, but we needed to know what was happening. We were limited to radio reports, and we sat arguing among ourselves about what to do. That evening we learned that British troops had taken up positions on the Falls Road. We were raging, feeling impotent in our isolation. I wanted to see what was happening.

'You can't go down the road! There's British troops, there's British fucking troops!'

'Why is there British troops? Why?'

'Did you hear the statement from Callaghan?'

'Did you hear the last news?'

'Can you phone anyone?'

'Don't be using the phone!'

There were reports of shooting in the Clonard area once again. All this time we were sitting in this house, away from the action. What use were we? I decided that I would go down on to the Falls again to see what the score was.

I sat in the passenger-seat of a borrowed car as we travelled through a surreal streetscape. There were very few other vehicles on the road. By now there were barricades on every street corner and on both sides of the road. Eyes watched us the entire length of our journey as we moved slowly and carefully, suddenly strange and vulnerable in our once familiar surroundings. I saw my first British soldiers on the Grosvenor Road at the bottom of Leeson Street. They were mere shadows in the dusk, but the sight of them angered me in a way which I couldn't fully comprehend. By the time I got to see Jimmy Sullivan, I was furious.

'What are we going to do about the soldiers?' I demanded.

We were going to sit tight, he told me. He also asked me would I go around different areas to sound out the situation on the ground. I went first of all to Ardoyne, and apart from the people who lived there, I was probably one of the first to come into the district from outside to find out what was going on. From some of the older republicans I heard criticism, even outrage at the failure of republicans to provide defence. But the people of the area, whom I met in the schools and in the streets while they were milling around looking after refugees and seeing to their own defences, were just concerned to know what was happening over in the Falls Road. In the same way as we had been greedy for information, they too were looking for accurate reports. Rumours swept the place. I went to a number of republican houses in Ardoyne and in the Bone to meet and talk to people and to get as detailed a report as I could. It was safe enough moving around by this time, although there had been constant sniping a few hours beforehand.

I went into Clonard looking for Kevin Hannaway. Someone told me where to find him, and I went as directed to a house off the Kashmir Road and knocked at the door. I was bundled inside, and a gun was put to my head. Here were assembled some of those who had valiantly defended the Clonard area. They were very angry as they gave me a first-hand account of the events of the past hours. The whole area, especially the Clonard church and St Gall's Catholic school at the rear of the monastery, had come under concerted attack. Geraldo McAuley, a fifteen-year-old member of the Fianna, the republican youth organisation, had been shot dead defending Bombay Street, and the street itself was ablaze. The fighting here had been at very close quarters, yet the poorly armed defenders had repelled a large, much better armed group of attackers. What particularly incensed all of us was that Bombay Street was burned despite the presence of British troops who had been deployed around the area sometime beforehand. They made no effort to intervene to prevent or halt the pogrom.

The presence of the British troops totally and absolutely outraged us. In our view the British government had been using the RUC and the unionists to uphold and disguise the nature of their rule in this part of our country. We experienced a sense of victory in having exhausted and defeated their first line of defence – the RUC. Although the unionists were still in charge, it was now the British soldiers who were holding the line for the British government, and so that government could no longer absolve itself so easily of responsibility for what was happening in the Six Counties. Despite this sense of having moved the situation on, we felt very emotional about the actual presence of the British troops on our streets. In at least one situation, in the Clonard area, when troops had been sighted after the battle of Bombay Street, one of the defenders of that area had opened fire on the Brits, wounding one of them.

I left Kevin Hannaway and the Clonard area, went to one or two other places and then reported back to Jimmy Sullivan. For the next few days I was engaged in helping to resolve some of the many problems which arose. My role was a functionary one; I was told to go into an area, to organise it, to issue bulletins, to mobilise co-ordinating committees or relief committees.

People responded over those August days with great fortitude and resilience, and they showed a remarkable ability to organise collectively. So spirits were good despite the situation. Young people who had never been responsible for anything now found themselves guarding the property of displaced families, organising and minding barricades, securing supplies and so on. It was a heady and a testing time, but it was also uniquely and unforgettably fulfilling. People who had long been regarded and treated as the lowest of the low now proved themselves to be capable and resourceful and strong. The biggest forced movement of population in Europe since the second world war had resulted from the loyalist pogroms, and people had responded by opening up their homes behind the barricades to refugees. Working people had taken control of aspects of their own lives, organised their own districts in a way which later deeply antagonised and traumatised the Catholic middle class, particularly the hierarchy of the Catholic church. It was an experience of community oneness, of unselfishness at every hand.

I did not see my parents for most of this time, but I heard that my da had been elected to chair a committee at a meeting called to debate the defence of the area. They had organised patrols in all the Ballymurphy streets, and my da and others had liberated a lorry-load of bread from Barney Hughes's bakery.

With virtually no guns in nationalist Belfast and no sign of any guns coming from the IRA leadership in Dublin, whole areas were defenceless against further loyalist attack. Meanwhile, Catholic families continued to flee from the Grosvenor Road, Donegal Road, Tiger's Bay, York Street, Sandy Row, Highfield and Greencastle. Some fled south, but more moved into safer areas of West Belfast, particularly Andersonstown and Ballymurphy. Relief committees were established in most of these areas. Sometimes these functioned separately, though in liaison with defence committees, some of which had been organised initially in the summer in areas like Ardoyne and Unity Flats which were threatened by loyalist mobs.

In the Andersonstown area, where I spent a short time after the August days, the people opened up their homes to families who had been forced out of other districts; and in the upper Andersonstown area, around Rosnareen and Tullymore, people just emptied their houses of blankets and clothes and gave up their beds to those who had been forced to flee. Earlier in August we had housed some refugees in an almost completed building site and, with the aid of local tradesmen, makeshift electricity, water and other facilities had been installed. St Teresa's school was the main centre for co-ordinating relief efforts in the area, and other schools were used as temporary points either for shelter for refugees or as collection and distribution points for relief supplies. There were considerable difficulties in terms of supplies of food for children, posed by the suspension of normal transport into the twenty-seven barricaded areas of nationalist Belfast. In West Belfast, where I was to spend all of my time, emergency provision of dried milk and other necessities had to be organised, first of all to be distributed to the areas, and then within the areas, and that had to be done on the basis of need. A lot of organisation was required in difficult circumstances, but the local people of all the areas which received refugees responded marvellously to that challenge.

During this time, five or six of us were living in a basement flat thrown open to us by its owner, and a woman across the street, who was a republican, fed us. We were living a crazy existence, unkempt and half asleep, running from pillar to post, all the time on the go.

Republican activists constituted a separate layer from the defence committees and the relief committees, though republicans were involved in all levels of this activity. They came naturally into area leadership positions because they had standing in the community or because of their previous experience of agitational activity in unemployment and housing action and civil rights campaigning. There was also an organisation of former republican activists who had come together earlier in 1969 and, with the permission of the republican leadership in Belfast, formed an organisation known as the Auxiliaries. These older men saw themselves as providing back-up to the local IRA and volunteered their services to organise defence. In some areas where there was no IRA presence or where the IRA had only a small number of activists, they became a semi-autonomous force. They provided the backbone of the wider defence committees, which were initially made up of local people, mostly male, who volunteered to staff the barricades.

All of the areas of West Belfast had their own barricades. On each side of the Falls Road, every street had its own barricades. In the housing estates, which didn't have the same street pattern, where there were green areas and wide entrances and where barricades were impractical for the entire area, they were set up at main entrances, at vulnerable points and at vantage points, sometimes with a lean-to or a hut from which people kept watch.

The organisation of the defence committees developed naturally. People living in one area or in one part of an area went to keep watch on another part, simply because it was seen to be too vulnerable. Out of the natural spontaneous responses of people, there emerged a sort of structure, the sophistication of which depended on the ability or the number of people involved. Defence committees armed themselves with petrol bombs and stones. People living in the area who had British army backgrounds brought their expertise to bear also, and indeed an organisation known as the Catholic Ex-Servicemen's Association was formed.

In Andersonstown, for example, which was one of the big areas of dispersal for refugees and where there wasn't any great risk of loyalist attack, the work here was mostly devoted to co-ordinating the relief operation. There were also frenzied efforts to get weapons, and an amazing arsenal of old sporting rifles and shotguns, of .22s, and ill-assorted items from old IRA dumps was soon being ferried into and around Belfast city.

There were all kinds of other defensive experiments. Crates of petrol bombs and stones, usually from broken pavements, were stockpiled near barricades, spikes were hammered into the roads, and trenches were dug. In one case during an alert I came across a group filling a trench with petrol. Not only was this a particularly dangerous ploy, but they were surprised some time later to discover their trench empty again, the petrol having evaporated.

There were regular alerts, some serious, others the results of rumours which were both widespread and frequent. As the defence committees organised, some of them arranged set-piece contingencies for particular barricades, usually under the tutelage of a local republican. Former British soldiers assisted in this, and petrol bombs or stones were the main weapons. The graffiti coined by a wit in Derry, 'Throw well, throw Shell', applied also in Belfast.

The petrol bombs came in all shapes and sizes, and strenuous efforts were made to improve the product. One evening a few men brought what they described as a self-igniter – a molotov cocktail – to the barricades. When they announced that they were going to throw it to see if it worked they were quizzed thoroughly by the lads on the barricades.

'I experimented with some of that sodium stuff.'

It was the older of the two men who spoke. He had a large envelope in his hand, which he opened to reveal rows of pink blotting paper.

'You soak the blotters in sodium. Blotters are the best. Newspapers are too thin. Once they get wet they disintegrate. I dried these out in the oven. Don't worry, I didn't have it lit. I heated it on a low heat and then I turned it off and put the wet blotters in. Otherwise it would take years to dry them out.'

His companion had a paperback book. It was about guerrilla warfare in Cuba and it opened easily at a well-creased page. He explained how he had come across it in a bookshop in Smithfield weeks before. It contained the writings of Che Guevara and described how molotovs could be made. It also had diagrams for spigots. These contained the means whereby such petrol bombs, which looked remarkably like Halloween fireworks rockets, could be propelled by way of a shotgun. Our two amateur scientists had ignored this since they had no shotgun. The only problem was that the book said that acid was required, but didn't specify the type.

'So we got some sulphuric and we want to go and test it now. Only we wanted yous to know. If it works yous can have it, like. We could make enough for the whole district.'

It was decided to test it against a blank wall across a stretch of waste ground. About forty people, mostly men, some children and two stray dogs followed at a safe distance.

'Che's people came from Cork,' someone remarked.

'Well, we'll soon see if he was spoofing or not.'

The young man threw the bottle overarm at the wall. It somersaulted and turned in the air before disappearing into the evening darkness. There was a dull clunk.

'You missed the bloody wall,' someone laughed.

'No, I didn't.'

'Yes you bloody well did.'

The two advanced cautiously to where the bottle had landed in a patch of grass and nettles, inches from the wall.

'Dead-eye Dick,' the older man chuckled, as he examined his missile. It was a screw-top Lucozade bottle wrapped in blotting paper which was fastened with elastic bands. It was intact.

'Do you want another go?' he asked.

'Aye,' his friend said.

'No chance. Watch this.'

He threw the bottle underarm. It arced easily away from them. 'See . . .'

The words were lost in the breaking of glass and the whoosh of ignition which accompanied it. For a few seconds the entire scene was illuminated by the bright ball of fire and the little streamers of flame which cascaded from the wall. Then there was a brief whisper of smoke and a hint of scorched grass.

The children cheered. The two dogs fled.

'Aha,' someone exclaimed. 'Old Che Guevara was right!'

For days after 15 August, in fact for almost a week, sniping continued into Catholic areas, but as the situation generally quietened into a stand-off and as the nationalists withdrew from the statelet in behind their barricades, the foreground was taken up by frenetic political manoeuvrings between the British government and the Stormont regime, and the role of the B Specials and of the RUC in the disturbances and the killings came more and more under scrutiny. The demands of the civil rights struggle were reiterated repeatedly by its spokespersons and also by the nationalist MPs to Stormont, and Prime Minister James Chichester-Clark and members of his cabinet were called to London for urgent talks with Harold Wilson, the British prime minister, James Callaghan, the home secretary, and other members of the British cabinet.

Harold Wilson emerged after these talks to announce a number of major changes in the role of the Stormont government. These included the appointment of two senior British civil servants, who were to be assigned to represent the British government directly in the Six Counties. The other was that the British military were to take effective control of all security matters and to supervise the gradual demobilisation of the B Specials. A declaration of rights was published also, and a visit by the British home secretary, James Callaghan, was announced for later that month.

The unionists, of course, were outraged. Harry West and the former minister of home affairs, William Craig, declared that the Stormont government had no authority to agree to terms of this sort. 'I for one and I am sure a large number will call for their immediate resignation. As for the action of the British government, it seems to be an unwarranted interference with the government of Northern Ireland, and represents a going back on the agreement that was entered into when this state was founded.'

From the nationalist side, while there was some general satisfaction about the pending demise of the B Specials, there was some considerable scepticism, a distinct feeling that the promised reforms did not go far enough, that what was coming out of London was too little, too late. Behind the barricades, Radio Free Belfast had been established. A silk-screen printing press was churning out posters. The local Citizens' Defence Committees were beginning to network and a Central Citizens' Defence Committee (the CCDC) was soon to be established in Leeson Street, representing all of the areas behind barricades in nationalist Belfast. This Central Citizens' Defence Committee brought together a very wide representation of the Catholic people of Belfast city, including republicans, local IRA people, the Stormont MPs Paddy Devlin and Paddy Kennedy, representatives of the Catholic middle class, local church leaders and ordinary people concerned that there would be no going back to the old days. As James Callaghan flew into the north on a fact-finding visit and as the internees were released, a *céilí* band on the back of a coal lorry in Leeson Street played to thousands of men, women and children. There was a sense and a reality of a popular uprising.

Behind the barricades in the weeks after 15 August, I learned to drive in an old Volkswagen car and involved myself in the production of a one-page news bulletin, *The Barricade*. We had a fairly well developed support base in the Andersonstown area, particularly the top estates where a number of us were active. As the last of the internees were released and the Belfast republican leadership regrouped once again around Liam McMillen, operating from behind the barricades in the Leeson Street area, I was sent back into Ballymurphy to act as organiser.

By now, the republican role in defence of nationalist neighbourhoods had been taken over by defence committees, and while the IRA was to provide them with back-up, as well as training and general guidance, in Ballymurphy, as elsewhere, life behind the barricades had settled into a routine of sorts. The people who were on barricade duty organised themselves in shifts. Local shops contributed cigarettes for the vigilantes, and a rota system of tea making from house to house, from street to street was devised. There were also some houses that everyone used as meeting places and information points, and various local people just opened up their houses, providing food, stew and soup, at all hours of the day and night.

At the end of September loyalists attacked Unity Flats and were repelled by one armed IRA volunteer. They turned their attention on Coates Street, a tiny Catholic street between the Falls and the Shankill, and burned it down. The present reality and the continuing threat of further loyalist pogroms, and the rumours of political change, the posturing of the unionist government, the setting up of commissions of inquiry and the reports back from the Cameron Commission, unnerved people. From Ballymurphy guns could be seen in windows and at barricades across the Springfield Road in New Barnsley. Many people involved with the defence committees flocked to the IRA, which speedily mushroomed out of all proportion to its previous numbers.

Life behind the barricades was a great equaliser. As in times of adversity everywhere, people got to know each other and began to realise that collectively they were a very talented group of people. Naturally, people like my father or Frank Cahill – who had been a community leader for some time – who were elected into the leadership of the Ballymurphy committee, and others who had some political experience, provided in the initial stages the catalyst to get certain things done. Once people realised what was required, however, a momentum all of its own developed.

In the short few weeks of that summer of 1969, the situation in Ballymurphy, as in most of nationalist Belfast, and indeed many other nationalist areas of the Six Counties, had changed for ever. Even where the change was yet to manifest itself in organisation, or even in any visible form, there was a definite change of mood.

Ballymurphy had been flooded with refugees who were shell-shocked and in some cases hysterical after being burned out. A group of local women organised to provide food and clothing, bedding, medicines, communications and transport. Food was collected door to door from residents. The local women had initiated the organisation of relief and also assured local Protestant families that they would be protected. There was by this time a well-organised co-ordinating committee and a defence association also. Ballymurphy was the centre of the greater Springfield area, which took in Dermot Hill, New Barnsley, Moyard, Springhill, Westrock and the Whiterock. There was also a sizeable number of refugees living in temporary dwellings or chalets at the top of the Whiterock Road. New Barnsley overlooked Ballymurphy, as did Springmartin, and within the nationalist area, each of the separate parts was fairly well organised, though there was little formal co-ordination or communication between them.

The British army had taken over the Vere Foster school and the Henry Taggart Memorial Hall just above Divismore Park. The troops stayed outside the barricaded areas, patrolling the Springfield Road. The officer in charge communicated fairly often and negotiated with the local defence and relief committee leaderships, but as in all other parts of nationalist Belfast, we were refusing to take the barricades down. Apart from their defensive use, and people in Ballymurphy were well aware that the flats in the loyalist Springmartin estate provided a perfect vantage point for sniping down at them, there was also some sense of political leverage in retaining the barricaded areas. There had been a move earlier in the Falls Road to take barricades down, following an intervention by Bishop Philbin, and I was among those who protested to the bishop and who helped to build them again. More barricades were to come down following a meeting between the CCDC and Jim Callaghan in London. Jimmy Sullivan, who was on that delegation, reported back to republican activists that there would be an amnesty for all of those who had been involved in the defence work over the August period.

Side by side with the growth of the IRA, there was also a rapid rebuilding of the Sinn Féin organisation, though in some areas this was very much a secondary concern. In the Murph there was a considerable growth of Sinn Féin, of which I became the local chairperson, and we developed Sinn Féin cumainn, or branches, in each of the recognisable communities within the greater Ballymurphy area, while Liam Hannaway built a Sinn Féin cumann in his area, and people in Ardoyne did the same. In Ballymurphy a co-ordinating committee, which I usually chaired, was established. It began to take on the character of a people's council, bringing together as many as fifty people representing every street to talk about what was happening and decide on issues as they arose. We also organised open meetings. Rather than being structured around agendas and dominated by speakers from platforms, these meetings, which were attended by between sixty and one hundred people, were held in such a way that anyone in the district was free to raise any issue that was of concern to them. We published a local newssheet, *The Tatler*, and energetically began building a strong republican base in the area. I immersed myself in this organisational work, and we quickly built up good contacts throughout the greater Ballymurphy area. There was really no great risk to this area, except on the Springfield Road flank, where from Corry's timber yard into Springhill or along Divismore Park into Springfield Road itself, it was overlooked by New Barnsley. Springfield Park on the other side of the Springfield Road was, however, a particularly vulnerable area, and a defence group supported by others from the Murph was set up there. With all this intense activity I was rarely at home for long periods. In fact, after that summer I hardly ever slept again in Divismore Park. I did call into the house regularly and I was in frequent contact with my parents, but it was usually only for a few minutes at a time.

While we busied ourselves behind the barricades, others were busy also. In October the Hunt Report was published. Its recommendations – for the abolition of the B Specials and the disarming of the RUC – led to loyalist riots on the Shankill Road, which left three people dead, including one RUC man. In the aftermath of these riots the British army launched large-scale searches on the Shankill Road and seized guns and ammunition. A week later a member of Paisley's Free Presbyterian church died while planting a bomb at an electricity plant in Ballyshannon, County Donegal.

Within republican ranks, the political fall-out of the insurrectionary events of August was settling on the leadership. The situation had developed rapidly. The civil rights movement had demanded rights which were taken for granted in western Europe, rights which existed in the rest of the so-called United Kingdom. They were, in themselves, unremarkable, simple, moderate; yet they had evoked a ferocious response from the state and its supporters. If the consequence of that response had left the authority and stability of the state in tatters, it had also shaken the authority and stability of the republican leadership. The Goulding/Mac Giolla group in Dublin had got it wrong. Their failure to provide adequate defence combined with the mishandling of an almost unprecedented opportunity to move the entire situation on was bad enough. But when circumstances dictated and cried out for a leadership capable of unifying or encouraging the maximum unity of progressives, anti-imperialists, socialists, republicans and nationalists, the republican leadership dithered.

The republican movement of the 1960s had proved incapable of responding adequately to events as they evolved in the Six Counties. The spontaneous popular uprising of August 1969, unco-ordinated, locally organised, lacking any general plan, and the subsequent effects in the Twenty-six Counties, found republicans ill-prepared and unable to cope with the needs and the potential of that period. Failure and inadequacy did not relate only to the question of the defence of beleaguered nationalist areas. Indeed, lack of guns was not a primary problem: once the pogroms were over, this lack was made up quite rapidly. The primary problem was the lack of political awareness and acumen, a shortcoming which I shared and which was to remain even after the guns had become plentiful. The political weakness of all tendencies in the then disunited republican ranks arose from an inability to understand what was happening on the ground, its causes, effects and possible consequences. Many of those who warned quite correctly of the need for armed defence contingencies, many of those who were strident in their condemnation of the republican leadership's failure to provide such necessities, did not understand the political requirements of the time. The leadership also was clearly lacking in political understanding, and this led to their failure to prepare properly, on all fronts.

As the crisis within the northern statelet deepened, differences within republican ranks were exacerbated by events and by the return of some lapsed members who had disagreed with the general direction of the movement in recent years. Under these pressures, the loosely united tendencies which made up the republican movement came sharply into conflict. This might have occurred anyway, in time, because of the underlying strategic and ideological strains, but the civil rights struggle and the backlash from the August 1969 pogroms in Belfast dictated the timing and to a large degree the sharpness of the divisions. Latent personality conflicts were given a new vigour by the emotive events of that time.

A lot of this went over my head. To a large extent, my political world was Ballymurphy. I was busy enough there without worrying about the rest of the struggle. There were three broad tendencies within republican activism in Belfast, anyway: first, the leadership; second, the older people who had come back in response to the crisis situation, and the new membership; and third, the younger people, like myself, on the ground. My feeling was that neither the leadership nor the older people had got it quite right.

A crucial, fatal mistake was made by the Dublin leadership when it proceeded to implement the commission which it had been mandated to establish at a previous Ard Fheis, the Sinn Féin national conference. This commission was to consult with grass-roots activists on a number of issues, including the establishment of a National Liberation Front, the ending of abstentionism and the development of electoral politics.

I had been at a number of hearings organised by the commission in Belfast, including one in the Felons Club which was addressed by Seamus Costello, and which Kevin Hannaway was also at. Roy Johnson was another visitor from Dublin who had addressed a number of meetings in Belfast. These were vitally important issues for republicans everywhere, touching crucially on matters of principle embedded in Sinn Féin's constitution. The abstentionist refusal to recognise the right of the British parliament to rule in the north-eastern six counties and the refusal also to recognise the legitimacy of the Leinster House parliament in Dublin were cornerstones of republican belief. As it happened, I favoured the development of a National Liberation Front, in which republicans would join in common cause with all organisations and individuals which opposed the British imperial intervention in our country. Although I was opposed to dropping the traditional abstentionist policy, I had no objection in principle to developing a debate on electoral strategy or abstentionism, though this clearly possessed great potential for division between people with deeply held opposing convictions.

However, all of this discussion and the commission had been initiated before the August pogroms. The pogroms changed everything, demanding unity of purpose and clarity and resoluteness of action. At the very least, the leadership should have recognised the need for urgent new priorities and suspended its pursuance of the new departure in republican strategy until a more settled time. To come before the membership, as it did now in the autumn of 1969, with findings recommending the ending of abstentionism and the development of a wider and demilitarised, broadly anti-imperialist movement, was not only anathema to some of those now involved once again, or newly involved in republican politics, it also, and more importantly, showed a fixation with these ideas and a blindness to the real needs of that moment. There was already considerable opposition to the dropping of abstentionism nationally, and it was obvious that some people at national leadership level, including Seán Mac

Stiofáin, Ruairí Ó Bradaigh and Dáithí Ó Conaill, were running in an organised way against this proposition.

I knew none of these leadership figures. I had a very close personal relationship with the prominent Belfast republican Jimmy Steele, which went back a number of years. A fresh-faced, sharp-featured little man of cheerful disposition, Jimmy had served long periods of imprisonment and had been part of a celebrated jailbreak in 1943. During one of his court appearances a judge had described him memorably as 'morally upright, politically suspect'. A particularly devout Catholic, he was a prolific writer whose poetry was favoured by republicans of his generation; he worked as a bread roundsman but was on the point of retirement. Jimmy was an opponent of the Dublin leadership, having spoken in a very forceful way against them in Mullingar the previous year. Before August 1969 he was very much in a minority position, certainly among activists. Now, however, it was the Goulding loyalists who were in a small minority in Belfast, being confined to the ranks of the Belfast leadership and to parts of the local organisation in Leeson Street and the Markets. In a matter of weeks, a newly engaged, active community in Belfast had mobilised around the republican position. Most of those now in local and more central leadership were opposed to the direction of the Dublin leadership, and some were actively opposed to the Belfast leadership of Billy McMillen and company.

I was in a strange position, one of a small cadre with contacts in both factions. Apart from my work locally in the Murph, I retained social contact with Kevin Hannaway, Francie McGuigan, Joe McCann, Anthony Doran and others. I was particularly close to Kevin Hannaway, and we frequented Proinsias MacAirt's house regularly. Small, thickset and swarthy, Kevin was a motor car enthusiast. Even as early as 1966 he had a car, and while I was messing about on bikes, he was engrossed in motor cars and already had a special ability to coax an engine, no matter how decrepit, into life. Trained as a joiner, he was a good driver, a fount of knowledge on all matters mechanical or practical, and could turn his hand to most things. Although obstinate if his temper was roused, he was very obliging and generally easygoing. He was also renowned amongst all of us for his ability to sleep in any circumstances and for the depth of his slumbers. Billy McKee, who had come back into the picture, having played a very crucial role in the defence of the Clonard area, also used MacAirt's house extensively. Under the pressure of events it was almost as if there were two leaderships: the formal leadership of McMillen and the informal leadership provided by McKee, Joe Cahill, and others.

I hadn't known Billy McKee before 1969, but I had seen Joe Cahill at *céilís* and other gatherings. The two of them, like many of the older activists, were friends of my parents, and they and my da had been imprisoned at the same time. Joe was a particularly well-known Belfast republican because he had been one of a number of young men arrested alongside Tom Williams after a shoot-out in a house in Clonard in 1942 in which an RUC man was killed. Sentenced to be hanged, all but Tom Williams, the leader of the IRA group, were reprieved after a widespread protest campaign. The hanging of Tom Williams at the age of eighteen had had a profound effect on republican Belfast, where black flags had adorned the streets, and since then there has been a continuing campaign for the repatriation of Tom Williams's remains from a prison grave in the Crumlin Road to the republican plot in Milltown cemetery.

Balding and fresh-faced, with a good sense of humour, Joe Cahill was married with a young family and worked as a foreman for a successful local building company. A long-time ally of Jimmy Steele, he had spent many years in prison, but he had resigned in the mid-1960s in protest against the trends in republicanism at that time; later he told me that he considered his resignation to have been a mistake. Joe delighted in the republican resurgence which followed 1969, and in this he mirrored the attitude of all republicans of his generation, who had spent most of their lives in isolated struggle. Now they saw that the situation had mushroomed into a popular uprising.

Billy McKee possessed a reputation for being a deeply religious man, and he was certainly very conscientious, but I never found him in any way sanctimonious. A bachelor, he was of his generation, conservative in political outlook but fond of a bit of *craic* and an occasional drink with close friends. Indeed, all of these older men mixed easily with us younger ones.

The Auxiliaries, then under the leadership of Seamus Twomey, who was later to play a decisive role in republicanism, also worked more easily with the McKee faction than with the McMillen faction, so in Belfast the division was two-edged. Resentment was widespread towards a leadership which had failed to provide defence for nationalist areas. The other edge was against the political direction of the Dublin leadership. While the latter was not to come to a head until later in the year, the former was already creating serious friction. This became a critical issue when the Belfast leadership gave an instruction that all the arms in Belfast city should be brought to a central point to be stamped and authenticated. Not only was there understandable resentment and suspicion about this within republican ranks, but there was also the question of the Auxiliaries, who were well established with their own network in all the nationalist areas.

I was perturbed and perplexed to find that extreme criticism of the Belfast leadership was being expressed most of all by republicans whom I didn't know or had only recently met. It was one thing, I felt, for me, and for others like me who had been active before August '69, to criticise, but I wondered where these people had been. A large meeting of republicans from all over Belfast passed a vote of no confidence in McMillen and the Dublin leadership. I had mixed feelings about this development: although I had little confidence in the McMillen leadership, I did nevertheless feel a certain loyalty towards it; there needed to be major changes in Belfast, but I had had neither the opportunity nor indeed the inclination to work these out.

Now, however, a delegation conveyed to McMillen the motion of no confidence. At a tense meeting he accepted the news quietly and undertook to relay it to the Dublin leadership. He was sharply informed that the Belfast republicans wanted no truck with the Dublin leadership. The ensuing row lasted for some time as different views were put concerning a wide range of issues: the national leadership and its handling of the overall situation; the Belfast leadership's role in this; the question of abstentionism and of an IRA convention which was coming up. Other, more local, but equally important issues were discussed in relation to the handling of the 15 August situation and developments since then, some of which centred on the fact that some of those who were known to be dissident had been cut out of the normal democratic processes and had rarely been consulted by McMillen.

The meeting argued all of the issues back and forth until eventually a compromise resolution was accepted. Belfast was suspending its contact with Dublin until further notice; there would be no attendance from Belfast at the forthcoming army convention; there would be wider consultation and representation, and some of the senior people who were opposed to the leadership would now be involved in decision-making, which would henceforth include a council made up of local leaders.

There was also widespread discussion in republican circles about the important question of the contact which had been established with the Dublin government, who had for some time been offering equipment and training for the defence of beleaguered nationalists, without concrete results. I and a number of others felt that this was a string-along designed to create a situation which the Dublin government could control, and we argued that no arrangement should be entered into which had any strings attached. The contact with Dublin had been developed nationally by the Goulding leadership and in Belfast directly under the leadership of Liam McMillen; relief money was paid into a bank account controlled by McMillen's finance officer; discussions about the provision of arms and money were held between Dublin government contacts and northern elements of the Goulding leadership of the IRA. Later, as the situation developed, this contact extended to wider groupings of Citizens Defence Committee people gathered from throughout the north, and it was at this point that John Kelly (later to feature in the

Dublin Arms Trial) became involved. As it transpired, a limited amount of training was provided at an FCA camp.

This issue of the Dublin government's contact with republicans, and particularly with republicans in the north, was used after the split in the republican movement by elements of the Goulding leadership in an attempt to justify their own stance; indeed, some of their propaganda blamed the government for setting up 'the Provisionals'. Such propaganda allegations were totally without foundation: the initial contact was made before the split and with the Goulding leadership, not with the dissidents who later became known as the Provisionals.

As the stormclouds of division gathered nationally over republican Ireland, back in Ballymurphy we were continuing to organise, to regroup and to expand. Then, disaster. On my way back from County Leitrim with Liam McParland, Mickey O'Neill and another friend in November our car crashed on the M1 motorway; Liam died later from his injuries. Understandably shaken, I was further shocked when in the aftermath of the accident I was suspended from my local leadership role in Sinn Féin by the Belfast leadership, who were eager to impose their authority on the Ballymurphy area. The local activists rejected this ploy and a period of some aggravation followed, in which I found myself in a state of limbo: although I remained active, I had no status.

I got the chance of temporary work with the Ulster Brewery and I spent two weeks before Christmas delivering wine and spirits to public houses, mostly in rural areas. During this time I was pressing Jimmy Sullivan for a tribunal into my suspension and I was summoned by him one evening to a public house in Leeson Street where he told me that my suspension had been lifted. The larger debate about where the republican struggle was going was now being waged intensely, and I asked Jimmy Steele how he thought it would develop. He answered that he thought everything would be sorted out quite soon. He refused to elaborate, which was of little consolation and somewhat disconcerting to me. A short time later the mystery was solved when news broke about the holding of an IRA convention and its outcome.

Meanwhile, Seán Mac Stiofáin came to Belfast and met with activists, canvassing their support. At this point I went to Jimmy Sullivan and suggested that he should come to a meeting of the Ballymurphy people to put his and the Goulding leadership's view to us. He did so, and we held a meeting of activists in the chalets at the Whiterock, the end result of which was that we decided we would not go with the Goulding leadership. Next day I went down to see Billy McMillen. On my way to his house I met Billy McKee and told him that we in the Murph had decided to remain separate until we saw what way things were going to break; that we were not concerned with the internal politics of the situation, but we were concerned to move the entire struggle forward. I then went on to McMillen's house where I had a lengthy discussion with him and some other people very close to him, during which I outlined my views in some detail. It wasn't an acrimonious meeting and we parted on good terms.

While for some people – the older people who had come back, and those who were newly into the movement – the reasons for the split were straightforward, to the core of activists who had been connected before 1969 and busy in the build-up to that period, the split was less clear-cut. Many of my age especially shared a sense of frustration at the presence of British troops – there were now 7,500 of them in the north, mostly in Belfast. To my knowledge the only area which formally debated and democratically decided the direction it was going to go was Ballymurphy; most other areas followed their local leaders.

A formal split in the IRA occurred at the army convention in December, when the Goulding leadership pressed ahead with its proposal to drop abstentionism and the dissidents, outnumbered, walked out. For many of the dissidents the issue was not abstentionism itself but what it had come to represent: a leadership with a wrong set of priorities which had led the IRA into ignominy in August. The split now out in the open, a provisional army council of the IRA was established with Seán

Mac Stiofáin as its chief-of-staff, and a period of intense regrouping ensued in the army.

But not yet in Sinn Féin. We were preparing for the Ard Fheis which was to be held in January. I realised that the majority of Belfast Sinn Féin members were opposed to the Goulding leadership, and I proposed to Proinsias MacAirt that we mobilise this majority to attend the pre-Ard Fheis meeting of the Belfast *Chomhairle Ceanntair* of Sinn Féin, which would decide on how the Belfast delegates would vote. I was disappointed that there was no great sense of a need to do this, which derived partly from the fact that Sinn Féin was seen by many as the poor second cousin to the army. Having failed to win many people over to my view, I went myself to the meeting in Cyprus Street, much to the surprise of some of those in attendance. The meeting was chaired by Malachy McGurran, northern organiser of Sinn Féin, and none of the Belfast areas which had opted to support the provisional army council were represented. I opposed the leadership motion as to how we should vote at the Ard Fheis and was quite surprised to receive substantial support from those at the meeting, who included my friends and comrades from the housing and unemployment campaigns. As well as Joe McCann, many of them gave me a very sympathetic hearing. Indeed, the motion was carried only on the casting vote of Malachy McGurran, and I felt that an important opportunity had been lost by the failure of some of my other comrades in Sinn Féin to attend.

When I tried to enter the Ard Fheis in the Intercontinental Hotel (now Jury's) in Dublin, I was blocked at the door by Malachy McGurran, who informed me that I could not be allowed in because I didn't have proper accreditation. In travelling to Dublin I had intended to attend both the Ard Fheis and an anti-apartheid march which was being held that day to protest against the South African Springboks playing at Lansdowne Road rugby football ground. So I left the Intercontinental and joined this protest.

At the Ard Fheis the Goulding leadership's position was

defeated, having failed to achieve the required two-thirds majority for the removal of a provision of the Sinn Féin constitution, but then stupidly the Goulding leadership put a motion expressing confidence in the army leadership. But the army leadership was split.

Seán Mac Stiofáin went to the microphone. He pledged his allegiance to the recently elected provisional army council, which he said was the only leadership entitled to call itself the IRA. At the end of his contribution he concluded: 'Now it's time for us to leave.' The split was complete.

Six

The delegates who had walked out of the Ard Fheis met afterwards. Later that evening they announced the formation of a caretaker executive of Sinn Féin with Ruairí Ó Bradaigh as acting president. Back in the Murph we formed a revamped cumann for the whole greater Ballymurphy area and called it after Liam McParland. There was less pressure now on republicans to take care of defensive arrangements. These were catered for by and large by the Auxiliaries or by the defence committees, which had become well established. Although it was more difficult now to get the constant patrolling that had marked the August and September period, there was also less need for this type of manoeuvring. However, there were standbys in areas which it was felt were vulnerable. This was particularly the case in Springfield Park, that long finger of a street mostly inhabited by Catholics on the opposite side of the Springfield Road from Ballymurphy.

The split had caused some friction and tension within my family. My sister Margaret had gone with the Officials; with whom her fiancé, Michael McCorry, was a prominent activist.

Most of my time was spent working as an organiser in the Ballymurphy area, though I still maintained my contact with Kevin Hannaway and others from outside the area. Proinsias MacAirt's house was a particular point of social contact for us all.

MacAirt was a bachelor, a Gaeilgóir, a *sean nós* singer and a very sociable and socialist republican, and his small two-bedroomed house was always open, becoming the centre for the production of *Republican News*, the Belfast newssheet. The small core of full-time activists used to touch base at MacAirt's, as much for the social contact and *craic* as for anything else. I particularly enjoyed going there early in the morning; if Kevin Hannaway and I were together, we bought baps for breakfast and brewed tea while MacAirt regaled us with stories of the adventures of the night before. MacAirt had been particularly close to Liam McMillen. Now the two had parted company with, I think, a great deal of sadness on both sides.

In the course of my organising work in the Murph I met Tom Cahill, a younger brother of Joe Cahill, and we became good friends. Tom ran his own small milk delivery business, and he got me a few weeks' casual shift work in Kennedy's Dairy in Tates Avenue. None of us was subsidised in any way for our full-time republican commitment; we didn't expect to be, but it meant that we were dependent on our family and friends. Since I had no income whatsoever, Tom's good deed came as a timely boon.

Most of the work in Kennedy's was conducted in a huge cold, wet room of clanking conveyor belts, clinking bottles and hissing hose pipes. There was none of the warmth, closeness or conviviality of the Duke's. It was a very new experience, and a tediously boring one. My first job was to stand guard on a conveyor belt, which bore serried ranks of dirty milk bottles through the first stages of a cleaning and sterilising process and to watch for cracked, broken or unwashed bottles. Occasionally the conveyor belt would jackknife and send glass splintering and crashing everywhere. Noise and the working conditions limited camaraderie between workers, and there was fierce competition for overtime, which made me recall what my da had said when mildly scolding my annoyance years before at his stepping in the muck.

By now Belfast had returned to some sort of normality, on the surface at any rate. The RUC were being kept out of nationalist areas, but the British army were starting to make their first, tentative incursions, feeling their way gingerly into the stronger districts. There was still a lot of nervousness around, and although it was now possible once again to go into the city centre and young people had resumed visiting the picture houses and public houses and dance halls, most returned quickly after nightfall to their own areas. Everyone listened in to the British army messages and the transmissions by the RUC, which could be picked up on most ordinary wirelesses or even transistor radios, and some people went further by obtaining scanners. The place was frequently swept by rumours.

Number 11 Divismore Park stood directly in the view of the British army post at the Henry Taggart, but as it was a gable house we could come and go at our leisure on Glenalina Road out of sight of the British army. They had organised a disco in their garrison and invited local girls. We organised a picket, made up mostly of women from our Sinn Féin cumann, in opposition to this, and in the course of organising these pickets I met and became friendly with a group of women activists of about my own age, including Colette McArdle, Dorothy Maguire and Marie Vallely. We aimed quite consciously to prevent collaboration with the British forces and were successful beyond our expectations. What started off as a peaceful picket quickly deteriorated into shouting matches between British army squaddies, who were incensed by the protest, and the local women, who were incensed by the attitude of the British soldiers. The idea of the disco was quickly dropped, but it had given us our first opportunity to agitate publicly against British troops, and we continued this low-intensity agitation through the spring of 1970.

In March the local commander of the British army's Royal Scots regiment informed an incredulous Frank Cahill that at the end of March a loyalist Orange parade was scheduled to proceed from the New Barnsley estate down the Springfield Road. No parade had marched down that route in any previous year and now, after eighteen months of pogroms and tension, was no time to be promoting a new exercise in sectarian triumphalism. As secretary of Ballymurphy Tenants' Association and co-ordinator of the relief centre, Frank Cahill had worked strenuously to prevent Catholic youths who had witnessed the pogroms from becoming involved in confrontations with their Orange contemporaries in New Barnsley. He now faced the undoing of all his efforts.

The parade would march in clear view of Divismore Park, and negotiations between residents in Ballymurphy and the Orangemen led to an agreement that no music would be played while it was passing Ballymurphy. The parade duly started, but when it came on to the Springfield Road, the band ignored the agreement and struck up a sectarian tune. In the protests that ensued, the British soldiers on duty attacked the people from Ballymurphy and escorted the Orange march on its way. Absolute bedlam followed. There were fist-fights between people in Divismore Park and British squaddies, who retaliated with batons and then with CS gas. The British army had taken over the RUC's role as protectors of triumphalist marches and had become involved in their first major clash with nationalists. Many who had been ambivalent in their attitudes to British troops until now became unambiguously hostile. The fierce rioting which followed lasted for four days, during which time the British army saturated the area with CS gas and used brutal violence in an effort to establish full-scale military occupation of the estate.

The behaviour of the British army was quite stupid, and they acted as an oppressive occupying force, trained, as they were, in the arts of war rather than policing. The first huge mistake they made was that they poured CS gas into the area, affecting everybody and uniting against them people who were already fairly co-ordinated in terms of dealing with refugees and defending their area. It was an estate with no common basis except that the people in it were generally of Catholic proletarian stock with big families, and some of them were ex-service people.

When British troops came out of Henry Taggart barracks, they looked down on Divismore Park, which lay at a lower level. One particular soldier became an object of special hatred, because when he was part of a snatch squad which seized a rioter, he used to stand out in the middle of the road and hold him up as a prize, whereas other troops would just beat the shit out of rioters and drag them into the barracks. But when the soldiers came in as snatch squads to catch rioters and take them away, they could quite easily be diverted into cul-de-sacs. After all, they didn't know the area, but we had grown up here, moving daily and easily up and down back entries.

My father and Frank Cahill put barbed wire in behind British soldiers when we lured them into the Glenalina Road, so they couldn't get out. Soldiers often found themselves stranded in the middle of an area, trying to find their way out again, and it was then they encountered their greatest difficulties. Residents armed with hurling sticks went out against soldiers in furious hand-to-hand combat, or stones and bottles rained down on them from the rooftops. On a number of occasions British soldiers kicked their way into houses and beat everyone in them, yet they could not defeat the local community.

By their approach the British army had generated in the residents of Ballymurphy a willingness and an eagerness to meet head on the violence of the soldiers who now strutted their streets with riot shields, batons, helmets and guns. No one could look on and passively accept having their doors kicked in, their houses wrecked, their family members beaten up. As military intervention in the neighbourhood increased in frequency and intensity, so the local people, out of their own feelings of self-respect, outrage and resistance, organised more and more their own response to the military presence. The attitude and presence of British troops was also a reminder that we were Irish, and there was an instant resurgence of national consciousness and an almost immediate politicisation of the local populace.

People born and brought up in West Belfast deeply resented the sight on their own streets, the playgrounds of their childhoods, of armed and uniformed young men who jeered and taunted them in the accents of London, Glasgow and Birmingham. The use of Scottish regiments, amongst whom support for

Orange bigotry was strong, guaranteed that provocation and abuse would be directed against residents. The nationalist people of West Belfast were no more saintly or pacifist than people anywhere else, and during the spring of 1970 even some of the mildest of them took up sticks, stones, petrol bombs and bottles as they took on the British military on their own streets.

It was during this time, in April 1970, that General Freeland, the British officer in charge in the Six Counties, made a belligerent television declaration that the honeymoon period was over and that in future petrol bombers could expect to be shot dead.

The relatively sophisticated organisational structure in Ballymurphy welded the population of the estate into a formidable body of insurrectionaries. The network of organisation included street committees, women's committees, a revamped Sinn Féin, youth groups, the relief co-ordinating committee, the tenants' association and the co-ordinating committee; we were in effect operating a whole, organic system of local democracy. We published a newsletter and we developed 'hen patrols', squads of women who followed British patrols around when they came in. We also launched bin-lid brigades which sounded warning whenever troops were raiding.

Mine was a background role, but the Brits already had my name as the local subversive and they concentrated a great deal of attention on our house in Divismore Park, even though I wasn't living there. As they came down the hill from the Henry Taggart, the Brit squaddies shouted my name, and every dinnertime, as a regular routine, they used to pull up in front of the house, sometimes driving their Saracens through the front garden and right up to the hall door.

The house was constantly under attack. CS gas was fired into it, and neighbours had to come and rescue the children, wrapping them in blankets. My youngest brother Dominic developed a speech impediment in the trauma of that time. For days afterwards no one could go into the house because it reeked so strongly, and every time a blanket or cushion was lifted it would give off more of the acrid, choking gas.

One day Scotland Yard plainclothesmen in tin hats and overcoats came looking for me; I wasn't there, but they gave the menfolk who were in the house a hiding. My sister Anne was about to be married, and seeing the presents lined along the wall, they insisted that they had been stolen. A detective finally accepted the obvious evidence that they were wedding presents.

On another occasion a fire bomb was thrown at the house from a Saracen and hit the post of the porch. If it had come through the window, all inside would have been burnt to death. Once my young sister Deirdre, coming back from the shops with eggs, found that she couldn't get back into the house because everyone in it was under arrest.

Bishop Philbin paid a rare visit to Ballymurphy to attack the people for their involvement in the riots. I went around to Tess Cahill's and asked her if a busload of women might go over to the bishop's house to let him know how they felt. As it transpired we could have had a fleet of buses. And these were neither anti-clerical women nor were they all republican women, but in no time there was a well-organised picket over at the bishop's palace objecting to what he had said.

On 27 June a similar situation to the Easter riots arose: the loyalists again insisted on parading down the Springfield Road, and this time the conflict reached the intensity of a pitched battle. In the process local people succeeded in forcing the RUC to abandon permanently their barracks on the Springfield Road, and temporarily drove the British army out of their base in the Henry Taggart Memorial Hall. Captured army jeeps were driven out of the fort, then sent careering driverless through army lines. The riots went on continuously, night and day.

Professional soldiers, trained to kill, found that they were facing women and men who looked like their own mothers, sisters, fathers and brothers, and the women were breaking them with their tongues, screaming at them and abusing them, and sometimes hitting them. After a particularly intense period of rioting, I walked up the Springfield Road, as far as the Alvarno Hotel, where I saw people sticking flowers into the muzzles of the guns of young British soldiers, who were sitting crying, totally and absolutely shattered. That night the officer in charge shot himself dead, and the following day they had to withdraw the regiment and bring in other, harder regiments. I always felt sorry for the man who killed himself.

In late June 1970 my father was arrested and received a fierce beating by British troops after coming home to Divismore Park from the funeral of republican veteran Hugh McAteer. I arrived on the scene when he was just being put into an ambulance, which was parked at the green box. His face was a mask of blood, and hospital examination revealed a hairline fracture of the skull. He was subsequently beaten quite badly on a few more occasions, and once the paratroopers hammered him very badly as he was coming out of mass in Corpus Christi in Springhill. In his own day he had been a robust, stocky little fighter, and they gave him a very hard time. Our Paddy was also arrested on a riotous behaviour charge, and Liam narrowly escaped from the snatch squads on numerous occasions.

But a great deal was happening in a very short time. On the same day, 27 June, as the Orange parade marched down Springfield Road, riots broke out in Ardoyne just after another march had passed. In this instance the IRA were ready and waiting, and in the ensuing gun-battle, three loyalists were killed. There was also a defensive action by the IRA in Clonard against the Orange parade. There had been a build-up of tension there over a core of the Mackie's workers shouting sectarian insults on their way to and from work about Bombay Street being burned out and people being killed in the area.

On the other side of the city unionist crowds were launching a determined attack with gunfire and petrol bombs on St Matthew's Catholic church at the entrance to the small, isolated Catholic enclave of Ballymacarret. When an opposition MP demanded that the British army intervene to protect the area, they refused.

The 'Provisional' IRA, in their most important action since the split, engaged the loyalist attackers, who were bent on visiting a new pogrom on apparently defenceless Catholics, and succeeded in driving them off, in the process establishing a new credibility for themselves. One volunteer, Henry McIlhone, was killed and Billy McKee was wounded in an intense gun-battle; two loyalists were shot dead.

I was living a crazy life at this time, up till dawn every morning, dossing till noon, because every night there was some kind of alarm or excursion. I was in Clonard on Friday, 3 July, when news came that the British army were raiding heavily in the Falls, and that there was a big build-up of troops throughout the area in what was the first major offensive by the British army. At 4.30 pm they started searching for arms in Balkan Street, an area in which the Goulding/McMillen faction were active. They found a small number of guns, but they also found that they were being met by the resistance of the local people, who feared that they were going to be left defenceless to face further loyalist pogroms. In the ensuing riots a group of squaddies were stranded in the midst of a hostile crowd and large quantities of CS gas were pumped in. Then 3,000 soldiers piled into the area with jeeps and Land Rovers, supported from the air by helicopters.

General Freeland sealed off an area of about fifty small streets of tightly packed terraced houses in the lower Falls. From helicopters hovering over the rooftops, loudspeakers broadcast a message of war, declaring a curfew which confined the local residents to their homes for an indefinite period while thousands of troops went on the rampage.

His troops attacked, firing 1,500 rounds in the narrow streets. They killed one civilian in his fifties at the front door of his Falls Road home. Another in his sixties they shot close to his home in Marchioness Street; he died seven days later. They shot and killed an English/Polish photographer in his twenties, who was visiting from London, and a man in his thirties was deliberately crushed to death by an armoured car. Dozens more were injured in the British army assault on the lower Falls.

For thirty-six hours the troops had the area under total military occupation and curfew while they carried out a house-to-house search. They broke down doors with pick-axes and rifle butts; they ripped out fireplaces, pulled up floorboards, smashed kitchens, walls, ceilings and religious statues. They arrested 300 people. In all, fifty-two pistols, thirty-five rifles, six automatics and 250 rounds of ammunition were found – a small enough haul in the context. Meanwhile, of a total of 107,000 licensed guns in the Six Counties, 80% were in the hands of unionists.

The military siege was lifted by a march of women, organised by republicans and led by Sinn Féin's Maire Drumm, who brushed soldiers aside as they barged through the military blockade carrying food and milk to relieve the area. When word of the violence that had been inflicted on the people of the lower Falls was carried back by these women to areas such as Ballymurphy, Andersonstown and Turf Lodge, a second march was spontaneously organised, a great tide of 3,000 women pouring into the Leeson Street area that evening and forcing the British army finally to abandon their curfew without having completed their search for arms. In addition, many of the women on the march had brought prams and in these they were able to take out large numbers of guns. The Goulding faction had most of their leadership arms dumps in that area, and most of these now wound up with the 'Provos'.

The curfew was completely illegal, yet no one in the British army was ever charged with any offence in relation to it, and no attempt was ever made to bring any of the murderers of any of the people killed to trial.

There was another engagement in Andersonstown that night to draw attention away from the lower Falls, quite a sizeable gun-battle with the British army, which was a bit of a botched operation but was nevertheless the first engagement in which the British army were attacked by the IRA. There was also an attempt to engage them in Ballymurphy, but the Brits pulled their patrols back to avoid becoming stretched and the engagement was aborted.

For many Catholics the Falls curfew was yet another turning

point in their attitude to the British government and its forces, and the fact that following this 'rape of the Falls' the British army brought two unionist politicians in the back of a Land Rover on a triumphal tour of the devastated area was seen as hugely insulting and provocative.

Nearly a year after the August pogroms had traumatised the entire nationalist population, any hopes that some had harboured that the British army might prove a less brutal force than the RUC had been dashed. The curfew had been undertaken partly as a search for arms, principally as an exercise in military intimidation of a whole community; but although respect had never been shown to it by the government, this was a community with a strong sense of self-respect, and it was not about to submit. Irrespective of their political views, people's sense of justice and fair play was outraged. Thousands of people who had never been republicans now gave their active support to the IRA; others who had never had any time for physical force now accepted it as a practical necessity.

At about this time a mandatory six-month sentence was introduced for 'disorderly behaviour', which covered being present at a riot even if not participating. Frank Gogarty of NICRA was, on 1 August, one of the first victims of this new law.

In July 1970, 1,500 refugees fled over the border as a result of pogroms launched by loyalists. It wasn't that Catholics were entirely innocent of displaying any malice to Protestants, but there was no real threat to the Protestant inhabitants of streets or housing estates; no pogroms were launched against them. In fact, Protestant families have lived in Ballymurphy throughout all the troubles, valued and welcome members of their local community. However, it suited loyalist politicians to suggest that Protestants were in imminent danger of being burnt out of their homes just as the Catholic residents of Bombay Street and other streets had been.

In New Barnsley, Paisleyites intervened, the same people who had intervened previously to bring an end to the joint action of Catholics and Protestants over the erection of safety railings. Now they sought to convince the Protestants of New Barnsley that they were about to be subjected to a pogrom by Catholics and they brought in lorries to assist in what soon became a full-scale evacuation.

We therefore became the reluctant inheritors of almost an entire housing estate. As I walked up into the estate on a very still morning, it was eerie to see these empty streets painted red, white and blue. Some windows were open, their curtains fluttering. A few cats looked on warily.

Then we discovered that some of the houses had been booby-trapped, the gas left on and candles burning in the attics of some, while in others inflammable liquid had been placed up the chimneys. Others were flooded: their water taps had been left on. We had to check every single house, and it was strange to go through these houses, many of them still with a few personal effects proclaiming lives that had been lived there until hours before.

We decided to use the estate to rehouse refugees who were still living in people's houses or in the chalets on the Whiterock Road. Some of those who had initially fled to the Twenty-six Counties had by now returned. We called a meeting in St Thomas's school, and in a very democratic way those houses were allocated on the basis of people's need.

I addressed the meeting, asking everyone to help to allocate the houses in a fair way. I told them: 'We don't want to be getting involved in doing the Housing Trust's work for them. If you can work it out between yourselves, we're happy enough with that, we'll leave it to you. Let's go through it, and if there's any dispute then we'll come in and try and settle it, but we would far rather that you just worked it out yourselves. Everybody here is in the same boat.'

To the credit of the people involved, that speech ended Sinn Féin's involvement. They didn't need us to do what they could do themselves.

As the fighting between the people of Ballymurphy and the British army intensified, we sought to anticipate how they would act. A local man who had served in the British army in Aden warned us that they were liable to start shooting at any time. He told us that they would bring out a squad of soldiers in box formation with riflemen and they would have a banner and a megaphone; an officer would announce, speaking first in the English language and then in the language of the natives, that the riot was over and that they would open fire if the crowd did not disperse. Then the officer would pick out people, tell the riflemen to shoot this fellow in the red shirt, and so on. Eventually, things happened as our local veteran had predicted. But when the British officer stepped forward to tell us the riot was over, a guy called Herbo Gibson, who had got his hands on a British army megaphone, reduced everyone to hysterical laughter when he stood up and responded, in a very crisp, officer-class British accent: 'Disperse or we will throw stones!'

Herbo was always in the thick of the riots, as was his dog Bo. A true rebel and a proud Ballymurphy mongrel, Bo would attack British soldiers on sight and would continue to harass them, no matter how many kicks they landed on him. Sometimes he would also chase stones thrown at the Brits and bring them back.

One day in Divismore Park a riot was in progress when someone threw a nail bomb, which landed near a Brit riot squad. Bo, busily engaged in the riot, spotted the nail bomb, picked it up in his mouth and ran off back towards Herbo, his tail wagging with pleasure.

The crowd scattered wildly, leaping over fences and hedges, while Herbo, the dog in hot pursuit, sprinted up Glenalina Road, screaming 'Drop it, Bo! Drop it!'

Poor Bo didn't drop it, and that night he was buried in Herbo's back garden, local children providing a guard of honour for the fallen hero while Herbo himself sounded the 'Last Post'.

Incredibly, the Brits later exhumed him for forensic tests.

At times Ballymurphy could be quite surreal. One night when the Brits shone their searchlight down into Divismore Park, near our house, two guys waltzed into the spotlight with their faces blackened and began to sing 'Are You From Dixie?'

On a number of memorable occasions, and to the delight of the masses, rioters attacked British riot squads with CS gas canisters. While the riots were deadly serious, there was also an element of contest in them, and when the rioters scored a point the community applauded. There was also a contingent of spectators at every riot, especially in Divismore Park.

In this context it constituted a new turning-point when the British army shot nineteen-year-old Danny O'Hagan dead during a minor riot in the New Lodge Road on 31 July. That night when the riot squad formed up outside the Taggart, a very large crowd of us marched right up to the marksmen in protest at the O'Hagan killing. The officer in charge was quite nervous and was shouting at all the riflemen to arm their weapons. Barney McLoughlin, one of our long-time activists, pulled his shirt apart, all the buttons flying off, and he pushed his chest right up to the muzzle of the gun of the rifleman.

'Go on!' he shouted. 'Give us another fucking Sharpeville!'

It was obvious that troops would engage in shooting; it was, after all, what they had been trained to do. For their part these, mostly young soldiers, who had joined the British army for a host of reasons, none of which had to do with a wish to be stranded in a fortified barracks in the midst of hostile residents in Belfast, must have experienced frustration, confusion, anger and boredom.

For people of my generation in West Belfast the killing of Danny O'Hagan came as dreadful confirmation of the fact that what had started as a peaceful campaign for civil rights was now resolving itself into a violent confrontation between the armed forces and the ordinary people. The experience of the pogroms had been traumatic enough in itself, but now the British army was behaving as a conquering colonial power. The riots had been expressing a vigorous physical opposition to the arrogant behaviour of the soldiers but they had stopped well short of a full military confrontation. Now, however, it seemed we were heading inexorably towards war. Bitterness at the violence with which our demands for justice had been met crystallised for many around the death of our young contemporary, and a steely determination entered many hearts, a feeling that if it was war they wanted, then it was war they would get.

Local republicans got involved in the Ballymurphy riots, which continued for months, very consciously and deliberately in a serious attempt to create a situation of popular conflict with the British occupying forces. The republican leadership on the other hand were against it and sent up a group to stop it, and these IRA people from outside were actually stoned out of Springhill by the young people, who resented their intervention. However, as the fighting continued, we local activists had been finding that the Brits were going wild with frustration at their inability to suppress the riots and, instead of backing off and letting the violence subside, they were coming in aggressively looking for trouble, seeking to fly the flag in a classically macho military fashion. As they were heavily armed and the rioters were not, we feared for the outcome and knew we had to get the rioters off the streets before there were multiple fatalities.

The 'Provisional' IRA leadership were opposed to the riots because they wanted to avoid being drawn into armed conflict. By mid-1970 they had built up a good number of volunteers with some degree of training and capability. Then, after the Falls Road curfew in July 1970, recruitment had been massive. But republicans still faced a dearth of arms. At first old and cheap Springfield and Lee Enfield rifles, which were readily available in the US, were obtained. These increased the IRA's defensive capacity, but they were not yet ready to engage the British army.

The pace of events was being set on the streets, where rioting continued, despite the jailing of many young nationalists for mandatory six-month sentences. Opposition politicians were aware that they were having little impact on the situation and were perceived as having little relevance. Southern business and political leaders and the Dublin government were concerned about a situation that was spinning out of control, and they assisted at the birth, in late August, of a new party, the Social Democratic and Labour Party (SDLP). This brought together a wide range of individuals, three of whom had been elected as independents, one as a Northern Ireland Labour Party member, another as a Nationalist and another as Republican Labour. Including John Hume, Paddy Devlin and Austin Currie in their ranks, they appointed Gerry Fitt as their leader, and a couple of months later they acquired a party following when the National Democratic Party joined them.

Paradoxically, the street-fighting in Ballymurphy suited neither the IRA leadership nor the British army, and the hierarchies of both forces wanted it stopped. In late January a senior British army officer asked Liam Hannaway for a meeting to discuss this matter. The British army and some senior republicans authorised by the national leadership held confidential discussions, and agreed that if the Brits stayed out of Ballymurphy, republicans would quell the riots. And so, after seven months of continuous rioting, we local republicans got hold of some of the key people involved in the riots and succeeded in calming the situation down.

It was also agreed with the Brits that there would be no RUC or British military activity in Clonard, where the talks occurred, while they were going on. However, Ian Paisley revealed the existence of the deal, and on 3 February the British army, for reasons of political expediency, broke the agreement and launched an invasion of Clonard by the Second Royal Anglians. After conducting violent house-to-house raids, the soldiers remained in the area, provoking riots by their wild and oppressive behaviour, and at lunchtime they were joined by loyalist workers from Mackie's engineering works, who mingled with the soldiers, throwing bolts, ball-bearings and other missiles at the local residents. Later in the afternoon the British army cleared the residents from the streets by driving jeeps at high speed up and down and assaulting people at will.

Rioting continued for two days and nights in response to these continuing interventions. Although the whole exercise had been launched in order to appease Paisley and the unionists, there were further complaints from the unionists, who claimed that the British army had no idea who the Provisionals were. A spokesman for the military then announced on television the names of five republicans, including Liam Hannaway and his son, my cousin Kevin, without mentioning that some of these were the people with whom the ending of the Ballymurphy riots had been discussed.

Hopes that the situation in Belfast could be calmed by agreement being established between republicans and the British military had been sacrificed by the British on the altar of political expediency, in the form of appeasing the unionists. On the day after the television broadcast, the IRA killed a British soldier, the first British Army fatality, and on the following day Prime Minister Chichester-Clark announced that 'Northern Ireland is at war with the IRA Provisionals'.

In November my Granny Adams died. I was in the Whiterock when I got the news. I had seen my granny very little for some months now. Even when I called to the house, and I had done so a few times since August '69, it was always only for a few minutes. She was always in good form, and maybe I thought she would go on for ever; or maybe I just didn't think. She had always been there for me.

Now the Adamses assembled from Dublin, from Canada and from throughout Belfast for her funeral. Neighbours from Abercorn Street called to the wake. On the day of the funeral the removal was delayed so that my Uncles Sean and Francis, who flew in from Toronto with Aunt Rita and my Canadian cousins, could attend. The burial at Milltown was particularly emotional, and my Uncle Sean broke down very badly. For my part I felt a little detached from the collective grief. My head was filled with Granny Adams – happy thoughts and fond memories of a wonderful woman.

After her funeral our Canadian *clann* stayed for some time, dividing their days between Divismore Park and the rest of the family.

By this time the Provisional army council had regularised the IRA's position. In November a statement announced that the Provisional army executive and council had gone out of office and that an army convention, held in accordance with the IRA's constitution, had elected a regular executive and council. While this formally brought an end to the 'provisional' phase, the title stuck and was used especially by the media to differentiate the IRA from the Goulding faction, who were referred to as the 'Officials'. Both factions at that time engaged in armed actions, though the 'Provisionals' were much more active. (Incidentally, I have always disliked the description of either the IRA or Sinn Féin as 'Provisionals' or 'Provos'.)

Following on the split, a number of feuds arose from the very existence of rival armed republican groups, and the first fatality occurred when Charlie Hughes was shot dead on 8 March 1971. There had been some friction between the two groups in the Falls, the Markets and Ballymurphy; most of it happened simply when rival groups or individuals ran into each other and one word borrowed another. There was a row in the Falls area in which people involved in the 'Officials' tried to evict people whose families were involved in the 'Provos', and that led to arms being produced, and then there was a gunfight. Charlie was shot dead and another person was injured coming from a house in Cyprus Street. Tom Cahill was very badly wounded on his milkman's round a few hours after I had left him home. There was a series of shooting incidents, and in one of these a young man called McGuinness was wounded with his own weapon in a mêlée with two local activists. He was hospitalised for a long time and died subsequently. Many people felt torn by conflicting emotions during these feuds. Proinsias MacAirt, for example, was very close socially and personally with both Billy McMillen, the leading figure in the Officials, and Charlie Hughes of the Provos. For my part, Tom Cahill and I were close friends and I was very angry at the situation in which he had been shot down premeditatedly. Yet my sister was in the Officials. MacAirt suggested that I could help end the feuding, and I found myself witness to a meeting between Billy McMillen and Billy McKee, at which an arrangement of sorts was hammered out.

The Officials were still in the field, but the Provisional IRA rapidly moved from principally defensive concerns to a substantial offensive against the British presence and the Stormont regime in all its forms. Indeed the IRA's capability increased so dramatically that by mid-1971 they were able to carry out as many as 125 bombings in just two months. Brian Faulkner became prime minister in late March, and in May he gave the British army carte blanche to fire 'with effect' on anyone acting 'suspiciously'; but he balanced this politically in June by offering positions on Stormont committees to the SDLP, whose enthusiastic response suggested that he might succeed in bringing the Catholic middle class on board.

The British army could now open fire 'at will', in its own jargon, 'on male persons of military age'. That at least was the instruction given to its soldiers, whatever about the niceties of the matter as enshrined in civil law or stated in military regulations. The purpose was clear: to terrorise the local community by killing any available person 'acting suspiciously' in the vicinity or in the wake of an IRA operation, especially one against the British army. That was the message brought to local communities after the Brits killed obviously innocent people. 'Tell the IRA to stop,' they said, 'and we'll stop.'

On 8 July 1971 the British army shot dead, in Derry, Seamus Cusack and Desmond Beattie; both were unarmed Catholics. The deaths of these first victims of shooting 'with effect' marked a critical turning point. Sinn Féin held a massive rally in Derry at which Ruairí Ó Bradaigh, president, and Maire Drumm, vice-president, both spoke. Nationalist Derry was in wholehearted revolt as queues formed to join the IRA. The SDLP had become associated with the regime by its acceptance of involvement in the committee system, and now the mood of its constituents meant that it risked losing all credibility with them. On 15 July the SDLP withdrew from Stormont. What had been primarily a battle between beleaguered nationalists and the Stormont administration for equal rights was now a battle between beleaguered nationalists and the British establishment.

Ma, Gerry and Margaret in Greencastle

Gerry and Paddy, Divismore Park

Gerry, Margaret, Anne Murphy (cousin)

front row: Frances, Liam, Maura
second row: Paddy, Margaret, Anne, Gerry, Sean (in Gerry's arms)
back row: Da, Granny Adams, Deirdre and Ma

front row: Deirdre, Gerry, Ma, Dominic, Da, Maura, Sean
back row: Liam, Anne, Paddy, Margaret, Frances

Kevin and Liam Hannaway, August 1969

On the streets of Belfast

Press conference, 13 August 1971: Belfast city councillor Eugene McKenna,
Joe Cahill, Stormont MP Patrick Kennedy, John Kelly,
Belfast city councillor and member of the Police Committee John Flanagan

Volunteer on sentry duty in Ballymurphy, 1971

Frances and Patrick Mulvenna

In Long Kesh.
front row: Tom Cahill, Tommy 'Toddler' Toland, Gerry
back row: Jimmy Gibney, Tomboy London, Brendan Hughes,
Terence 'Cleeky' Clarke, Bobby Sands

In Long Kesh: Cleeky Clarke, Gerry

In Long Kesh: Gerry and the Dark

After the burning of Long Kesh

Gearóid and Gerry near Ughtyneill, Co. Meath, 1977

Tom Hartley, Gerry and Collette

Seven

The British and unionist search for a military victory intensified. On 23 July 1971 almost 2,000 troops carried out dawn raids on the homes of people believed to be republicans; it was a dry run for internment.

Kevin Hannaway and I were in a house in Panton Street in the Falls area. We decided to cut through to another house at about four o'clock in the morning, and on our way round four Brits on a surveillance mission stopped us in Merrion Street. They brought in more soldiers and a senior officer arrived, brandishing a Browning pistol, which he placed at my head.

Kevin Hannaway was being covered by a soldier with a rifle, and Kevin looked as if he was ready to fight.

'If you don't take that rifle out of my face,' he said, 'I'm going to ram it right up your arse!'

By now the street was practically crowded with British soldiers and I most certainly didn't want to fight.

'Pay attention to what he's saying. You can see we've got you surrounded,' I told the Brit, trying to get Kevin to shut up.

The Brits proceeded to abuse and threaten us. Lights were coming on in windows in the houses all around and people were leaning out to look.

We assumed we were going to be arrested, but to our surprise they let us go. We walked around the corner and then we ran like mad.

'There definitely isn't going to be internment,' Kevin said to me when we got indoors somewhere safe.

'Kevin,' said I, 'there definitely *is* going to be internment.'

On 6 August British army troop levels (excluding the Ulster Defence Regiment) were increased to 11,900. We got definite word that internment was being introduced a couple of days later. Late on 8 August, Kevin and I went running around telling people to stay out of anywhere they were known.

In the early hours of the morning of 9 August, we parted company and I went up into a house in Springhill.

I woke up at 4.00 am to hear people running around shouting 'Internment's in!' It sounded strange to me, as if internment was a person who'd come to visit. Before I could get dressed, a number of local women activists, including Colette McArdle, arrived. I was wearing Paisley-patterned underpants, which occasioned humorous comment even in the circumstances. I went out of the door of the house, and at the top of Springhill Avenue I could see the British army. Across the river I could see our house, from which my father was dragged that night. Our Liam was taken too. At Girdwood barracks they discovered that he was too young, so they took him and threw him out of a Land Rover far from nationalist West Belfast.

By now the entire area was in a state of insurrection. The Brits had been forced back to the outskirts, mostly along the Springfield Road and into their barracks at the Taggart Memorial Hall. There was also fighting on the Whiterock Road at McRory Park. A pitched battle was raging at the top of Springhill Avenue, and from the Murph people had advanced on the Henry Taggart barracks to which many of those lifted in the swoops had been initially taken and where they were being brutally beaten. Whatever anyone could lay their hands on was being flung at the base. The British army replied with rubber bullets and later with lead ones.

In the meantime loyalist crowds gathered in Springmartin and began taunting the people of Ballymurphy and Springhill, chanting 'Where's your daddy gone?' in imitation of a pop song of the time. Then they started throwing rocks at the houses of Catholics beneath them in Springfield Park. Father Hugh Mullan, the thirty-seven-year-old local curate, intervened to prevent nationalist youths from responding to the taunts and telephoned the RUC and the British army. After several hours of rocks and bottles raining down on to houses, Father Mullan advanced up to the Springmartin ridge to ask that the loyalist crowd have some consideration for the young children of Springfield Park; they told him to 'Fuck off, you Fenian bastard!'

As the missiles continued to rain down, residents of other parts of Ballymurphy gathered in Springfield Park to support their neighbours, and by a couple of hours later a pitched battle of stone-throwing was raging.

When shooting started from Springmartin, the IRA replied from flats in Moyard. British troops immediately opened fire on Ballymurphy from the Henry Taggart, then moved into Spring-martin to join loyalist gunmen in firing into Moyard and Ballymurphy. Through back gardens residents of Springfield Park evacuated their houses and made their way towards Moyard community centre, children being shepherded by adults across a piece of open ground in front of Father Mullan's house.

At the height of the fighting Colette and Maureen McGuinness made their way to number 11 Divismore Park to check on my mother. Soldiers of the Parachute Regiment had wrecked the house, and because of the ferocity of the shooting outside and the state of the house, my mother was preparing to evacuate the younger children. Following the trauma and the savagery of the raid and the arrest of my da and our Liam, everyone was distressed; my mother was obviously concerned also about me and our Paddy and our friends. She and Colette and Maureen bundled up the smaller children and left the house. As they did so there was an extremely long and loud staccato burst of heavy gunfire.

'Jesus, Mary and Joseph!' my mother cried.

That was the last time she was in Divismore Park.

When the family tried to return later, the Paras were in occupation, and when they eventually left, the house was uninhabitable. The Brits had rammed the house repeatedly with an armoured vehicle. Inside, not only had they smashed furniture and sinks, they had also destroyed personal effects and bric-à-brac, family papers and photographs. Ceilings had been pulled down. My da's beloved partition and other doors had been smashed. The beds were soaked in urine and shit, as were the clothes in the wardrobes.

Years before, my mother had kept ornaments on the mantelpiece and on top of the TV. These were generally small presents which she had received, mainly from us, her children. As would be expected in a household as large and boisterous as ours, these ornaments were knocked over and broken from time to time. Chipped and cracked, they were given to my da to repair. Once while so engaged and in a moment of inspiration he had glued all the ornaments to the mantelpiece and to the top of the TV.

'They'll not break these again, Annie,' he had told my ma.

Shortly afterwards she had been greatly embarrassed when the television had broken down and had to be taken away for repair by the hire purchase firm, ornaments and all. Now, years later, that was one of the images in Colette's mind as she surveyed the wreckage of the house. Amidst all the other destruction, only the stumps of the ornaments remained on the mantelpiece, but from the TV set even as it lay on its side amid the other debris on the floor, my ma's ornaments projected, still intact.

There was trouble also in other areas. Loyalists used the confusion of the internment swoops as cover for launching a sniping assault on the Ardoyne, but were met by a strong IRA reaction. Fighting was strongest in Belfast, but broke out also in Derry, Newry, Armagh, Lurgan and Strabane. Residents now combined with IRA units to a greater extent than ever. As the Brits used armoured cars and bulldozers to shift barricades, people overturned vehicles and set them ablaze to create new barriers.

We arranged a meeting of West Belfast activists, but before this I walked up into the Murph, down through the Whiterock, down the Falls Road into Beechmount, down the lower Wack, as we called the lower end of the Falls Road, up into Clonard, then back into Andersonstown. It was like being a spectator at something which I was involved in. When I cut down through the Whiterock, I could see that the Brits had tried to bring up a bulldozer to move a barricade, and here they had killed a man.

I met local republicans down in Beechmount and they said I shouldn't be walking about, so they got me a driver and a Morris Minor car, which we parked on a street while we went into a house there. When we came out of the house, we found that the local people had built barricades at each end of the street, and so our car was useless. I went, on foot again, down into Leeson Street. There were quite a few of the Officials in Leeson Street, and I chatted briefly with some of them before making my way to Kevin Hannaway's house. There I learnt to my dismay that he had been arrested; the house itself was a wreck.

Internment was brought in under Section 12 of the Special Powers Act, which allowed people to be held indefinitely without charge on the authority of Brian Faulkner, prime minister of the statelet. Faulkner announced that 'The main target of the present operations is the Irish Republican Army.' But he also deliberately included anti-unionist political activists committed to entirely peaceful means: people, as he put it, 'who would have called meetings to protest against internment'.

Faulkner, the architect of internment, had been described by former unionist Prime Minister Terence O'Neill as 'devious', 'treacherous', 'scheming' and 'totally untrustworthy'. Maybe he was all of these things, but his popularity among unionists had always rested on his penchant for coat-trailing, and his introduction of internment, exclusively directed as it was against anti-unionists, was undoubtedly extremely popular with his party.

Internment was an act of mass political violence directed by the state against its nationalist and civil rights opponents. That it was a political exercise was made clear by the fact that General Sir

Harry Tuzo, General Officer Commanding Northern Ireland, opposed its introduction, insisting that the British army did not possess sufficient information to be able to intern the 'right' people, and that interning only Catholics would make matters worse by uniting them against the state.

In the dry run on 23 July, British troops, backed up by the RUC, had concentrated on address books and documents. Then plans had been laid to conduct internment swoops on 10 August. However, when a man on his way to work was shot dead by a British soldier outside Springfield Road barracks and his passenger dragged from the van by soldiers and brutally beaten, as a consequence of the rioting which followed, a decision was taken to bring forward internment by one day.

Operation Demetrius, as it was named, was carried out noisily and was well signposted. Defence committees and local residents observed the advancing Saracens and furniture lorries used by the British army to transport prisoners and raised the alarm with bin-lids and whistles. Soldiers smashed in doors and fired live ammunition and rubber bullets. In Derry local people drove the Brits off before they had completed their intended arrests. The way the operation was handled, with the heavy-handed intimidation of the entire nationalist population, cemented that community's opposition to British rule even further.

The people who were lifted were many of the best of their generations in the communities from which they sprang and to which they contributed; and they came from several different generations. Liam Mulholland was seventy-eight, one of about fifty older men who were lifted simply because they had been interned before. Then there were young student members of People's Democracy and a few members of NICRA. Some people were perhaps picked up because they were related to political activists; others, completely uninvolved people, were just in the wrong place at the wrong time. There were local community and tenants' association activists, and there were republicans, but despite the fact that the first killings had been the loyalist killings in May and June 1996 of Peter Ward and others in Malvern

Street, the first explosions had been caused by the UVF, and the first RUC man had been killed by unionists, no unionists were interned.

One of the consequences of the internment operation was that it removed from the nationalist community many of its most articulate, energetic and socially committed members. In particular, because the intelligence information on which the operation was based was out of date, many of the older community, political and civil rights activists were interned, while few of the younger generation were. Thus the responsibilities of leadership within the community fell upon young shoulders. At the time, my contemporaries and I, who with the benefit of hindsight may be said to have stepped precociously into older and wiser people's shoes, knew only that there was an urgent need to meet the immediate challenges facing us on the ground.

As it happened, all the many arrests carried out by the British army that internment morning were illegal, because even under the draconian Special Powers Act the soldiers should have been accompanied by members of the RUC. The crimes of the powerful pass unpunished, often unremarked.

After our West Belfast meeting and when all the different contingency plans had been discussed and agreed, I returned to the Murph where the fighting continued, with the British army unable or unwilling at that time to risk coming back into the area. The shooting continued all night. The next day, to make matters worse, refugees from loyalist and British army attacks in other parts of Belfast started arriving into Ballymurphy, where efforts were already underway to organise the evacuation of terrified children. Then late that night everything quietened. We knew to expect the worst.

On 11 August the Paras advanced on Ballymurphy. Coming down the mountain loney, some behind a herd of cattle which they moved in from the fields around, they fired indiscriminately on reaching the houses. Moving through the area, they kicked in doors in every street, took men from their homes, beat them brutally and handcuffed them to railings and fences. Some men they tied to their Saracens as human shields. By 8.00 am they had the area under total military occupation. Faced with overwhelming odds, and anticipating an all-out assault, the IRA had faded away, leaving a small number of individual volunteers placed throughout the area in relatively safe positions to offer token resistance and to create distractions and diversions.

In a house close to the top of Glenalina Road, I and a few other local people sat up all night. To our horror when the Brits came they kicked in the first door in the street and occupied the front bedroom. They skipped the next house. Smashed into another one. Further down the street a woman came to a bedroom window. A British soldier screamed at her, another discharged his rifle. Then there was a burst of shooting. Soldiers clumped together in the front garden of the house we were in. We lay on the floor.

Colette McArdle was with us. 'If we get out of this, I'm going to marry you,' I whispered to her.

Upstairs we could hear the woman of the house anxiously and stridently hissing at her children not to move.

Outside we heard the running feet of British soldiers, the crashing and screams as they smashed their way into houses, occasional shots. They were into the house next to us. We barely breathed as we heard the thumps and shouts through the dividing wall. Miraculously they came no closer than the front garden and porch of our house.

After some time the area became deadly quiet. I asked Colette to go out and check the area. She slipped outside.

The quietness continued. Then we heard female voices and footsteps on the path. It was Colette and the other women. She tapped on the window. We nervously let her in.

'It's OK, they're away,' she said.

I sent her off to double check before venturing out myself. Meanwhile, others arrived with reports of what had been happening in the area during the chaos of the last couple of days, and when Colette returned she, too, had further reports. We compared notes, trying to make some sense of events.

On the night of 9 August, it seemed, as Father Mullan and

others had moved to evacuate children from Springfield Park, they had come under fire from British troops. As nineteen-year-old Bobby Clarke had moved across the open ground to guide another child evacuee to safety he had been shot in the back from the Taggart. Waving a white handkerchief, Father Mullan had left his house to administer the Last Rites. Finding that the fallen man was not dying, he had turned to go back and ring for an ambulance. In a fusillade of shots from the Taggart, two bullets had hit him, one in the heart.

Frank Quinn from Moyard, aged twenty, had also moved into the open area to help Bobby Clarke and was also shot dead by the British army.

Every time over the next few hours any attempts had been made to recover the bodies, firing had opened up again. However, a Jordanian student doctor had eventually succeeded, waving a white helmet, in dragging each of the three bodies to cover.

Meanwhile, before the shooting had started, Joan Connolly had left her house in Ballymurphy Road. Fearing for the safety of her children with the riots going on up at Springfield Park, she had gone in search of them. When she reached Springfield Road opposite the Taggart, she had exchanged greetings with a group of about seven men, who included Daniel Taggart, Joseph Murphy and Davie Callaghan, as they stood at the entrance to an old house called the Manse. Just then the British army had opened up from the Taggart base. Joan Connolly, aged fifty, was hit once, rose to her feet to get away, and was shot again in the head with such force that her body was thrown into a field, not to be discovered until the following day.

Also shot by the British army that night of 9 August was twenty-year-old Noel Phillips, whose body was also found the following day, in the stream between Ballymurphy and Spring-hill.

Davie Callaghan and Joseph Murphy had been injured; Joseph Murphy tried to escape across the fields with Danny Taggart and two other men, but the British army had caught up with him. A forty-one-year-old father of nine children, he had been hit in the leg, and the soldiers had then fired rubber bullets into him at close range, causing severe injuries to his liver and kidneys. They had brought him in an armoured car to the Taggart, where he was laid on the floor with the dead, and every time soldiers passed they had lashed out with their boots at both the living and the dead. Days later we learned that he had been removed to hospital where he was put on a kidney machine, but doctors were unable to perform a necessary amputation of his leg because of the injuries caused by the soldiers' beatings. Gangrene developed and he died nearly two weeks later.

Danny Taggart, a forty-four-year-old father of ten children, had also not succeeded in escaping the soldiers on internment night: his body had been found with thirteen bullets in him.

Davie Callaghan, a fifty-nine-year-old retired postal engineer with chronic asthma, had been hit by a piece of flying masonry as bullets fired from the Taggart had slammed into the gateposts of the Manse. He had been dragged by soldiers to an armoured car, beaten with rifles and thrown in. In the Taggart soldiers had held his legs apart and over and over again kicked him in the testicles.

Eddie Butler, aged eleven, had been shot from the Taggart as he tried to climb through a hedge between Springhill and Ballymurphy. As he lay screaming on the ground, the soldiers continued to fire. A man with an artificial leg courageously pulled a door from a shed and used it to haul the young boy to safety. IRA volunteers provided covering fire. I witnessed that event myself, and as I heard the child's cries they reminded me inescapably of the rabbit I had shot years before up at Glenavy.

The man the Brits shot near a barricade close to McRory Park was Eddie Doherty, aged twenty-eight. At Whiterock Road Corporation Yard they shot dead John Lavery, twenty; they tied his brother Terence to railings and proceeded to cut up his clothes and shoes with knives they had stolen from a butcher's shop.

Many of the killings on the night of 9 August had taken place in the vicinity of the Taggart, including and close to Divismore Park and our house. This area around the base had obviously been designated a killing zone. As we registered the information coming in and assessed it, we could see no reason for all those deaths other than that soldiers had been told to shoot whoever entered that zone.

And in the British army's brief saturation of Ballymurphy this morning of 11 August, they had shot Joseph Corr of Divismore Crescent, then taken him away and beaten him up although he was already seriously wounded (he died fifteen days later in Musgrave Park military hospital).

Now I walked down a deserted Ballymurphy Road into Springhill. It was eerie. I went into Corpus Christi and sat quietly in prayer. When I came out more people were starting to move around. A middle-aged woman greeted me.

'The bastards! They didn't stay long enough to fight. They could only kill women and children.'

In the immediate aftermath of internment, rioting and gun-battles took place all over the north; people died but the world wasn't watching and the media were full of the alleged great success of the operation. Military bases and RUC barracks came under attack from enraged citizens who had witnessed the internment raids. In nationalist areas British troops fired wildly, using lead and rubber bullets and CS gas, kicking in doors, wrecking countless houses and assaulting countless people in their homes and on the streets. In addition to the rampaging British troops, loyalist mobs roamed borderline Catholic streets burning out nationalist families. In the immediate aftermath of intern-ment, there were 2,500 forced evacuations. Thousands of refugees streamed over the border, 6,000 alone winding up within two days in five refugee camps established by the Dublin government.

In the four days from 9 to 13 August, twenty-two people were killed, nineteen of them civilians; others died later of their wounds, and scores were injured.

News began to reach us about the treatment of people lifted in the internment operation. Of those who had been arrested in the internment swoops, twelve – one of them Kevin Hannaway –

were singled out for special attention as the British engaged in a grotesque exercise to test techniques, new and old, of torture.

Kevin had been in bed when the Brits raided at 4.30 in the morning, smashing in the front door and racing up the stairs to the bedroom. His older child, aged a little over a year and a half, was screaming in terror, and when Kevin's wife went for one of the soldiers with the child's bottle, he fired at her, the bullet lodging in the ceiling.

Told that he was being arrested under the Special Powers Act, he was marched at gunpoint to Mulhouse Street barracks, then put on a lorry, his hands tied in front of him, and driven to Girdwood barracks. Here he was photographed and put sitting on the floor of the gym for several hours with 100 or more other detainees, who were called out one at a time to be questioned by a member of the RUC Special Branch. Kevin told me later that my father received particularly vicious treatment. Soldiers and RUC men alike told detainees that hundreds, even thousands of people were being killed all over Belfast.

After some time they were all taken outside to run a gauntlet between two lines of Military Police while being beaten with fists, boots and batons. Kevin was thrown into a helicopter with its rotor blades already rotating. Threatened that he was going to be killed, he was pushed backwards out of the helicopter, only to find that they were just four feet off the ground. This performance was repeated several times, and he had to run the gauntlet again, being batoned and kicked as he ran. He was brought out in his bare feet with others and forced across a square covered with barbed wire and glass, being beaten all the time. His nose bleeding and misshapen and his teeth protruding through his lip, he was beaten from Girdwood barracks by a back entrance into the adjacent Crumlin Road prison, where he was thrown into a cell. A fellow prisoner did his best to bathe his wounds.

Twenty-four hours after British soldiers had smashed down the door of his home, Kevin was taken from his cell and beaten back to Girdwood barracks by members of the RUC and the Military Police. Here he was forced again to run over the obstacle course while being beaten, punched and kicked by soldiers and bitten by a guard dog. After being put into a room and told to lie there on a camp bed, he was taken out and had a black hessian bag placed over his head and was handcuffed. The square-shaped bag, made of doubled material which effectively kept out all light, extended down over his shoulders as far as his chest. Handcuffed to other hooded detainees Joe Clarke, Francie McGuigan and Archie Auld, he was forced to run out of the building while again being beaten with batons until he was again thrown into a helicopter, where the handcuffs attaching the detainees to each other were removed but each person remained tightly handcuffed at the wrists.

During an hour's flight his guards tightened the hood so that he could hardly breathe and pulled at the handcuffs, making them cut into his wrists. When the helicopter landed he was thrown into a lorry and beaten with fists, boots and batons.

Dragged into a room, he was put in the search position and left there until he was taken to another room where he was stripped of everything except the hood and medically examined. He was weighed, registering 12st. 3lbs; asked by the doctor about his health, he explained that he had had a heart condition since childhood and named the specialist he was attending. Given an oversize pair of overalls, he was put against the wall again. Now unremitting noise pounded in his head, an amplified sound resembling that of a fan or drill. He lost track of time. Whenever he tried to stretch and ease the aches in his limbs he was kicked, kneed and beaten.

After a long time he was taken out, thrown in a lorry and brought to the helicopter. After an hour's flight he was taken by Land Rover to a building where he was seated in a chair and the hood was removed. Two guards stood on either side; one man faced him and gave him a piece of paper and told him to read it, but he couldn't because after so many hours in the hood his eyes were unable to focus. He was hooded again and placed against the wall; they beat his head against the wall, before taking him out again to the helicopter for another hour-long journey, at the end of which he was returned by lorry to the room with the mind-numbing, mind-wrenching noise, and put against the wall again. Whenever he could stand no longer, he was beaten again and taken away for questioning; placed on a chair, the hood was removed and a bright light was shone into his eyes as questions were fired at him by three inquisitors. Then he was brought back to the wall, back to the high-pitched noise and to the beatings again; taken for questioning again, brought back again, beaten again, questioned again . . .

He didn't know how many days and hours had passed; in fact, he was unable by this stage to calculate time at all. His mind was completely confused, and he was conscious only of his aching, bruised body. Then he lost consciousness of his body, and felt he was going insane, becoming aware only of thoughts and visions of his wife and babies, his friends, those who had died before him. He prayed for God to take his life.

Eventually, on Monday 16 August, a week after his ordeal had begun, he was offered tea and a cigarette by a Special Branch man who said that he could take off the hood. He washed and was given a thorough medical examination. He now weighed 11 stone. He was photographed in the nude before being taken back to a small room where he was given his clothes. He was hooded again, brought to the lorry, then to the helicopter. Convinced he was going to be thrown out of the helicopter, he shook with fear during the flight. On landing he was brought by Land Rover to the front door of Crumlin Road jail, where he was formally admitted.

He had been subjected to inhuman torture, cruelly injured in mind, body and spirit. He was in need of urgent specialist treatment and long-term care. Yet far from being admitted to hospital, he was kept for three months in Crumlin Road jail, then transferred to the internment camp at Long Kesh.

The experiment conducted by the British allowed them to refine and develop a wide range of methods of torture for use in Ireland against republicans and others over the succeeding years. Amongst these methods were:

Use of the 'search position' for long periods, one finger of each hand on the wall, legs stretched apart and back, on the toes and with knees bent;

Heavy punches delivered to the pit of the stomach of men in the 'search position';

Kicking the legs out from under people in the 'search position' so that they fell and hit their heads on the wall, the ground or the radiator;

Beating with batons on the testicles and kidneys while in the 'search position';

Kicking between the legs while in the 'search position';

Placing a powerful radiator or electric fire under a man in the 'search position' and stretching a man over benches with two electric fires underneath and kicking him in the stomach;

Punching in the back of the neck, banging the head against the wall, delivering a crescendo of hits to the head with a baton, and slapping ears and face;

Twisting arms behind backs and twisting fingers, hitting the ribs from behind while punching the stomach at the same time;

Squeezing testicles, shoving objects up the anus, kicking knees and shins;

Using electric cattle prods, injections, and electric shocks delivered by a machine;

Burning with matches and candles, sleep deprivation, urinating on prisoners;

Russian roulette, firing blanks, beatings administered in darkness, blindfolding and hooding, white perforated walls in cubicles, threats to prisoners and to their families . . .

The effects of the internment exercise on those who were lifted were in many cases both long-lasting and severe. The worst brutality was inflicted upon the hooded men, but others who received less intense torture (or 'ill-treatment' as authorities prefer to term it) were also afflicted by a wide range of symptoms, including long-term disturbance of memory function, depression, recurring headaches and nausea, ulcers, anxiety states and insomnia. Many of the effects experienced by those who were interned were also experienced by those who were interrogated, even when they were not also interned.

The effects of the internment exercise on the nationalist population of the north were deep and long-lasting. Through the networks of community there were few who did not know someone who had been subjected to intimidation and internment. Indeed, the entire operation had quite consciously been directed by the British against the nationalist community as a whole. But, far from intimidating them, it had stiffened the people's resolve to resist oppression.

On 13 August, four days after the swoops, Joe Cahill, introduced as Belfast commander of the IRA, gave a press conference under the noses of the British army at St Peter's school in the Whiterock. The organisation was intact, he reported, had not been seriously affected, and only two members had been killed during Operation Demetrius.

After the press conference I brought Joe out down the back of St Peter's, and Joe slipped into Beechmount. Later that evening as darkness fell, a friend and I collected him and brought him back along the route we had used after the press conference. We were bringing him to meet journalist Vincent Browne for an interview in the Whiterock. Now, however, instead of going through the school we cut our way across the all-weather playing pitch. We knew we were in clear view of look-outs posted on the high ground above us, close to Corry's wall and at the back of Westrock, on alert against loyalist or further British army attacks, and they had been told that we would be coming that way. As we crossed the playing pitch we chatted quietly together. Suddenly there was a crack of a low-velocity shot. Then another. The second punctured the grey surface of the pitch. The three of us dived earthward. There was another crack, closer this time. From where I was stretched the football pitch looked enormous. We three were sitting ducks. We couldn't even see the firing position. Then there was a shout.

'Who goes there?'

We jumped to our feet. There was another shot.

'It's us! It's fucking us!'

Our companion ran bravely headlong towards the firing position, shouting and gesticulating at the hidden gunman. Joe and I advanced more cautiously behind him.

Afterwards a rumour went around the district that three loyalists had been killed trying to attack Westrock. The valiant defender of St Peter's playing pitch was profoundly embarrassed; for our part we were delighted by his bad shooting. Later, when the true story emerged, he became known as 'Rifleman' after a popular television series of the time.

Internment had been undertaken to smash the IRA, but, far from succeeding in its aim, it confirmed the IRA in its role and boosted popular support. Just two years before internment the IRA had been disorganised, almost completely unarmed, unable to play the role it had played in the pogroms of the 1920s and 1930s of defending the areas under attack. In one or two instances individual republicans had attempted to hold off attacks, but the IRA had been in no shape to offer any organised response. In the months after the August 1969 pogroms, republicans had worked frantically to procure arms, to raise money and to reorganise the IRA to meet the demands of a situation of armed siege. Streets, people and even churches had come under attack, and IRA volunteers had put their lives on the line to protect them. At first, sticks and stones, petrol bombs and unsophisticated guns had been used against the forces of the state, which were equipped with the most up-to-date weaponry. Meanwhile, in the midst of rioting and skirmishes, the IRA had been training, screening and attempting to instil discipline into new recruits.

In a remarkably short time, a people's army had taken shape; closely knit with the nationalist community, it was made up of the sons and daughters of ordinary people, its members indistinguishable to any outside observer from the rest of the community. Therefore, when the government struck with the weapon of internment, they struck against the entire community, for whether people in the nationalist areas agreed or not with the IRA and all its actions, many saw it as their army, knew for the most part which of their neighbours were volunteers, and referred to it simply as the 'ra'.

Some years later I tried to capture in a short story something of the harsh reality of the campaign waged by the IRA against Britain's armed forces as they patrolled the streets of my home town.

Seán, uncomfortable with squatting for so long in one position, eased himself carefully up on one knee and slowly rubbed his cramped limbs.

Below him, back gardens were crisscrossed by fluttering, flapping, shirt- and nappy-laden clothes-lines stretched between back-to-back houses. Seán, above the clothes-lines, hedges, coal-holes and back doors, had a clear, wide-angled view of the street.

He could see ten, no, twelve houses on one side and fourteen on the other side of the street. He could easily see the windows of number 36, where the blind was drawn on the front bedroom window. He reminded himself to check that blind every few seconds. No use getting lackadaisical.

The kids in number 40 were late going to school; they must have slept in. He watched three youngsters dashing out of sight along the street. When, he mused, they got to the lamp post they would be 140 yards from where he was perched. His eyes searched and found the white rag tied, waist high, to the lamp post, then swung back to check the blind on number 36. It was still drawn. Other windows stared back blankly at him.

Number 36 seemed different. The drawn blind, like a dropped eyelid in the face of the house, was almost winking at him – one of those conspiratorial winks that seem to go on for a long time.

The sound of a shovel scraping coal into a bucket swung his attention once again to the back gardens. He chided himself for not immediately tracing the source of the noise, in fact for not seeing the source before it scraped its way into his attention. Mrs O'Brien, he smiled to himself, as the smoke curled lazily from her chimney to be lost against the haze of the Black Mountain.

Mrs O'Brien paused, coal bucket in hand, and peered over her hedge into the neighbouring garden. Her voice, raised to a shout, carried easily to where Seán crouched: 'Are you there Maggie?' Twice she shouted, before the door opened and Maggie came out. They stood, Mrs O'Brien with coal bucket in hand, on opposite sides of the dividing hedge, chatting. Seán's gaze swung away from them up towards number 36 again. It remained as before, the blind in the same position.

All these homes could do with a new coat of paint, he decided. Especially that one, the red one with the cracked window. Like the brown one below that, it definitely deserved a fresh coat. His gaze paused momentarily at a neat row of green vegetables. Jimmy Graham's lettuces seemed to be coming along well, and Da Grogan's spuds. He smiled to himself, then watched intently as a black and white cat picked its way stealthily towards an open dustbin where a few scrawny starlings quarrelled over bread wrappings and discarded tin cans.

The sound of a motor-car brought him back to the street and to number 36. The blind was up. The window with its bright curtains glared glassily back at him. Forgetting the cramp in his legs, he checked the piece of wood which held open the slate, forming the slot through which he peered. Hurrying now, he eased a round into the breech of the heavy rifle which straddled his legs. He raised it up so that the muzzle nosed through his slated peep-hole. He squinted along the sight, zeroing in on the white rag which bandaged the lamp post and thumbed off the safety catch. One hundred and forty yards, give or take a few feet. He had checked it himself, scrambling over hedges and wire fences to pace out the distance. Beneath him, in the innards of the house, a door bell rang. Seconds later, a head appeared at the open trap-door.

'It's dark in here,' a voice complained. 'Where are you Seán?'

Seán didn't turn round. The transition from daylight to the gloom of the attic would have upset his vision. 'I'm here,' he muttered.

'The car's below,' said the voice, relieved at seeing Seán's dim shape wedged below the roof tiles against a heavy joist.

'OK,' Seán replied, 'I won't be long.'

'I'll wait below,' said the voice, but Seán's attention, now that the car had arrived and his run-back was clear, was riveted to the street before him. His heart pounded heavily against his ribs. The cramp in his legs had returned, and as he strove to exorcise these distractions a quiet stillness seemed to settle on the deserted street.

It was a feeling he would never get used to. The whole area, the houses, unanimous in their silence. The gardens, even the streets themselves, seemed to be holding their breath. Every time he got the same feeling. How many times was this?

He smiled grimly to himself. Concentrate. Don't let your attention wander. That's the way to get yourself killed. Maybe that would be better than killing? He was surprised at the suddenness of the thought.

He squinted again along the length of the rifle as he considered this question and his response to it. It was a question which had come into his head off and on during the last few months. Not about getting killed. He wasn't into getting killed. No way. If it happened it wouldn't be by choice. He surveyed the scene before and below him. Nothing had changed. Was it right to kill?

No, he told himself, it wasn't right to kill. But there was no choice.

Of course there was a choice. No one forced him to do what he was doing. He could leave now. Leave? What good will it do, staying there? No one would know and no one could complain. He'd have done his best.

He swung his attention back to the task before him. It might or might not be right to kill, but sometimes it was necessary. He considered that proposition. The people he was trying to kill were better armed, better equipped, better trained than he was. There were also more of them.

And they would have no compunction about killing him. He settled himself back, pushing the doubts and imponderables out of his consciousness. They should not be here, he reminded himself. It was his country, not theirs. They didn't belong. They were the enemy. They gave him no choice except to fight. And in fighting it was necessary to kill.

He crouched now, blocking out thoughts of everything but what he was to do. Though he knew these other thoughts would return. Maybe it was good that they did. He could smell, or thought he could almost smell, the tension. They would certainly be able to sense his own fear.

There would be scores of British soldiers. He tried not to think of that. He was well covered. Better not to worry. It was too late now anyway. It would not be long.

Then into view came the first of a patrol of green-uniformed soldiers. They moved cautiously forward on both sides of the street, covering one another, snuggling into their flak jackets and arching their rifles to point at the grey jerrybuilt houses which mutely and sullenly surrounded them. The leading soldier was walking by number 36. Seán studied him with a vague disinterest and waited. A second soldier appeared, an officer. Seán gently nuzzled the rifle-butt against his cheek. The officer edged his way forward and then stopped, outside number 36.

'Move on,' hissed Seán, 'move on.' A half-panic started to flutter in his stomach. He breathed in as the officer reached the lamp post, and held his breath as his finger tightened on the trigger. First pressure. He let his breath out almost in a sigh and whispered 'second pressure'. The heavy flat thud of the rifle exploded his words, sending the black and white cat scampering from the garden and the starlings from the dustbin.

Seán prised the piece of wood from between the slates, and closed his eyes as the lowered slate shut out the daylight and returned the attic to its usual gloominess. He scrambled from his perch.

The car whisked him away. Behind him the back gardens, crisscrossed by fluttering, flapping, shirt- and nappy-laden clothes-lines, stretched between the back-to-back houses.

The twelve houses on one side and fourteen on the other side of the street remained silent and undisturbed. Against the solitary lamp post the white rag cushioned the pale staring face of the officer. His patrol, scattered into gardens, lay hugging the ground. The starlings returned to the open dustbin and the cat, as stealthily as before, picked its way towards them.

Mrs O'Brien, oblivious to all this, bade her neighbour good morning, eased the coal bucket to her other hip and shuffled her way indoors.

The British officer's expression, staring unseeing at the clear Irish sky, was curious, surprised.

For many people the issue of force is an academic one, since they rarely find themselves in situations where they have serious choices of this kind to make. Even when they do it is generally in a defensive situation when they or perhaps their families are under attack, or it occurs in wartime when they are the foot soldiers in a larger enterprise. The big decisions are generally made by others and most people accept, even reluctantly, that in these circumstances force is justifiable. There are those who are against all violence as a matter of both principle and practice, but for the majority it is a measure of last resort.

Whatever the arguments about physical force in general, there can be no doubt that the conditions and causes of conflict have existed in Ireland for as long as there has been British involvement in Irish affairs. From these circumstances of conflict the questions then arise of legitimacy, of tactics and of strategy. But foremost in the questions raised is the need and the responsibility to remove the causes of conflict; to end the cycle of repression leading to resistance leading to reaction, and to develop alternative forms of struggle. No one in positions of power or authority can hide behind a smokescreen of selective condemnation or denunciation and expect to have any positive effect on any conflict situation.

In Ireland the physical force tradition is very strong, and those who are part of it, especially on the republican side, have a huge responsibility to bring it to an end, to embrace other forms of struggle and seek to develop these in place of armed struggle if this is possible. No one should be dogmatic about armed struggle as a tactic. Nor should it be romanticised. I have lost many good friends, and their families' loss, like my own, is, I know, reflected also in the loss experienced by those who have suffered because of the armed actions of the IRA.

In the days and weeks after internment, however, in the state of military occupation which was in force in nationalist areas throughout the north, armed resistance was seen as a legitimate tactic by most nationalists. The honeymoon period immediately after the arrival of the British troops was well and truly over. For the first time in the Six Counties there was the combination of armed struggle and mass, popular struggle. Behind the barricades there was a sense of euphoria, which was perhaps naive, but it was nonetheless real. The civil rights campaign continued, albeit on a smaller scale than previously. Most Catholics had withdrawn from the institutions of state and, when internment came, they all withdrew. On 15 August the SDLP announced a campaign of civil disobedience, including a rent and rates strike, which had already begun in working class nationalist areas. On 22 August, 130 anti-unionist councillors resigned.

In the midst of everything Colette and I decided that we would get married. There was a war raging all around us; the community was in a state of popular insurrection. Young people like us who were active in the struggle had a sense that we were going to prison or to our deaths; we were being hunted by the British and we could hardly know what the future held for us.

I had got to know Colette early in 1970 when she and her friends had come to a meeting in the Whiterock and I had seen her again a number of times in the weeks and months after that at co-ordinating meetings for the greater Ballymurphy area. In the first half of 1971 we saw each other more often, but always on political matters; I was keeping company with a number of different girls during this time, all separately! But in July of 1971 I asked Colette to go out with me, and for the following six weeks we saw each other every single night. Usually we met late at night when I had finished my work and went for a walk around the area or stood or sat outside her front door or on her stairs. Once we went to the pictures. And once in that six-week period we made an arrangement not to see each other. She went out with a friend, but when she returned, I was there anyway, waiting for her.

After this whirlwind six-week courtship, I spoke to Colette's father, as was the tradition then, nervously asking if I could have his daughter's hand in marriage. Jimmy McArdle, God rest him, was a good-humoured, at times extremely funny little man. He was also extremely reluctant, though he did not say so, to let Colette go. Instead he gave us his blessing. My own father was still interned, and indeed I think he was rather upset that we didn't wait until he was with us, but the spirit of that time was to seize the moment. My mother responded bravely when she realised I was serious about my proposal for marriage.

Our friends bunched up and gave us a few bob, and the day before the wedding Colette went shopping with a friend of mine for shirts, underpants and socks for me. I always thought that Tony was very lucky: he was merely driving the car, but for every item that was bought for me, Tony came back with its brother. I got a new shirt, Tony got a new shirt. I got new socks, Tony got new socks. I got new Y-fronts, Tony got new Y-fronts. Tony had been with me the first night I had left Colette home. We had met by accident in a house where a gang of us came together for a *scoraíocht*, an informal session of talk and *craic* and fun. It was 11 July, and there were standbys all over nationalist Belfast in case of trouble from the Orangemen. Afterwards, in the very early hours of the morning, Colette and I and Tony had walked the long road home, up Divis Street, the Falls Road, and up into the Whiterock. Tony lived in Beechmount and on some pretext or other, because he was intent on going as far as the Whiterock, we got him to leave us at Beechmount. Then Colette and I had walked the rest of the way up towards her house together. That was the first night that we kissed, as we walked up the Whiterock Hill.

Only a small number of close friends and comrades attended our wedding. At the last moment, and as a security measure, we went to St John's chapel on the night before the original date. A number of the lads from Ballymurphy, including our Paddy, scouted out the church and some of them sat at the top of St James's, watching for any possible raid by the British army. I was at a meeting in Andersonstown up until a few moments before mass was to begin and I dashed to the chapel, arriving late, and making my way down beside Colette in the middle of the ceremony. After the mass, when the church had cleared, we went into the back of the chapel and, accompanied by Colette's brother Paddy and Annemarie, a friend of ours, we were married by

174

Father Des Wilson. Colette's mother was in the church, along with two of Colette's sisters, Maire and Leah, and Leah's daughter Geraldine. My mother and two of her friends, Annie and Mary Shannon, were in the chapel, too, but Jimmy McArdle was too upset to attend. No photographs were taken except one of Colette as she emerged after the wedding ceremony and was presented by Geraldine with a horseshoe.

The McArdles were a very large family of eight daughters and four sons, some married and all adults by the time I joined them. The parents, like most parents of that era, had a difficult time providing for such a big brood, but they had done so valiantly and with good humour. Maggie McArdle, Colette's mother, was the rebel. A contemporary of Joe Cahill's, she was a quiet but unrepentant republican. She was also great fun, a ready singer of humorous songs and a teller of stories. She and Jimmy and all the McArdles – when they all eventually heard that Colette and I were married – welcomed me into their family with open arms.

After the wedding we had no reception, though the best man, bridesmaid and the rest adjourned to the Rock Bar to spend the money we had given them for the priest and the altar boys. Father Des, fair play to him, had refused to accept his stipend.

'Well, Father,' said Paddy McArdle, 'I'll drink to that.' And he did.

Meanwhile Colette and I went to the Whiterock to pick up Tony and another good friend of ours, Alex, who had agreed to let us ride with them to Dublin. We stopped in Dundalk in a pub for one celebratory drink, and Alex played 'Blueberry Hill' by Fats Domino on the juke box. Then we continued in high good spirits on a memorable journey of slagging and humour. It was after midnight by the time we booked into the Belvedere Hotel in Gardiner Street. I ordered tea and sandwiches for the four of us. We were starving, and when they arrived the two boys took great delight at what seemed to us to be the exorbitant price charged. To add insult to injury, the two of them then ate most of the sandwiches. It was in the wee small hours of the morning before we eventually got rid of Tony and Alex, who seemed intent on staying for the entire honeymoon.

We stayed that night and the next in the Belvedere before returning to Belfast again. On the day we left, Colette and I stood on the fringe of a large anti-internment protest meeting outside the GPO in O'Connell Street. Our meagre funds had dried up, and as we waited for the lift back home we bought one coke between us and I asked the guy in the café for two straws.

That night in Belfast I was back on the run and Colette was back with her mother. When I had first met Colette, I had been drawn to her large green eyes and her ready smile. In the craziness of that time she seemed to be very stable and steady. We talked when we were alone together about everything except politics, and I relished her company. Our short courtship had been conducted mostly on the stairs of her mother's house, and it was there that I left her on the night we returned from Dublin. Only three nights before, as we sat on those same stairs, on the eve of our wedding, I had warned that ours could not be a normal marriage.

'We'll work at it,' she had said.

Life on the run is a strange experience. During the post-internment period and through the days of the barricaded areas, one could move relatively freely within the areas of Free Belfast. Later on, it became necessary for survival to keep all movement to a minimum, and as I then went from house to house, as was common practice for everyone involved, only a small group of very close associates was aware of my movements. But in late 1971 and early 1972, it wasn't quite as restricted, and I spent all of that period in the Whiterock, Springhill and Ballymurphy area.

During this time we almost always got warnings from local people about the whereabouts of British troops. Occasionally, despite best efforts to avoid them, I and others on the run were stopped by British patrols. It was relatively easy and absolutely crucial, though always nerve-racking, to establish quickly whether these were random chance encounters or planned ones. I was always lucky enough to be able to bluff my way out of random encounters. Planned ones, however, could only be avoided by being alert, getting some forewarning or, if all else failed, by running like hell, and many people on the run had close, at times near-miraculous escapes.

By the late 1970s most hunted people carried false ID. In the early '70s, however, this was rarely necessary unless travelling outside the area or making a journey by car to Dublin or Derry. At all times the important thing was to avoid contact with the British forces. For their part the Brits patrolled extensively and raided continuously. These raids, planned on the basis of information which they had received or because of surveillance work, could be huge, sometimes lasting for days, with whole regiments deployed and hundreds of houses being hit, or they could be sudden operations using small groups of soldiers, including undercover agents. At times – and sometimes very often – there would be random raids on houses of known republicans or their relatives at meal times or in the early hours of the morning. Patrolling took the same pattern: sometimes a very wide net of roadblocks was established for a short duration only or foot patrols stopped people at random for spot checks; at other times there were meticulous intelligence gathering operations and screening of entire areas.

As time went by, undercover surveillance, high tech back-up, the use of helicopters and computerisation became more and more important as the British built up unprecedented amounts of information on the nationalist population. Local people responded valiantly to these new challenges. Street names were removed, bin lids were rattled at even a hint of the sight of a British soldier; patrols were confronted, usually by women, whenever they stopped local people, usually young men. Because of this and other tribulations which they suffered, as well as the calibre of the individual soldiers or regiments, the British patrols could generally be avoided if one were careful.

On one memorable occasion, Tony, Colette and I were not careful. In the early hours of the morning, we three were travelling through Ballymurphy on a motorbike, with Colette as the passenger, me driving and Tony on our shoulders, when we drove around a corner straight into a patrol of the Parachute Regiment. They must have heard us laughing and yahooing before they saw us, and the entire patrol exploded into laughter at the strange sight in their midst. Tony with great dignity climbed down from his elevated position to be frisked, and then as the Paras quizzed Colette and me, he climbed up again on our shoulders. For a moment the senior Para looked as if he was going to come the heavy, but then one of the others chortled.

'Fuckin' Irish!'

All dissolved again into laughter. Tony retained his dignity, gazing down on them from his lofty perch.

'Go on,' the officer smirked.

And our little trio on the Honda 50 chugged happily and very slowly away down the street.

Internment came as a crucial indication that the road to reform was blocked off and had a major effect in making people conscious participants in the struggle. There were even those in British political life who recognised that events had crossed a vital threshold. After a visit in November 1971, Harold Wilson, leader of the opposition Labour Party in Britain, called for a conference of all major parties in Ireland and Britain, stating that 'the situation has now gone so far that it is impossible to conceive of an effective long-term solution in which the agenda does not include consideration of, and which is not in some way directed to, finding a means of achieving the aspiration, envisaged half a century ago, of progress towards a united Ireland'.

On 4 December McGurk's Bar in North Queen Street was bombed by loyalists, killing fifteen people. Seamus Twomey, who was very badly wanted at that time, came to my billet with the news. Seamus, a remarkable individual who was the father of an almost grown-up family, was slightly older than my father, probably the same age as Joe Cahill, and he had also been active in the 1940s. Now here he was thirty years later on the run in his own city. Once in Leeson Street, Seamus and I perched on a yard wall for an hour while the Brits raided houses close to us. As we clambered down when they had departed, he said, 'I'm too old for this carry-on!' But he wasn't. Seamus's quick temper, which reduced him at times to incoherence, was legendary. He certainly didn't suffer fools gladly, but if he was in the wrong he was always repentant, and indeed he was conscious of his quick temper, which he tried to curb. A keen sports fan, Seamus loved Gaelic football, hurling and horse-racing. During his long years on the run, apart from the desire to go home to Rosaleen, his wife and family, he longed to spend a Sunday evening watching a game in Casement Park and having a pint afterwards.

Now he had to face up to the responsibility of giving leadership to young people at an extremely dangerous and risky time.

In the same month as the attack on McGurk's Bar, our Paddy was arrested and interned. That Christmas Colette and I stayed in my Aunt Kathleen's house, while she was away. On Christmas Day, however, my sixth sense told me that it was time to move. Colette and I went back to the Murph and later heard that Kathleen's had been raided.

We faced into the New Year in good spirits, but brutal confirmation of the obstacles to reform came with the shooting dead of unarmed demonstrators in Derry on Bloody Sunday, 30 January 1972.

I was on my way back from a trip to Dublin with Colette when we first heard that people had been killed in Derry, and as we drove north the numbers of dead in the news reports on the car radio were rising. I stopped in Dundalk to see if we could get more detailed news. People were incensed and had no clear notion of how the deaths had occurred. I drove then pell-mell back into Belfast.

The Paras had been deployed against a civil rights march from Creggan through the Bogside to the Guildhall Square. I have no doubt but that the killings were a deliberate military operation designed to strike terror into the hearts of all Irish nationalists living under British rule through the exercise of murderous violence against unarmed civilians. The Paras, the shock troops of the British army, trained for the most aggressively demanding of

179

military encounters, were deployed against a largely working-class demonstration of 20,000 people seeking civil rights. Some have suggested that the Paras ran amok, that they were out of control, but perhaps the most disturbing truth is that this was a controlled, deliberate exercise, decided and planned in advance at the highest political and military level. This was a cold, predetermined, intentional massacre of civilians, a disciplined assault upon a non-violent demonstration. The march having been stopped by the troops, a small riot had developed, young fellows throwing a few stones; but the vast majority of the large attendance were listening to speeches when the Paras suddenly started shooting, firing coldly, repeatedly and deliberately at 'males of military age' in the crowd; they continued to fire on people as they fled, and they fired, too, at those who sought to go to the aid of the wounded. Thirteen innocent civilians were killed that day by the Paras, another died later; twenty-nine were injured.

It was no accident that the events which marked the beginnings of the troubles had occurred in Derry, for if the north was a time bomb, then Derry was its detonator. For despite its Catholic majority Derry held a special place in Unionist mythology and could not be allowed by them to pass out of their control. The most blatant malpractices were employed to keep Catholics in their place. Yet it had little history of republicanism; there were a few spinal republican families or personalities, but essentially the politics of nationalist Derry had been dominated by middle-class Catholic values. More than Belfast, Derry was a rural place with a busy port which provided a natural point of departure for many who could not make a living there. Cut off as it was by the border from its natural hinterland in Donegal, it was a place apart. While there was no real tradition of radical struggle, there had been an absence also of the more extreme outbursts of sectarian rioting with which Belfast is associated.

The Battle of the Bogside, when the people of Derry defeated the RUC and the B Specials, changed everything, liberating the entire west bank of the city. It was a people's uprising involving women and men, young and not so young, and they achieved it against all the odds. They also had a sense of having achieved it fairly. Bloody Sunday, by complete contrast, was a foul set-up, a crude effort to put them back in their place, to let them know who was in charge and to frighten the rest of us. It was the same old story: unarmed civil rights marchers became 'armed terrorists' and the injury inflicted that day remains an open wound even now.

Ireland was convulsed by Bloody Sunday, which had happened, unlike the killings in Ballymurphy, publicly in daylight in front of the media. The television pictures, about which there was a kind of terrible, mournful stillness, could not be ignored. There was a very widespread feeling now that really the British government had gone too far. Tens of thousands of workers left their jobs to march in protest all over the Twenty-six Counties. Even church people and the Dublin government reacted. The day of the funerals in Derry was a day of national mourning. In Dublin three days of marches and riots climaxed in the burning of the British Embassy in front of a crowd of 30,000. In the north riots, barricades and strikes followed Bloody Sunday; 50,000 people joined a NICRA march in Newry. At the British parliament at Westminster Bernadette Devlin attacked Home Secretary Maudling, hitting him in the face.

Money, guns and recruits flooded into the IRA. In the six or seven months after the internment swoops, the armed struggle was waged with greater intensity than ever and with major support and tolerance from the nationalist community. The huge gun battles which became a feature of life in the Murphy and other nationalist areas didn't mean that a lot of people were killed; nor were there necessarily two different factions fighting each other. On many occasions it was a case of the British army fighting the British army. Sometimes the IRA engaged to a small degree and then withdrew, discovering to their complete surprise that the shooting then continued and intensified. But amongst older nationalists, who had previously been aware only of small-scale and largely defensive actions by the IRA and who had been largely unaffected by the particularly unsuccessful border campaign of the 1950s, it was a matter of amazement, wonder and pride to see the younger generation in their neighbourhoods building an IRA campaign of such a magnitude that they had large numbers of professional and well-equipped regiments of the British army on the run. Some of these gun battles drew audiences who stood usually just outside what they judged the range of fire to be, generally around the corner from the action. At times as many as a hundred people gathered to watch.

The IRA campaign was dominated by Belfast where a series of attacks was mounted on all the British army and RUC barracks in West Belfast, the most celebrated of which was on Hastings Street. It had been attacked unsuccessfully initially, but the IRA were back in action very quickly and blew the barracks up. As the campaign gathered force and momentum, Faulkner made occasional announcements to reassure his constituency, saying that 'we have the situation under control'. The IRA then responded with alacrity to each such claim, and this had the effect of boosting popular identification with the IRA. Hastings Street barracks became something of a popular symbol, because everybody in the Falls knew that only the exterior walls remained. However the IRA had placed the bomb, the sand-bags acted to direct the entire blast inwards, blowing the whole place to smithereens.

By now the Brits knew that Colette and I were married. One day they arrived to Colette's family home.

'You know who your daughter is married to?' they said to her father.

'No,' he lied.

'Gerry Adams,' they said.

'Well, God help him!' said Jimmy.

Colette and I, unknown to them, were actually sitting watching this whole business from a house in the street. We saw them again, as they used to call to her house regularly and we used to watch them.

The Paras were in the habit at the time of going around at

night shouting my name. 'We're looking for Gerry A. Come out, Gerry Adams, you bastard!' Some nights I'd be awoken by the noise they made, which every one of my comrades thought was great *craic*, except me.

One day in 1971 the Brits had killed Mickey, our red-haired collie-type mongrel, and our Dominic cried for a week afterwards. Now they captured my dog Shane, but one day not long after, I saw him going up the street with a patrol. They had him on a lead and I waited until they were a good distance from me before I whistled him, the way I always whistled for him: one long, three short, then one long whistle, all in the one breath; he went mad, broke away and came to me.

I had become particularly attached to Shane when at about nine months old he had fallen very ill and the vet said he might have to put him down. Every night for a week I sat up spoon-feeding him with scrambled eggs, milk, rusks and water. I gave him penicillin tablets, force-fed him honey to bring the phlegm up, and washed the mucus from his nose. He survived both my ministrations and the illness to become my constant companion. Inevitably, however, I found it difficult to spend much time with him once I went on the run, but our Liam or our Sean would walk him down to wherever I was and I'd have an hour or so with him.

Colette and I were given the use of a house in Springhill and Shane moved in with us, but in 1973 he vanished, captured by the Brits, though I was to meet up with him briefly later. Our new home was a three-storey house like most of the Springhill homes of that period and we had no furniture except a few sticks friends had given us, but it was ours. For a very short time we lived in a kind of normality, the two of us and Shane in a huge, almost bare dwelling. However, one day I arrived home to discover that Colette had given it away, having met someone whose need was obviously greater than ours. I always admired her for that.

We found a new billet in the Whiterock, and Colette became pregnant in September. We were both delighted at this news. In the first weeks of her pregnancy, Colette took a craving for bananas and Walls vanilla ice-cream. The bananas were easy, but more than once as I toured Falls Road shops looking for Walls vanilla ice-cream – no other flavour would do – I knew that only the fathers or expectant fathers amongst my comrades would understand if I were arrested on such a mission. Mother Ireland sometimes had to take second place. However, as we lay in bed on the night of 23 October 1971, we heard a commotion outside. Down at the front door we learned that our friends Dorothy Maguire and her sister Maura Meehan had been shot dead by the British army after going into the lower Wack to warn people that the Brits were raiding. They had been very long-term friends of Colette's, having been reared with her, and when I was on the run I had been getting my dinner in Dorothy's house or staying in a house that she had arranged. We were all very close. Soon after that, Colette miscarried in Dublin. We were staying overnight in my Aunt Maggie's and Colette was suffering from dreadful pains. Aunt Maggie was more alert to this than I was, and at her prompting Colette went to the Rotunda hospital in the early hours of the morning. We were both shattered by the experience and returned home despondent.

By now the British army were threatening to shoot me, Brendan Hughes, Jim Bryson, 'Toddler' Tolan and a few others on sight. Indeed, once they called to Colette's mother to say that I had just been killed by a patrol down the Falls. I went to stay up in Beechmount for a while. I was always on the alert. Very rarely did I turn directly down a street; instead, I crossed the street and as I did so I would look down first. I avoided streets where there were stretches without doors. In Clonard Street, for example, there were blank walls; Beechmount Avenue was too long. One evening in Beechmount I walked into the marine commandos. I just couldn't avoid them: I was caught in the middle of the street and there wasn't a sinner about. They called me over; I contemplated running, but it wasn't on. I gave them my bum ID and I gave them a story and they let me go. I walked up the street, turned into an entry and ran like mad. Moments later they came running after me. I got into the house I was going to, but all that night I could hear them tramping and turning and chasing in the back entry and up and down the street.

Another time I was in a car which I parked in the grounds of Clonard chapel. As I stepped out of the car, the Brits nailed me. I had no ID except a dole card and the soldier quizzed me about how did I have this car, which was quite a good one, while I was on the dole. I replied that it was my father's. Then the caretaker of the chapel came out and tackled the Brits, saying that there was an agreement with the rector that people were not to be stopped in the chapel grounds, and they started arguing the toss. Meanwhile a few young children came along, and the ice of this tense situation was broken when I started chatting with these kids. I said I'd go into the chapel while the Brits and the caretaker worked things out; the Brits said OK and I walked into the chapel. After a while the caretaker came in and encouraged me to make a complaint.

'No,' I said. 'No, it's OK.'

But he insisted that he would support me: cases like this had to be fought, and there was no need for me to be afraid; people needed to stand up for themselves.

I just whispered to him then: 'I'm on the run.'

Suddenly he changed, nodded understandingly and quickly showed me the way out the back.

When the Brits realised what had happened, they went mad. Later, some of the lower Wack lads decided to try and get the car back. They did so, but when they parked it in another street the British mounted an extensive raid and turned that and neighbouring streets upside down.

I stayed in a very good house then for a while, which Colette could come to. Here the people of the house, Kathleen and Eamonn, were very good to us, and their home became ours. They told the neighbour that I was a schoolteacher and the only reason I was on the run was because my father was a mad dog republican and the Brits were messing with me to get at him. And the woman next door used to go for messages for me, getting cigarettes or milk. At one point the Brits did a house-to-house search, and as they came out of her house to come into where I was, I went out my back door and into her place. When I was eventually arrested, with the accompanying media hype, she was astounded.

The man of that house was a great character. The worst night of the week was the night before the bin collection, because if he had had a few drinks he used to persist in putting the bin out beforehand. His dog, a Yorkshire terrier, would accompany him and, glad of the sudden freedom, sometimes it ran away. The house was directly in line with the barracks and the Brits used to patrol a lot. So he'd be going along whistling for his dog at two or three in the morning and calling its name, 'Sweep! Sweep!' Then you'd hear: 'You all right, moite?' from a patrolling Brit, followed by a crazy conversation punctuated by the yelping of a Yorkie. He used to say that he thought the Brits could see in the window from the barracks, and one night I was woken by the sounds of knocking at the window to find him hanging there, saying, 'No, they can't see it.'

At the same time the situation was militarising into a conflict between the IRA and the British army. There were fewer public manifestations now. The militarisation was partly the IRA's fault, but it was also a natural consequence of the fact that republicans had been forced underground by laws which made even our peaceful political activities and organisations illegal and banned our newspapers; by bans and baton charges on demonstrations by the forces of the state; by internment, and by the use of combat troops to shoot people dead in the streets.

The IRA had equipped themselves with more up-to-date weaponry. By 1972 they were getting plenty of Armalites; these were lightweight and with a collapsible butt, making them easy to conceal, and they fired high-velocity bullets. 'God made the Catholics,' stated the graffiti of the time, 'but the Armalite made them equal.'

There was so much action in along the back entries of the warrens of houses in the Falls that on one occasion a group of IRA people went over a yard wall into an entry right into a British

186

army patrol. Two groups, both heavily armed, just stood, weapons cocked and ready, and looked at each other for a long, silent moment, and then both groups cautiously backed off and went about their business.

In a relatively short time the IRA had not only created a defensive force of unprecedented effectiveness, they had also carried out a massive offensive with overwhelming support from the nationalist people, which had succeeded in creating an intolerable situation for the London government.

It was obvious that the statelet could not survive the onslaught. On 22 March, Stormont Prime Minister Brian Faulkner met British Prime Minister Edward Heath, British Defence Secretary Lord Carrington and Leader of the House of Commons William Whitelaw. On being told that security powers were to be taken away from Stormont, Faulkner threatened to resign. After two days of discussion between Faulkner and his colleagues in Belfast, Heath announced the resignation of both Faulkner and his cabinet, the suspension of the Stormont parliament and government, and the appointment of Whitelaw as secretary of state for Northern Ireland.

For nationalists it was a time of complete and utter jubilation. At this crucial watershed the feeling amongst the nationalist people now was that they would never go back to unionist rule again.

Eight

Four young IRA volunteers were killed on 9 March 1972, shortly before the fall of Stormont, by the premature explosion of their own bomb in a house in Clonard Street: Tom McCann was twenty, Tony Lewis sixteen, Gerry Crossen and Sean Johnson nineteen. The whole house had been destroyed in the explosion; people frantically searched the rubble, not knowing at first how many had been killed. The story began to circulate that Tom McCann hadn't been there. We went around his usual haunts, but once he didn't surface in the first few hours I feared that the story was wishful thinking and that he was dead. Even so, it came as a terrible shock when, after much searching, someone found Tom's scalp in amongst the rubble of the destroyed house. He had dark hair with a very distinctive white patch on the back of his head, and now this was to identify him.

In the preceding two years a good many of my friends and associates had been killed. The list was growing longer. Belfast republicans were in the midst of the storm and, whether in armed actions or accidents, or as victims of British or loyalist assassination, they were paying a heavy price. Many British soldiers and RUC men had died also. So, too, had civilians – innocent non-combatant victims of bomb attacks, and the crossfire of British,

IRA and loyalist actions. The IRA had also killed informers. The death toll was rising, at times on a daily basis.

By now Colette had moved into a house in Harrogate Street in Beechmount, a small, good house which had been recommended to us because the owner was living in Dublin. I contacted him, and he was happy that Colette should get caretaker tenancy until the estate agent had rationalised matters. One of the principal problems of being on the run was the instability and insecurity of living arrangements, which was obviously more difficult for married couples, especially those like us who had no base of our own. The place was in need of a massive job of cleaning out, and we had no money and no furniture. But someone gave me a tenner and I went into Hector's shop and spent some of it on two knives, two forks and two plates. Somebody else had given us a king-sized bed as a wedding present, and we cheerfully installed it. I had few hopes of being able to establish some element of settled pseudo-normality. I knew I would not be able to spend long in the house, and I hoped to use this time so that Colette and I could at least establish some domestic stability, but we were hardly there when the house was hit and I was arrested in a dawn raid on 14 March. I was suffering from the after-effects of the shock of the death of these four young men and I failed to exercise my normal caution about not staying too long in the one place.

On my arrest I gave a false name, but they brought me to Springfield Road barracks and were obviously acting on information of some sort. They weren't sure it was me: I had them nearly convinced that I was Joe McGuigan, and I certainly convinced the two British soldiers who were escorting me. However, they then brought in Harry Taylor, who was one of the very few RUC men who actually knew me. I wasn't ill-treated in the barracks, but once he had identified me the whole mood changed. I continued to deny my identity, but in vain. I was taken to Palace barracks in an armoured car. By then it was daylight.

The British officer who had arrested me said I'd be better coming clean, and obviously he said it tactically, but I felt he said it with great sincerity, which made me feel all the more despondent about the fate which awaited me. Towards the end of the interrogation, one of my tormentors said to me, 'Republican propaganda has done such a great job that you people usually break before you even get in here.' It struck me that this was what the senior Brit had been doing.

I had seized upon the device of refusing to admit I was Gerry Adams as a means of combating my interrogation. By continuing to assert that I was Joe McGuigan, I reasoned that I would thwart the interrogation by bogging it down on this issue.

In the interrogation centre they brought me into a very large room in a barracks–style wooden hut, and this room was divided up into open cubicles; men were seated facing the wall in these cubicles. I was placed in one and left there facing a wall made of board with holes in it which had the effect of inducing images, shapes and shadows in front of my eyes. Soldiers or branchmen kept coming up behind me, kicking the chair from under me, shouting at me, hitting me on the back of the head. There were steel food trays, quite deep with lids and handles, and they dropped them beside me; I was terrified at first, but I found after a while the desperate, clanging noise didn't affect me much. I also discovered that when they came up behind me, I could see their shadows, and although I was frightened I could anticipate their shouts and blows and kicks, which made it easier to take. But some others undergoing the same treatment in other cubicles close to me were in states of total terror and showing it by their shouts and screams.

In the interrogation room they employed the 'good cop, bad cop routine'. I got a fairly lengthy hammering, and then a berserk man came in trying to shoot me, yelling and pulling a gun while the others jumped on him. Also, while I was being interrogated by Harry Taylor, they tried to administer what they called a truth drug. The one time I was really frightened was when they took me down to get my fingerprints taken, going to very elaborate lengths to make sure I saw nobody or nobody saw me. A few times, on the way, they ran me hard up against a hut or through an open doorway until someone passed. It was clear that they were trying to fluster me. Eventually we reached the fingerprint-ing room. I was resisting having my fingerprints taken and demanding that they provide proper authorisation. They had my arms outstretched over a table. Suddenly the ferociously scream-ing and shouting figure of an apparently deranged man reared up and came at me wearing a blood-stained apron and holding a hatchet high. This succeeded in unnerving me momentarily, to the great glee of my tormentors.

They took me back to another interrogation room and put me up against a wall, spreadeagled, and beat me soundly for hours around the kidneys and up between the legs, on my back and the backs of my legs. The beatings continued for the period I was in Palace barracks. The beating was very systematic, quite clinical; there was no passion in it. It was as if they and I were drawing second wind, as if we both knew that we each had a good bit to go yet. We had measured each other and now it was down to stamina or stubbornness. I was bruised and sore but I was aware that I wasn't being subjected to the tortures that Kevin Hannaway and some others I knew had suffered; in this I was benefiting, I felt, from the effects of the publicity that had emerged about the torture and brutality at the time of internment the previous August.

I had arrived in Palace barracks at the tail end of unionist control and the end of a period of truly brutal treatment. I was one of the last to be detained under the signature of Faulkner and one of the first whose internment order was signed by Whitelaw.

Just before the end of my interrogation I abandoned my assertion that I was Joe McGuigan when the Special Branch told me that I would be imprisoned under this name and that Colette would be refused visits to me. While I doubted that, this threat told me that my time in Palace barracks was coming to an end, so I gave them my correct name. Of course, my strategy had been reduced to a charade by this time, but it had given me, I felt, a crutch to withstand their inquisition. To remain silent was the best policy. So even though they knew who I was, it was irrelevant. I couldn't answer their questions, on the basis that I wasn't who they said I was.

At one point they even brought Eamonn McCaughley, my brother-in-law, arrested in the same period as I was, into my cell to prove my identity. Eamonn, sound man, said nothing.

Before I left Palace barracks I made a formal complaint about my treatment. My interrogators made serious efforts to ignore my repeated requests about this, and the uniformed RUC administrative people also tried to ignore my demand when I was handed over to them. Eventually, however, I was taken into a room to make a formal complaint, and there I was confronted by a number of large, baton-wielding British army redcaps who also sought to intimidate me.

From the barracks I was taken to the *Maidstone* prison ship, a terrible, dismal place. It was a relief to be among friends, and especially to get a visit with Colette, but this was short-lived in the awful conditions of the boat. We were held below deck in the bow section. The fold-up bunks were in tiers of three, and there was no space at all. There was a small recreational room. Light struggled in through small port-holes. I arrived just after a successful and celebrated escape, and security was so tight it was paranoid. Amongst the prisoners I knew was Liam Hannaway, my uncle; his brother Alfie Hannaway had been interned in 1940 as a seventeen-year-old on the *Al Rawdah*, a troop carrier of the India Line at anchor in Strangford Lough. Here were Liam and I and 150 or so others on a British prison ship again.

The food was disastrous. The boat sat in its own sewage. British troops were also garrisoned on board, as well as the screws, and we were sitting on their sewage as well as our own. The toilets were constantly flooded. Soon after my arrival I had my first encounter with a prison doctor. I was badly bruised, especially about the ribs, after my Palace barracks sojourn.

'Is it sore?' he asked.

'It's sore when I breathe,' I answered.

'Stop breathing,' he declared without even a flicker.

Later I learned that after I was taken from the house the British soldiers took the place apart. Hilda Hartley, one of our neighbours and the woman who had originally let us know about the house, stayed with Colette during this raid. Some hours later an intelligence officer arrived in. He told one of the soldiers that an RUC Special Branch man had identified me as Gerry Adams, and the soldier told Colette and Hilda.

'I'm sorry,' he said to Colette. Then he began to talk to the two women about his family and about how he hated doing what he was doing.

Days later, when Colette was cleaning the parlour window, he passed on foot patrol and rapped on the window. She ignored him. To her embarrassment, the following day while she was walking with my mother, she heard a hissing sound from a garden. It was the British soldier.

'My name is Paddy Burns,' he said. Again Colette ostracised him.

Another day during a bomb scare in Harrogate Street when all the houses were evacuated, Hilda left a pot of potatoes boiling on the stove. Spotting Paddy Burns, she sent him up to turn off the gas.

Some time later, after his regiment finished its tour of duty, Hilda received a card. It was from Paddy Burns. 'Tell Colette I've left the army,' he wrote.

From the *Maidstone*, when you looked out of the port-holes from below decks on the side that was beside the dock, you could see into the visitors' area. For some short distance around the boat, they had military wire and security pillboxes; there were a couple of huts which constituted the visiting quarters, and then there was a gap of open space. When internees heard that someone had been arrested, they watched for the visitors' bus and for any convoy bringing another prisoner. It was a way of passing the time.

One evening there was a shout that a convoy was coming in. People who went to the port-hole saw a hooded figure being taken out of the back of a jeep; we could see the soldiers talking to him for a few minutes, and then they pulled the hood off him.

Immediately he ran, in a desperate, frantic fashion, and as he ran he saw the fence and then ran the other way. He was like someone or something demented, and I couldn't help thinking of the rabbit at Glenavy again. The guy was in a state of total terror, and we learned later that the Brits, before they took off his hood, had told him they were going to shoot him. As it happened he was not connected at all to any organisation, which made it all the worse for him, since he lacked the benefit of psychological preparation.

A friend of mine called John, who had been arrested some short time after me, arrived on to the *Maidstone*. In Palace barracks they had hung him up by his thumbs on coat hooks and left him stretched out like that for hours and hours while tapping him on the navel with a small rod, and now the entire area around his navel was a deep purple where all the blood vessels had been broken. Apart from that he showed little bruising, though he was obviously in physical distress. That was different from the type of torture that had been used for a long period on people such as those lifted in the original internment swoops, and the sight of him in that condition and the notion of men patiently tapping away at his flesh till it screamed sent a chill through me.

News came in of the shooting in Belfast of Big Joe McCann, my erstwhile comrade of the '60s. Soldiers of the Parachute Regiment shot him dead as he ran away from a patrol, presumably trying to avoid being arrested. The bitterness of the feud in which Charlie Hughes had been shot and Tom Cahill wounded and the emotion of the unresolved tensions of the split could not blunt the sense of sadness which enveloped me. Whatever the differences between us, I could not, and had no wish to forget the good times we had enjoyed or the common struggle we had joined before the pogroms of 1969 and their consequences separated us.

Conditions on the *Maidstone* continued to worsen. For days we were refused exercise. Some of us protested, and the British army came below decks in riot gear; in the mêlée one internee's arm was broken. As a means of resisting this conduct, we came up with the idea of a solid food strike. We needed to have some focus for mobilising opinion outside. I had started taking statements from people arriving battered from interrogations and writing a few letters and getting the odd statement out not long after my arrival. The strike picked up some support, with relatives putting notices in the *Irish News*, and it being reported, and it built up a little head of steam. In response to our protest the prison ship authorities brought down marvellous food to us: things like a whole side of ham glazed with honey; we were offered brilliant, over-the-top presentations, including wonderful desserts.

Outside the confines of our floating jail, a crescendo of fascist-style rallies was mobilising tens of thousands of loyalists, many of them in paramilitary uniform, to which the British army and RUC turned a blind eye. In February William Craig, former Stormont home affairs minister, had launched a new movement called Vanguard, and now he held a series of rallies at which he arrived with motorcycle escorts and reviewed lines of men drawn up in military formation. After reading a pledge to his audience, he would ask them to endorse it by raising their arms three times, shouting 'I do'. The echoes of Nuremberg were unmistakable. At a rally in March, Craig announced: 'We must build up dossiers on those men and women in this country who are a menace to this country, because one of these days, if and when the politicians fail us, it may be our job to liquidate the enemy.' In late April he elaborated further: 'When we say force, we mean force. We will only assassinate our enemies as a last desperate resort when we are denied our democratic rights.' A loyalist campaign of assassinations of Catholics had already begun in February. The UDA was making little or no attempt to disguise the fact that it was arming itself, and by May it was drilling openly in numbers with the tacit support of the British army.

We were concerned that the *Maidstone* could be attacked at any time. Stormont had fallen; Vanguard was on the move; we were moored on this dock in the middle of loyalist East Belfast; every evening we heard new reports about William Craig instituting the last Reich. So it was with some considerable relief that we were told by the governor that the *Maidstone* was being closed down. The prison ship was to be no more. We were elated at the success of our campaign and ended the protest after we heard a Stormont statement confirming the governor's message. A short time later we learned that we were being shifted to Long Kesh, the compound of Nissen huts, barbed wire, watch-towers and floodlights which had been built eight miles from Belfast specially to house internees.

I was the last one taken off the boat. They put me beside a guy who told me that he had been waiting in trepidation, praying that he wouldn't be next to me for fear of the hammering I would attract. His confidence that this would happen did little to help my nerves. They handcuffed the two of us together, but despite muttered threats from many of the huge number of British soldiers who evacuated us, our helicopter flight passed uneventfully.

We were delighted to get to Long Kesh despite its forbidding appearance. I was especially glad to see my da. Our Paddy, Kevin Hannaway and many others greeted us from their separate cages.

When we had been processed and brought to our new home, we were like young cattle being let out into a field after they've been cooped up in stalls. We were detainees under a new law and we were allocated to a new cage, where everything was shiny and new. We could see the sky, a view denied us below decks on the *Maidstone*. We were energised by our victory there and by our new surroundings. Mainly young men, some of us had spent months on the run. Now in Long Kesh we released all our pent up energies. Alarmed by our crazy behaviour, the authorities moved my uncle Liam Hannaway, at the suggestion of the internees' camp council, into our cage to try and sort us out. He started republican lectures, and he was very good, very relaxed, but the prison authorities were still concerned about our wildness and dispersed us to cages throughout the camp. It was a hilarious few weeks, a mixture of Brendan Behan's *Borstal Boy* and boarding school, in which we engaged in constant pranks, mayhem and craziness. Internees were supposed to go out and parade in front of the governor when they were making any kind of submission to him. We decided, however, to present a submission dressed only in our underpants and sitting on the floor. Every second day they had the British army up outside our cage to quell our boisterousness. We had water fights and – God help some of the older people in the cage – guys progressed from water bombs made with plastic bags to dustbins full of water, even to three-day water fights. Guys going out on a visit, cleaned up and in their best gear, would be set upon just as they got to the cage gate and someone would throw gallons of water over them.

My first intervention in internal discussion in the camp was to join others in arguing for escapes, but, probably because of all the giddiness, we didn't fight the issue very hard. However, Billy McKee was leading a hunger strike in Belfast prison for political status, and we argued very strongly that there should be some sort of solidarity action. This was resisted by the cage leadership and the older men, even though what we argued for was no more than a propaganda gesture rather than a serious hunger strike. I can now understand their reluctance, but eventually they changed their minds and having resisted the idea initially, now they wanted a full-blown strike. Liam Hannaway was one who went on the hunger strike, and he stuck with it, damaging his health as a result. I came off it on the fourteenth day. My most enduring memory is that, having eaten a first bowl of porridge to end my hunger strike, a burp of wind, which felt actually solid, developed low in my stomach and very slowly worked its way up my body and then came out, with great satisfaction for me, and stunned everybody else within about ten feet. I watched others coming off hunger strike going through the same thing, and their breath was absolutely stinking, foul.

I was only off the hunger strike for a day when I heard a shout outside the cage: 'Release! Adams release!' There were releases all the time. Indeed, my da and our Paddy had both been released on the same day earlier that month. By then my ma had secured a house back in the Murph near the top of the Whiterock Road after squatting for some time in Lenadoon. So it was to 183 Whiterock Road and not 11 Divismore Park that my da returned.

Gate fever was rife, and it wasn't unusual for people to mess you around by shouting out fake messages. You'd hear 'You're wanted at the gate', constantly followed by someone's name, but it didn't affect me at all because I had no reason to expect to be released. So when they shouted for me to go, I thought it was someone winding me up. Liam Hannaway came and told me to go, and when I reached the gate the governor confirmed that I was to be released.

'Are you sure?' I asked, nonplussed.

'Yes,' he said, 'you're for release.'

I still didn't believe that it was genuine. I thought it must be a trick and that I would be shot dead driving from the prison or else whisked off to some interrogation centre. I didn't want to go, and I didn't want to leave my comrades. However, Liam Hannaway told me firmly to catch myself on, and reluctantly and gingerly I stepped out of Long Kesh.

Dolours and Marion Price, two young republicans who had participated in the Burntollet civil rights march, were waiting for me. They drove me down to Andersonstown where I met with Francie McGuigan and learned the reason for my release: talks were scheduled to take place with the British and I was to take part in them. Seamus Twomey told me that Paddy Devlin of the SDLP would be taking me to a meeting in Derry and had a pass to get us through any British army checkpoints.

I was updated on recent developments: in March there had been a three-day IRA ceasefire; no good had come of it, but early in June Seán Mac Stiofáin and Dáithí Ó Conaill of the Dublin leadership, Seamus Twomey, and Martin McGuinness of Derry had held a press conference in which they had suggested that Whitelaw should meet them in Derry to talk about a truce. The British government had rejected the suggestion out of hand, but John Hume had opened contacts with the Northern Ireland Office. Our side had insisted that negotiations could start if political status were granted to republican prisoners and had sought my release to take part in talks.

By this time Colette had heard somewhere that I had been spotted leaving Long Kesh, and she and I were able to meet five or six hours later at my parents' house in Whiterock Road. It was great to see her and my parents, but we had hardly a moment together before I had to leave for Derry.

On 20 June in a large country house outside the city, Dáithí Ó Conaill and I had a meeting with two senior British officials, Philip Woodfield and Frank Steele. Dáithí was a tall, thin, angular man with slightly receding dark hair, whose soft Cork accent enhanced his very compelling oratorical style. The first time I ever heard him speak, at a commemoration in Monaghan for Feargal O'Hanlon, he enthralled the large crowd with his evocative retelling of the IRA operation on which O'Hanlon had been killed, along with Sean South, another IRA hero of the 1950s campaign. A schoolteacher and a married man, Dáithí was personable, articulate and affable, and he was more politically tuned in than many of his contemporaries. He and I never got to know each other socially, more on account of the times that were in it than anything else. He had come to Belfast secretly on a number of occasions, so that when I met him in Derry before the meeting with the British officials we already had a general sense of each other's politics.

At the meeting itself, which was straightforward and business-like, the late Paddy McGrory, a noted lawyer and a very good friend, had a letter of authentication and did the formal introductions. A number of things had happened just before, which were confirmed at that meeting. The prisoners in Belfast prison, a major concern for republicans outside, were to be given political status or, as the British termed it, 'special category status'. Political status was agreed not only because of the hunger strike, but also as part of the effort to create a climate for talks between republicans and the British government.

My role in the discussions was fairly minimal, but together Dáithí and I arranged what transpired to be acceptable conditions for both the British and the IRA leaderships. Our position was that a meeting between a republican delegation and the British would take place a certain number of days after the IRA had ceased operations. It was agreed that both the British and the IRA would make statements, and there was some discussion about how the British forces would respond. My main concern was to ensure that the political meeting would take place quickly, and I felt that many of the other elements of our discussion were distractions. We argued for talks to start seven days after the beginning of a truce; they argued for fourteen days, and we agreed on ten. Of course, this was only a draft agreement; neither delegation could go any further. Our terms had to go back, on the one hand to the British government and on the other hand to the IRA.

After the meeting we returned to Derry city, where I told Dáithí Ó Conaill, who was going back with this package to the IRA, that unless there was going to be a political agreement with the British, it was not in the republican interest to be involved in a long, protracted truce; that the British would then hook into issues which were secondary, such as the release of internees. He assured me that he would pass on my thoughts. Before going back home to Belfast, I spoke to Seán Mac Stiofáin by phone. Then I returned to Belfast and to Colette.

Seán Mac Stiofáin had an interesting and unlikely background for an Irish republican. A married man with a young family, and a keen Irish language activist, he had been born in London to an English father and Irish mother and had done his National Service in the RAF. Arrested in 1952 during an IRA operation in which arms were taken from the Officer Training Corps at Felsted school near London, he had served six years in Wormwood Scrubs as a consequence, following which he moved to Ireland. He had a distinctive English accent and slightly aloof air, and although he was well disposed towards the younger activists, I felt he found it difficult to relate to us, particularly those of us from Belfast. We met only very occasionally, and while he and I got on well I did feel a certain tension between him, Ruairí and Dáithí; there was no evidence of collective leadership on their part or of an appreciation of the need for this.

On 22 June the IRA announced its ceasefire, effective from midnight 26 June. Talks would go ahead in London on 7 July. During the intervening days I and other Sinn Féin activists worked to generate a political presence in Belfast, and I attended a sizeable Sinn Féin meeting in the Whiterock. Now that we were no longer compelled to be covert, we wanted to move quickly to set up an office and engage in open political work. Meanwhile, I took part in a number of internal meetings about the forthcoming talks in London, including one which received a submission which had been requested from Sean MacBride, the barrister and former IRA leader, former minister for external affairs and more recently former general secretary of the International Commission of Jurists. At a meeting with Martin McGuinness, Ivor Bell and others, I argued very strongly against the course of action which was being suggested, which appeared to see the pending negotiations as if they were a follow-through to the treaty talks of 1920, and which proposed a very formalised approach to our engagement with the British government.

Just as the truce came into effect, the loyalists stepped up their assassination campaign, giving deadly expression to the verbal incitements of Craig and Paisley, who had both warned that unionists would have to take the law into their own hands 'to execute vengeance' and 'take action against the republican community'. On 1 July the Ulster Defence Association set up no-go areas, and thousands of UDA members marched in Woodvale. Far from intervening against these displays of armed uniformed men, the British army sided with them, and on 3 July joint British army/UDA patrols were established in lower Springfield. Meanwhile, the same UDA was mounting attacks on nationalist areas. In its February bulletin a supporter had written:

I have reached the stage where I no longer have any
compassion for any nationalist, man, woman or child. After
years of destruction, murder, intimidation, I have been driven
against my better feelings to the decision – it's them or us ...
Why have [loyalist paramilitaries] not started to hit back in the
only way these nationalist bastards understand? That is,
ruthless, indiscriminate killing ... If I had a flame-thrower I
would roast the slimy excreta that pass for human beings.

The UDA had expressed their agreement with their readers' sentiments, and a campaign of assassinations in which many of their victims were terribly tortured and mutilated reached its height during the IRA truce.

It had been agreed that during the truce the IRA would carry weapons, but they wouldn't go outside their own areas, and the British army wouldn't go into those same areas. Some of the local units got a Land Rover, painted IRA on the side and began to patrol West Belfast. However, a dangerous situation arose when the British army broke the agreement by coming into the 'Bullring' at Divismore Park in Ballymurphy, and when Jim Bryson asked them to leave they refused.

'There's going to be the Battle of the Bulge down there!' I was told. Jim had responded to the Brits by arming everyone in the area with every gun of every kind he could find, and it had become a very tense stand-off. I got on to Paddy McGrory, reasoning that as a facilitator of the truce he might be able to get it resolved, and after various intercessions the Brits withdrew from the 'Bullring'. This open area in front of the shops had gained its name from the British army. Once after taking a serious pounding during the riots, a senior British officer had been interviewed on television.

'We were trapped,' he exclaimed, 'like bulls in the ring.'

It was a relatively settled time for me. I was a released internee; I was off the run. One of the reasons I had been chosen to be on the republican delegation for the talks was because I wasn't a wanted man. The Brits didn't want to meet with a wanted man in their early discussions. I continued to keep a low profile, but it was a period almost of normality, though a man was shot dead by the British army just outside my parents' house while driving past; we heard the gunfire in the dead of night as they shot him from the entry beside the house.

When it came to the talks in London, I consciously dressed down for the occasion. I couldn't have dressed up anyway, but there was a hole in my pullover, and I was aware of it. In my juvenile arrogance and ignorance, I thought that was appropriate.

When we reached Derry we learned that the night before the IRA had arrested some British soldiers. Contrary to speculation later, this had nothing to do with our meeting. The soldiers were not hostages, but they were extremely lucky that their incursion into Free Derry had happened at such a sensitive time. As it turned out, they were held until shortly before our return.

We were taken by bus, accompanied by British officials and plainclothesmen, one at least of whom was armed, as was Seán Mac Stiofáin and another of our group. On the way we were held up by a herd of cattle, and it occurred to me rather wryly that the best laid plans of government spooks could founder in the face of a herd of cattle and a farmer who wasn't going to be hurried by anybody. Then we were taken by helicopter on a trip which I naturally compared with the very different flight a few months earlier when I had been brought from prison ship to internment camp. This was a wonderful flight on a beautiful day over verdant countryside and the Glenshane Pass. On our arrival at Alder-grove, Belfast's civil and military airport, the plainclothesmen, anxious that we should not be spotted, tried to rush us on to a waiting military aeroplane, but we were not about to be rushed.

We landed at Benson RAF airport in Oxfordshire, and were then transferred to two limousines. At Henley-on-Thames we stopped: Seamus Twomey wanted to go to the toilet; I asked him to get me some cigarettes while he was at it. We meanwhile went for a brief dander. Seamus was away for what seemed to be a very long time and this caused consternation amongst our minders, who were frantically phoning and using their radios. Eventually Seamus strolled back, totally unconcerned and at his ease, remarking on how pleasant the place was.

We arrived at 96 Cheyne Walk, Chelsea, the home of Paul Channon, and entered quite a large house. I went into the bathroom, which was very untidy, with sheets in the bath, and I wondered whether the person who owned the house hadn't been given much notice. Whitelaw arrived late, and there seemed to be an effort to have the meeting proceed without him, but our side wouldn't have that. When he came in he struck me as florid and flustered; his hand was quite sweaty.

The two delegations were a considerable study in contrasts. William Whitelaw, 'Her Majesty's Secretary of State for Northern Ireland', was a Scottish landowner; Paul Channon, a millionaire Guinness heir, was minister of state at the Northern Ireland Office; they were accompanied by the civil servants Frank Steele and Philip Woodfield. On our side were Seán Mac Stiofáin, the ex-RAF republican; Dáithí Ó Conaill, a teacher; Seamus Twomey, a bookies' runner; Martin McGuinness, a butcher's assistant; Ivor Bell, a plasterer's labourer, and myself; we also had as notetaker Myles Shevlin, a solicitor.

There was a formal exchange of documents and a formal exchange of views. Whitelaw opened by announcing: 'I hope that the trust set between us is reinforced by this meeting. I record that the histories of our two countries give the Irish grounds for suspicion. I hope that in me you will see a British minister you can trust. Look on me as a man who will not make a promise that he will not keep.'

In the course of our meeting Seán Mac Stiofáin led the presentation of the republican position, supported by Dáithí Ó Conaill and the others. Seán read a prepared statement outlining our demands for Irish self-determination; a public declaration by the British government of the right of all the people of Ireland acting as a unit to decide the future of Ireland; a declaration of intent to withdraw British forces from Irish soil by 1 January 1975; pending this, the immediate withdrawal of British forces from sensitive areas; a general amnesty for all political prisoners in both countries, for internees and detainees, and for people on the wanted list. Our interim demands were for the release of internees; the repeal of the Special Powers Act; the removal of the ban on Sinn Féin; no more oaths of allegiance to the crown; and proportional representation for all elections in the north.

It was inevitable that there would be a certain amount of tension in the course of our discussions, and there were two small eruptions. In one Seamus Twomey, making a point with

204

characteristic forcefulness, shouted and thumped the table. The other came when Whitelaw remarked ridiculously that British troops would never open fire on unarmed civilians. Martin McGuinness laid into him strongly about the killings on Bloody Sunday. Martin was a year or so younger than I was, and even then he was well-known and highly respected in his own community. Although I didn't know him well, I was impressed by his straightforwardness; like me he had a lot to learn, but he was candid about this. Tall and with curly fair hair, he came from a large family in the Bogside. I had met him in Derry behind the barricades along with Seamus Twomey. Free Derry was practically a liberated area, and while the events of Bloody Sunday had had a profound effect on most Irish people, they had been particularly traumatic for Derry people in a way which was more than a normal consequence of such savagery.

As I recall, some of the best interventions in the meeting were those of Myles Shevlin. I played very little part in the meeting myself, but when they were arranging for the second meeting, I asked that we adjourn. We went into another room to discuss matters amongst ourselves.

'Jesus, we have it!' said Seán Mac Stiofáin.

But that was the complete opposite to what I thought. I argued that we should insist on less time before the next meeting. Following our adjournment an agreement was arrived at regarding the timing. The Brits said that they'd consider and meet again in a week. Meanwhile, it was agreed that the IRA and British army would both have the freedom of the streets and the IRA could bear arms – openly displaying them in republican areas only.

Whitelaw was stressing the need to keep our discussions private, and he said that if news of our meeting got out, 'All bets are off.'

Riled by his arrogance, I responded quickly: 'That means all bets are off, then.'

A British official accompanied us on the flight home and spoke more to Dáithí Ó Conaill than anyone else. He spoke about the unionists, asking what we were going to do about them. As regards their military operations in Northern Ireland he said: 'We can accept the casualties; we probably lose as many soldiers in accidents in Germany.' This, of course, was completely untrue, but perhaps it spoke eloquently of their attitudes to their own soldiers.

The meeting had been, I felt, part of the British government's exploratory approach, motivated by the fact that they had only recently imposed direct rule in the north. They had shown no sign of conceding republican demands, and I took a fairly absolutist position regarding these demands. I was conscious of the historical nature of the negotiations. We were in a direct line of descent from the republicans of 1920 – the last time such discussions had occurred – but they had represented a revolutionary government with massive support. A lot had changed since then.

Two days after the London discussions, the truce was breaking down. The UDA was mounting attacks on nationalist areas, and the RUC were assisting in intimidation, while the British army stood by, chatting with the loyalist paramilitaries. Catholic families, intimidated out of their homes in mixed and Protestant areas, were streaming into nationalist enclaves, some of them going across the border to the south to escape. In the Springfield Road area the UDA took over a street in which most of the inhabitants were Catholics; the British army talked to them about it and then withdrew.

Some nationalist families who had been hounded out of their homes by loyalist gangs, in particular the UDA, had been assigned houses in Lenadoon, a mainly nationalist estate with a loyalist fringe to it. Not content to have forced them out of their homes, the loyalists now blocked them from going into their new ones, and a confrontation developed, on 9 July, with republicans coming along to assist the families to move in. The British army joined the UDA in blocking a furniture van that was attempting to unload outside one of the vacant houses. A British army Saracen rammed the van, triggering off a riot, during which the

British army fired CS gas and rubber bullets at the nationalists. Dáithí Ó Conaill got hold of Whitelaw on the phone; he said he'd call back, but he never did.

The reason the truce broke down had to do with the background of loyalist assassinations and intimidation, and specifically the British collusion with the UDA, which came to a head in Lenadoon. It also broke down at the point that it did because Seamus Twomey, as the man on the ground, saw the British breaking the truce and he refused to accept that situation.

When it started to break down, the British seemed to be content. Having explored the republican position and perhaps concluded that they could not do business with us, either they engineered the situation or perhaps allowed it to continue because they were just happy to see the truce end. Rather than their coming back to us on the political points of our discussion concerning self-determination and British withdrawal, to which they would presumably be saying no, they preferred that the truce should break down in this way than for republicans to be able to stand on the high moral ground.

I was at a wedding when I heard that there was trouble down at Lenadoon, and a few hours later I heard that the truce had come to an end. It more or less crept up and took me unawares, and then I was off out of the house and on the run again.

The truce was over. Within an hour of the official announcement by the IRA, British army snipers opened up on Ballymurphy. Their preference for war could not have been made much clearer.

Firing from an observation post in Corry's timber yard, overlooking the Springhill housing estate, a sniper shot at two cars; as the occupants got out he fired about fourteen more shots, hitting nineteen-year-old Martin Dudley in the back of the head and seriously wounding him. Two seventeen-year-olds ran to help the injured man, whose body was lying in the street; a second sniper opened up, hitting Brian Pettigrew on the arm. As the two young men turned and ran back towards the Pettigrew home which they had just left, the snipers kept firing, hitting

Brian Pettigrew several times in the back before John Dougal, eldest child in a family of eight, was also shot and fell to the ground. Bleeding heavily, Brian Pettigrew made it into the house. John Dougal lay on the ground in the next-door garden, but for two hours the Brits maintained continuous fire and no one could reach him; when he was finally carried into the house, he was dead.

Margaret Gargan was a thirteen-year-old twin who helped in the community centre where her father ran the bingo; she didn't like to wear dresses, but she loved wearing trousers, and this day she was wearing jeans when she was shot by a third British army sniper.

On witnessing the first shooting, Paddy Butler, a thirty-eight-year-old corporation worker and father of six children, had run to get a priest; now he returned with Father Noel Fitzpatrick and David McCafferty. Hearing someone shout that a young girl had been shot, Father Fitzpatrick and Paddy Butler ran from the cover of a house. The first sniper shot and killed both men. David McCafferty, a member of the youth movement of the Officials who had just turned fifteen in April, showed great courage in trying to pull the bodies of the two men to safety, but as he bent over Father Fitzpatrick, he was shot more than seven times and died.

The British snipers continued for several hours to fire at anything that moved. An ambulance arrived to take Brian Pettigrew to hospital, but could not enter the street, and so his father and others who were in the house knocked a hole through a bedroom wall and carried him on a makeshift stretcher into the house next door, from where they were able to bring him down an entry and into the ambulance.

The IRA, including Ballymurphy volunteers, had been heavily committed to the gun battle at Lenadoon where the truce had broken down, and so were not in a position to react quickly in their own area. But they returned and began to direct heavy fire on the sandbagged British position. Next day the *Belfast Telegraph* carried the British army press office line, its leading headline declaring 'IRA launch big attack on army post in Belfast'; 'five terrorist gunmen,' they reported, had been hit. No doubt the British press copied.

The IRA hit back across the north over the next six days, killing eight soldiers and an RUC man, and wounding many others; bombs caused devastation in cities and towns. Loyalists meanwhile killed individual Catholics, slowly torturing and mutilating many of them as an exercise in terrorising a community. The British army all the time carried out punitive raids on nationalist areas. By 16 July, 5,000 refugees had crossed the border to the south.

As part of its response the IRA embarked on another bombing blitz. Whitelaw announced a ban on traffic in Belfast city centre, which the British army now declared to be 'bomb proof', and the IRA responded to their claims on Friday, 21 July. Between 2.15 and 3.30 pm, twenty-one IRA bombs exploded in Belfast. The British army claimed in a statement that no warning had been received in relation to two of the bombs, and Whitelaw stated that the IRA 'without warning were prepared to kill' innocent civilians. It was their claims which dominated media accounts of what the British swiftly dubbed 'Bloody Friday'. However, the Public Protection Agency later confirmed that accurate warnings *had* been received from the IRA for all twenty-one bombs, but in the case of two, at Oxford Street bus station and Cavehill Road, the RUC and British army were either unable or deliberately failed to act on the warnings. In relation to the first they had received thirty minutes' warning, in relation to the second seventy-three minutes.

That night Whitelaw reputedly remarked to Minister of Defence Peter Carrington: 'Right, now they have given it to us. We can go into the no-go areas.' Exploiting the propaganda opportunity, the British speedily produced and distributed 250,000 copies of a leaflet about 'Bloody Friday', *The Terror and the Tears*. The comparison their propaganda sought to draw between Bloody Sunday in Derry and the bombs in Belfast on 21 July was a specious comparison. In Derry the Paras had deliberately, knowingly and intentionally shot down fourteen unarmed civilians. In Belfast the IRA had set out to cause economic damage and had sought to avoid civilian casualties by providing at least thirty minutes' warning in relation to each of the twenty-one bombs. It is a moot point whether the IRA operations just stretched the British too far for them to be able to cope with the situation, or whether they deliberately failed to act in relation to two of the bombs, but it is clear that the IRA made a mistake in putting out so many bombs, and civilians were killed who certainly should not have been killed. This was the IRA's responsibility and a matter of deep regret. In all seven civilians and two British soldiers died, and many more were injured.

The events of the day and the breadth of the IRA operations provided the pretext for the British army to launch Operation Motorman. On 27 July, 4,000 more British troops arrived, together with heavy equipment. Four days later, 21,000 troops with Centurion tanks, helicopters and hundreds of armoured cars invaded the no-go areas of Belfast and Derry. They had given notice of coming in; clearly they didn't want to take casualties, and neither did the IRA try to meet them head on. I was lying low in a billet on the Falls Road reading *My Oedipus Complex* by Frank O'Connor when I heard the noise of heavy military vehicles moving into the district. The woman of the house, returning from early mass in St Paul's chapel, gave an account of the heavy British army presence. Later I strolled out on the streets, to have a look for myself.

From what I could see the Brits aimed to strengthen their hold in the heart of republican areas and to establish bases where none had existed previously. Thus they set about building a new fort in Andersonstown. They also took over a number of other buildings. In all cases they sited their new operations close to civilians, whether in schools, hospitals or in the midst of housing estates.

Operation Motorman failed to destroy the IRA; it actually increased recruits, but it forced them to change tactics. The difference in the situation was more marked in Derry than in Belfast, because in Belfast the British army had already been patrolling in large areas, particularly the main arteries such as the Falls Road, and in other districts they had been going in in raiding parties. But in Derry they hadn't breached the barricades at all. Now the Derry people quite correctly didn't offer any resistance when the British army went in and dismantled the barricades.

Motorman marked the beginning of a new level of aggressive activity by the British. Between 1969 and 1971 they had been coming to terms with the situation; in 1972 they explored and assessed the republican position via the Whitelaw talks, and concluded that the talks were going nowhere. By then they had got their own intelligence organised to a sufficient extent to encourage them to go on a generalised offensive. After Motorman the British army stepped up house raids and searches, mounting a major offensive against nationalist areas, taking over parks, schools, community halls and other buildings, and constructing forts from which they could enforce their military occupation. Ballymurphy was subjected to a violent campaign by the Paras, operating in patrols of between fifteen and twenty soldiers moving between back gardens while the streets were patrolled by Saracens with Brownings, Ferrets, Saladins – tanks mounted with 76mm cannons and machine-guns. In McRory Park they erected Fort Pegasus, a massive corrugated iron base, and they took over and fortified Casement Park, West Belfast's and County Antrim's principal Gaelic football ground. In all they erected nine such forts in the Andersonstown area alone in the wake of Motorman. The whole of nationalist West Belfast, now dotted with forts, was under military occupation.

Loyalists also claimed victims from amongst the people of Ballymurphy and other nationalist areas, and amongst those who died were my childhood friends and neighbours Packy McKee and Jimmy Gillen. In September they were caught in a loyalist bomb explosion in Conlon's Bar at the corner of Francis Street in Smithfield. Earlier that evening they had been in Kelly's at the top of the 'Rock, where the Paras had made one of their regular raids. While the Paras were looking for trouble, the lads just wanted a quiet drink, so they and some others left and went down town. The bomb exploded in Conlon's just before nine o'clock. The Murph lads emerged to find that Packy McKee was missing. Jimmy Gillen went back into the seriously damaged bar, where he discovered Packy still alive but half-buried in rubble. Jimmy began to pull him free, but as he did a wall collapsed. When the two of them were eventually rescued, Packy was so badly injured that he died later that night, whereas Jimmy lingered on for eighteen days. Those were sad times for Divismore Park and for the Gillens and McKees. Jimmy had survived a loyalist shooting attack in June when he was wounded while standing outside Kelly's Bar.

One of the most important elements of the British offensive was the use of counter-gangs such as the Military Reconnaissance Force (MRF), which they used in the way described in *Low-Intensity Operations*, the British military textbook by Brigadier Frank Kitson. Just before the ceasefire, on 22 June, four people in the Glen Road were hit by machine-gun fire from a passing car. It looked like a sectarian attack, but the RUC gave chase and caught the driver and passenger, who were armed with a Thompson, a non-army-issue sub-machine gun favoured by the IRA, and who turned out to be a Captain James McGregor of the Paras and a Sergeant Clive Williams, members of the MRF, which was attached to the 39th Infantry Brigade, and whose commanding officer had been until a few weeks before Brigadier Frank Kitson, but which was now under the direct command of the General Officer Commanding Northern Ireland, General Sir Harry Tuzo.

The MRF set up an elaborate undercover network for intelligence gathering, working from flats, offices and shops and using both women and men. Amongst the phoney businesses they set up were the Gemini Health Studios, a massage parlour on the Antrim Road, the Four Square Laundry in Twinbrook and an ice-cream parlour. The Four Square washed clothes not just as part of cover, but also to analyse them for traces of explosives, gunpowder or gun oil; even to check shirt sizes against those of known occupants of houses and thus identify possible safe houses.

The driver chatted with local women and observed the comings and goings of men in the houses he called to. Meanwhile, within the large van other operatives, in a hidden compartment in the ceiling, observed and photographed people on the streets.

On 2 October 1972 the IRA struck in Twinbrook, killing the driver of the van and two operatives in the ceiling compartment. At the Antrim Road massage parlour, they killed two more MRF operatives. It was a devastating blow, on a par with Michael Collins's actions against British intelligence in November 1920, except that the IRA then took their eye off the ball. The mistake they made was that having totally disrupted the MRF the IRA almost forgot about it, while British intelligence of course regrouped.

In addition to carrying out operations based on their own members, the MRF had recruited a number of agents within or associated with the IRA; they also recruited strongly amongst loyalists, and it was at this time that loyalist killings reached a height. They also carried out operations to bring the IRA into disrepute or to create anxieties within nationalist communities. They created a joint loyalist/republican counter-gang, some of whom were later arrested and, when in Belfast prison, declared themselves to the IRA as having been involved in the MRF. At least one of them said that there was a plan to poison republicans in the jail, which would cause major convulsions within republican ranks.

British intelligence also had its operatives south of the border, and in the same month of October the Littlejohn brothers, British agents whose brief was to provoke repression against republicans, to kill republican leaders and to carry out actions to discredit republicans, raided a bank in Dublin's Grafton Street. British intelligence involvement was also suspected in the case of two bombs which exploded in Dublin on 1 December, killing two people and injuring 127. The bombs had been timed to coincide with a vote in the Dublin parliament on draconian new legislation aimed at the suppression of republicans; in the hysteria following the explosions, the IRA was blamed and opposition to the passing of the legislation collapsed.

Brigadier Frank Kitson did not confine himself to military strategy in a vacuum; he recognised the importance of the legal structures in defeating the opposition:

'The Law should be used as just another weapon in the government's arsenal, and in this case it becomes little more than a propaganda cover for the disposal of unwanted members of the public. For this to happen efficiently, the activities of the legal services have to be tied in to the war effort in as discreet a way as possible' (*Low-Intensity Operations*).

In accordance with this perspective, the British parliament at Westminster adopted in December 1972 the Diplock report, which recommended the combination of extra-judicial measures ('executive detention') and juryless courts. Crucially, it also recommended that all confessions be admissible in the juryless courts, and replaced the standard of 'fairness' with the issue of whether 'torture, inhuman or degrading treatment' had been used. Bail was not to be permitted, and the onus of proof was to be shifted to the defendant in cases allegedly involving weapons. By thus suspending many of the cornerstones of the British judicial process, the state would now be able to secure convictions with some ease.

The republican struggle went through phases. In 1969–70 there had been a popular uprising, which was deep-rooted, profound and broad in its effects throughout Ireland. There had been a rent-and-rates strike, some elements of armed struggle, which were quite popular, and then there was the loyalist reaction against the Catholics and, to an extent, against the British. By late 1972 the popular uprising had receded to some degree. Three years was a long time to sustain a popular uprising, especially given the fact that the leadership was segmented if not fragmented. As a consequence of a mixture of sheer, hard repression and coercion by the Brits, and mistakes by the republicans, the struggle had entered a defensive mode.

On the political front, the Northern Resistance Movement (NRM) had been formed in October 1971, amongst its main instigators being Michael and Orla Farrell of People's Democracy. I spoke at a number of NRM meetings at which PD argued quite correctly for wider popular mobilisations, and it struck me that all of the potential for mobilisation was ours, while PD had the theory. I argued, and it was accepted, that republicans should support and be involved with the NRM. Quite sizeable demonstrations against internment were taking place, but the big weakness of our situation was that we created no political alternative to the SDLP. Neither did we seek any accommodation with them.

Sinn Féin was illegal, underground; it was a very difficult time even to consider open political activity. What strategic overview we possessed was a remnant of the policy that had led to the downfall of Stormont. The Goulding element had advanced a political strategy, looking for the democratisation of Stormont, but this had failed when tested by the speed and intensity of events on the ground. Maire Drumm was at the time the senior Sinn Féin person in Belfast, and she certainly subscribed to the view that republicans should stay away from electoral politics in particular.

In the spring of 1973 on one of my few trips to Dublin during this period I met her as she came out of a meeting to talk to Seamus Twomey, whom I was with, and she was clearly agitated about the fact that inside at the meeting they were talking about contesting upcoming Stormont elections. In March a British government White Paper had proposed the establishing of a power-sharing assembly at Stormont, and a Council of Ireland.

The view she held and which was shared by most republicans in Belfast was that we had succeeded in getting rid of Stormont and we just needed to keep up that momentum in order to get rid of the British altogether. To recognise the validity of a new Stormont assembly by contesting elections, even on an abstentionist basis, would be a definite step backwards. Seamus read the riot act, and Sinn Féin certainly then decided on a boycott. In retrospect this was short-sighted, but the reality was that, irrespective of elections, we were politically ill-equipped. We had failed to develop a means by which popular support could express itself, and the key failure of the leadership was the lack of an integrated strategy.

My own view of my political role was parochial, and I didn't see elections as having anything to do with me. I was in middle leadership and my focus was on Ballymurphy and West Belfast; sharing an outlook which was general through the whole movement, I thought that it was someone else's job to be thinking in broader terms than the local.

On the loyalist right Vanguard and the DUP vowed to join forces in contesting the assembly elections on 28 June, with a view to preventing any power-sharing with Catholics or any Council of Ireland. In the run-in to the elections, the government lifted the ban on the Republican Clubs but not on Sinn Féin, which chose to mount a propaganda campaign around our programme, *Éire Nua*, in opposition to the assembly elections. For lack of a republican political strategy, most nationalists in effect saw the SDLP as providing the politics, the republicans as providing the army.

The principal anti-unionist political success in 1973 did not derive from any initiative of Sinn Féin, but from the hunger strike undertaken by Michael Farrell and Tony Canavan of PD – who had been jailed for organising a protest march – and its associated demonstrations, from which was built the Political Hostages Release Committee. Their hunger strike began in July and ended after thirty-four days with the British being forced to make concessions, releasing both Farrell and Canavan as part of an amnesty.

During all this period since June 1972, I had been living underground. For a short period Colette and I were lucky enough to get the use of a flat outside West Belfast in the university area. It was difficult for me travelling back and forth and would have been highly dangerous if the loyalists or British intelligence had got wind of my whereabouts outside the relative security of my own turf. On the other hand, within the flat the two of us had domestic normality and we behaved like any other couple, leaving for 'work' in the morning, returning at night. By now Colette was pregnant again. We were being very careful and protective that nothing should affect her pregnancy. But then, on 19 July, my period on the run came to a sudden end.

The two weeks around the traditional Orangemen's day of 12 July were always very quiet in nationalist areas, apart from the disturbances which arose from the Orange marches themselves. Most Catholic citizens of Belfast who could afford to leave the city went to Donegal, the Glens of Antrim or Omeath in County Louth, and as a result most Catholic areas were remarkably quiet; quiet times like this were always difficult times for moving about on the run.

When I called to a house in the Falls Road, my sixth sense told me that there was something amiss. Brendan Hughes arrived soon after me and mentioned that he had noticed a suspicious car outside. When Tom Cahill came in, he, too, was concerned. So Brendan went out the back of the house to find some local people, and soon after his return we saw two republicans from the Beechmount area approach the car and speak to its two occupants briefly. Then, as we watched, the car drove off and the two lads stood for a moment on the pavement before they, too, left the scene. Little did we know that as they had approached the car, the passenger had threatened them with a machine-gun before driving off. Our two republican comrades, who did not know which house we were in, spent a frantic half-hour trying to find us. The people in the car were British military intelligence, and they had the entire area staked out. When their car was approached, they decided that the game was up, and moved to raid the house. Of course, we did not learn all this until later.

As we saw it, the raid seemed a very routine affair. A British patrol coming down the road stopped outside the house and one of the soldiers knocked at the door. This was not uncommon; many times in the past British patrols had knocked at houses where I was staying, and sometimes I had actually spoken to them. The usual routine was either to ignore such a casual visit or to send the least known of those present to the door. So, Tom Cahill went to the front door while Brendan Hughes and I went to make our way out the back and along the entry. But when Brendan climbed up on to the wall, he discovered that the back of the house was saturated with British troops. As we turned around we were confronted by a British soldier, heavily armed. He arrested both of us as his compatriots swarmed around the house.

I lit my pipe; Brendan looked at me. For months he had been a target for uniformed and plainclothed British troops, who had opened fire on him on at least one occasion. They had raided numerous houses looking for him, and he had experienced many a narrow escape. Now he was almost philosophical. Small and swarthy, as his nickname, 'the Dark', implied, Brendan had lived on his nerves for some time. Married, with two young children, he was a close friend of mine and a good-hearted, generous comrade. Quick-tempered but immensely kind, Brendan looked bemused as British soldiers crowded into the house.

'Is this it?' he asked as we were taken quite quickly to Springfield Road barracks which wasn't far from where we were arrested.

As local people gathered to protest, a decoy convoy was sent from the barracks and a news bulletin about our arrest declared that we had been moved to Castlereagh. We weren't moved, however, until the early hours of the following morning. In the meantime, we had been joined by Owen 'Daddy' Coogan, a friend of ours who had been arrested separately. We were beaten fiercely, though Tom Cahill's serious injuries, sustained when he had been wounded in a gun attack early in 1970, saved him on this occasion from the rough treatment meted out to the rest of us. We were separated, of course, but periodically when the cell door opened I could hear the shouts and screams from where the others were. I'm sure similar sounds issued from my cell.

All of the people who beat me were in plain clothes, and at one point there were three of them in the cell. After the first initial flurry and my first fright at the frenzy of the assault, the beatings

218

settled into a dogged routine, in which I was forced into the search position, palms against the wall, body at an acute angle, legs widespread. They tried to make me put only my fingertips against the wall but I resisted that, and those doing the beating stood behind and concentrated mostly on the kidney area and the sides of my stomach while also landing vicious kicks between my legs. They beat me, I fell to the floor. They flung buckets of water over me to revive me, pulled me back up against the wall, beat me until I fell again. When I passed out, my clothes were pulled from me. At one point I made a half-hearted attempt to defend myself, and this provoked my torturers to a frenzy. All the time they asked me for information on my associates, my family and my neighbours. After in the beginning replying with a polite 'I'm sorry, I can't answer your questions,' I gave up saying anything at all.

Once I was aroused from unconsciousness by a British army doctor. He examined me thoroughly and seemed concerned about damage to my kidneys. Apparently I had been knocked out for some time. Eventually after a thorough check he told my assailants that I was OK. They waited till he left the cell, then dragged me to my feet. The beating began again.

Hours later the beatings stopped suddenly, as quickly as they had begun. My main tormentor threw a last bucket of water over me and then pulled me into a squatting position in the corner of the cell.

'Well, Gerry, what was it you told Mr Whitelaw? All bets are off?' He smiled at me, placed the plastic bucket over my head and left. I sat in that position for I don't know how long. Two uniformed British soldiers, ordinary squaddies, kept guard. One of them stubbed his cigarette out on my wrist. I couldn't see his face: with the bucket over my head, I could only see his camouflaged trousers, his heavy boots. I could see my own wrists as I sat with my arms and hands draped over my knees. In my stubbornness I refused to flinch. His mate chided him, and when they left the cell I could hear the two of them arguing outside the door.

Some time later the interrogators returned. Their mood had totally changed: now they were very friendly. My clothes were being dried out, they told me. They offered me tea, which I refused. One of them combed my wet hair. They left again and then returned with my belongings, creased and slightly warm, parts of them damp. Then I and my two compatriots were taken to the back of the barracks, where it appeared the entire regiment waited for us. The Dark, Owen and I emerged, barely able to walk upright and very badly marked, black and blue all over our bodies. They lined us up against the wall and took photographs of us with our arresting party. For a short time a posse of British soldiers, individually and in groups, posed beside us here at the back of the barracks. We were to have confirmed what had only been a rumour until now: we were on an 'A' list – that is, a list of republicans to be shot on sight – and there was a bounty for the platoon or the soldier involved. Of course, we had been captured, not shot, but there was a bonus here, too, for the soldiers. The various regiments kept a book, as in a betting shop, on who would succeed in apprehending us. From the banter between the British soldiers, it was obvious that the lucky ones had won a considerable prize; hence the photographs to commemorate the event.

Somewhere, in some regimental museum or on the top of somebody's wardrobe, there are photographs of myself and the Dark, Daddy Coogan and TC. I'm sure we were not a pretty sight.

They trussed Brendan up hand and foot and, to his great annoyance, a British soldier flung him across his shoulder and bundled him unceremoniously into the back of a Saracen. I was handcuffed to the ceiling of the vehicle. A plainclothes man sat beside me, a heavy automatic pistol in his hand. They were all extremely nervous. He placed the gun to my head and told me that if our convoy was attacked, I was going first.

At Castlereagh we had a relatively easy time. We weren't beaten and we were barely questioned. We were not, of course, charged with any offence, but were served with our detention papers. As we made our way from the interrogation centre along playing pitches to the chopper which was to take us to Long Kesh camp, we were once again photographed and, indeed, videoed by a British soldier. By now we were certainly feeling the worse for wear. As we clambered clumsily and painfully into the helicopter, Long Kesh didn't seem to be such a bad place. After all, we had plenty of friends there.

Nine

Going back into the internment camp was in many ways a relief. I had survived on the run for thirteen months, mostly in a small area in Belfast, by being very disciplined about what I did. I hadn't socialised at all. Much of the time I had been confined to just one room of a house. I had, of course, been networking with people, moving around for a few hours each day, but I had rarely left Belfast. Only now in Long Kesh did I realise the tremendous strain which that unnatural lifestyle had imposed on me: waiting always for the knock on the door, waiting to be challenged or to be shot.

When Brendan and I, Owen and TC arrived in the Kesh, we were welcomed with open arms by the other internees. Even the screws appeared glad to see us. One, seeing my blood-streaked wrists, produced a penknife and after some effort cut through the plastic cuffs which fastened my hands together. The British soldier who had handcuffed me had done such a diligent job that the plastic had cut into my flesh.

We were examined by the prison doctor. For some time there appeared to be a dispute between the prison authorities and the RUC about whether the prison would even accept us into its custody until it had verified that our bumps and bruises had actually occurred before our arrival in the prison camp. The RUC for their part were reluctant to accept responsibility for our condition. I don't know how they eventually resolved this problem, but in any event the Long Kesh medics made detailed notes of our wounds before we were whisked off to Cage 6.

Here all round us were cheering, welcoming faces. We for our part were bent over, hobbling, walking wounded, stiff and sore from the beatings. But we were among friends. As I made my way into Cage 6, across from me I could see Kevin Hannaway in his cage. He waved excitedly at me and shouted a greeting.

'Are you all right?'

'Hard as nails,' I lied, spoofing with the rest of them.

As delighted as I was to see Kevin, I reflected later that night as I lay in my bunk, that during all that had been happening to me in the last year, Kevin had spent that time doing just what he was doing when he greeted me that morning: walking around a cage.

Long Kesh had grown since I had left it so reluctantly about a year earlier. Now there were over twenty cages, each with four or five huts, housing either internees or sentenced prisoners. The cages for sentenced prisoners were located at the top and bottom parts of the camp, separate from those of internees. All the cages were surrounded by wire and watchtowers. Two-and-a-half or three-and-a-half huts were for living and sleeping in; thirty men to a hut. One hut was the canteen; there was a washroom and study hut and a half-hut for 'recreation'. Most of the camp's draughty Nissen huts leaked; they were made of corrugated tin and had no proper form of heating, so all of them were bitterly cold in winter. We were strange-looking creatures, especially in winter, wandering around wearing overcoats and blankets, and big heavy boots, with socks on our hands for gloves. The washrooms were quite rough, completely inadequate for the numbers using them. The medical facilities were archaic, the hospital being simply a number of huts set to one side in their own cage.

We were a mixture of males from teenagers to old-age pensioners, with rural, urban, city or small town backgrounds, all herded into huts where there was no privacy. Some of us were republican activists, others might just have looked sideways at a British soldier once too often, and others had simply found themselves in the wrong place at the wrong time. The conditions were tolerable for those of us who were young, simply because we possessed the resilience of youth, but for some of the older people the circumstances were mind-bendingly hard and terribly lonely. In Cage 22 were people who had been in since August 1971, some of whom had also been interned in the '40s and '50s. There were people like Jimmy Drumm, who had spent many years of his life interned without trial, and Liam Mulholland, an almost blind old-age pensioner, who had first been imprisoned in 1919. Many of the older people had known each other in the '50s; some of them had known each other for thirty or forty years. My brother Liam was in the top end of the camp at the sentenced end. Our Paddy was in Cage 6, and the two of us were reunited in the half-hut.

Internment was very unsettling for prisoners, who didn't know whether they were in for twenty days, twenty months or twenty years. If you were sentenced at least you knew how long you had to serve and could settle down to doing your time, but with internment you never knew. This was especially hard to handle for those – and there were many – who had never done anything to warrant being imprisoned in the first place.

Raids occurred quite frequently, usually in the early hours of the morning when some Colonel Blimp would suddenly appear with a bunch of would-be commandos and a few regiments of combat troops and order us to 'put your hands on your blankets, look at the ceiling, then when told to do so you will get dressed and take your knife, fork and spoon to the canteen'. I've never been able to understand why we were ordered to bring knife, fork and spoon: after all, we never got fed during a raid. Instead, they would sometimes beat us, sometimes spread us on the wire, and always they would trash the hut.

After one such raid we were taken back from the canteen, as usual, between two lines of Brits. Sometimes they would belt us with batons, shout insults at us, and set their dogs on us, but on this occasion they confined themselves to the regular insults. Just as I turned the corner of our hut I saw Shane, my dog. He was about fifty yards from me, close to the gate of the cage, and accompanied by a small, stocky British army dog-handler. I shouted out to him but he didn't move. Then I whistled. He tensed immediately, ears cocked, head alert, his body on point. He jerked towards me and I thought he was going to break free as he lunged forward, jerking away from his handler, pulling and straining on his lead and howling out to me. Then a Brit shoved me around the corner and into our hut. I could still hear Shane crying. It was the last I saw of him.

Cage 6 stood in the very centre of the camp, and in our end of the cage were most of the recently interned men – in general a lively, rebellious young bunch. We came in for a lot of attention from the camp administration, particularly when we made a series of escapes and escape attempts. We felt a sense of having, by being captured, let down people on the outside, so we immediately rejuvenated the business of planning escapes. We also reckoned that we weren't going to be let out until internment was over, so we should meanwhile do everything we could to escape.

Within thirty-six hours of our arrival some prisoners in another cage sent a plan they had been working on down to Cage 6, which involved a prisoner going out beneath a rubbish lorry. Paul Marlowe, a former paratrooper, made a harness similar to one used by parachutists. Brendan Hughes, though his bruises hadn't even started to go yellow, was soon hanging from the harness to get him used to it, but as it turned out the escape didn't go ahead because it was considered too dangerous. However, the cage in which the idea had originated thought they could get someone into position under a lorry, so the harness was passed on to them. A guy from that cage, Mark Graham, did succeed in getting into the harness under the lorry, but as the truck went over a security ramp, his back was broken; he was paralysed as a result and was later released.

I was scarcely in a month when word came that Jim Bryson and

Patrick Mulvenna had been shot in Ballymurphy. Patrick Mulvenna, who died immediately or shortly after being shot, was married to my sister Frances, who was expecting their first child. The shadow of republican feuding fell briefly over our family again, as shortly before the shooting both Paddy Mulvenna and Jim Bryson had been placed under death threat by the 'Officials'. In the confusion of the time many people blamed the 'Officials' for their deaths, but it was the British army who killed them. Patrick's father, who was in the sentenced end of the Kesh at the time, tried unsuccessfully to get released on parole for the funeral.

Jim Bryson, who died from his injuries three weeks later, was a very brave individual who had escaped several times: once when he had been arrested by the British in the lower Falls but succeeded in fighting his way out of the back of a Saracen, another time when he escaped from Belfast prison, and, most notably, when he had escaped from the *Maidstone*. I had met Emerson, as he was also known, and his frequent comrade-in-arms, Tommy 'Toddler' Toland, the day after his escape from the *Maidstone*, and he had then gone to the Twenty-six Counties. He had been restless across the border, but when he returned to Belfast I had argued with him very earnestly, because he was very well known, that he needed to keep his head down; things, after all, had changed from the time when he could wander about the Murph at will. Just before Brendan Hughes, Tom Cahill and I were arrested, he had gone back to Dublin, but one of the first things I received when I arrived in the Kesh was a note from him saying 'I'm back'. He had obviously returned because we had been arrested and, over the next few weeks, we heard regular reports about his being around the Murph.

Tommy Toland was in with us, and he and I were together in the cage when we heard that Jim had been shot. Jim had been in Cage 6 himself at one time, and a cloud hung over the internment camp during the weeks leading up to his death finally in the Royal Victoria Hospital. When we heard reports of the deaths of friends and relations, naturally we were saddened, but we were also utterly frustrated at being locked away at such a time. A year after

226

Jim Bryson's death, I learned that my cousin Ciaran Murphy, the youngest son of my Aunt Kathleen in Ardoyne, had been picked up by loyalists, and his body had been found in a quarry on the Hightown Road in North Belfast.

Despite the failed escape which had left Mark Graham with a broken back, escape attempts continued, and within a short time Brendan Hughes got out. Observation of the routine of the bin lorry revealed that a whole mattress would be removed with the rest of the rubbish; one of the ordinary prisoners who was working on the bin lorry detail reported that there was no churning device inside the lorry, but that the screws spiked the rubbish. A prisoner in another cage had had a similar notion, and Cage 6 decided to mount the escape from the other cage, because our cage was always coming in for a lot of attention and scrutiny. Brendan would be slipped into the other cage. To aid the subterfuge he was kitted out in a distinctive anorak with a big coloured flash and a red and fawn leather hat with a big floppy rim. In the weeks before the planned escape, Brendan visited the other cage a few times, always walking a few feet ahead of the screws and not talking to them at all. On the appointed day, he went on a cage visit and he didn't return, but his anorak and hat came back on a different prisoner with a similar build. In the cage he was wrapped in a mattress cover and the mattress, tied around him, was thrown out of the cage for collection. The lorry came and the mattress was dumped into it.

He had an orange to suck on to help him with his breathing, but the mattress was full of sawdust and he nearly choked. To Brendan's dismay, as the lorry passed through one of the gates, the screws spiked the rubbish more thoroughly than anyone had expected. Inside his mattress, half suffocated with sawdust, he felt the edge of the spike as it was pushed again and again through the contents of the bin lorry. Finally over the third ramp was the last gate, and then he was out of the camp.

Arriving at the dump he clambered out and then hitch-hiked to County Louth, where he went into a pub called The Jolly Ploughboy. That evening there was a crowd of women down on a bus-run from the Falls, and when Brendan was recognised they had a big hooley to celebrate his escape. Meanwhile back in Long Kesh the following day, the decoy, who had kept the count in Cage 6 right, returned to his cage, where they had dummied the count. It was a good escape, and Cage 6 took particular satisfaction from having succeeded in diverting the focus away from itself.

Shortly after his escape Brendan Hughes placed an advertisement in the *Irish News* slagging off Davey Long, the senior screw in charge of security, whom we all took great delight in taking down a peg or two whenever we could. Another time, when a tunnel which was being dug had to be abandoned, a message was left for Davey, saying, 'You missed this ten times.'

Ivor Bell was arrested not long after Brendan Hughes's escape, and it was decided to try to get him out almost immediately. An internee had applied for parole to get married, and the plan was to have 'Ding-Dong' take his place. Ivor was with us in Cage 6 and the other guy was quite a distance away in Cage 5, separated by wire fences and gates. However, on the appointed day he succeeded in getting into Cage 5, another guy was smuggled into Cage 6 to make up the numbers, and the unfortunate fellow who had applied for parole was hidden.

Some time later Davey Long, realising that he hadn't seen Ivor for a while, came to the hut looking to see if he was there. Someone called down the hut: 'Ivor, you're wanted; are you there?' and someone else answered that he'd be out in ten minutes. We could see the intense relief on Davey Long's face. That felt good, especially later when Ivor's escape was announced outside.

A number of prisoners were intent on escaping and they systematically analysed escape opportunities. These divided into three categories: over or through the wire; under the wire; or through the gate. The third category became the most successful one; that is, escape by deception, decoy or disguise.

Escape tunnels were dug, but these suited perimeter cages better. Because of the time necessary, the problems involved in getting rid of the soil, and the real difficulties encountered in the actual tunnelling, many tunnels were discovered. Still, persistence sometimes paid off. The camp authorities countered efforts by increased raids and surveillance, and escapees were badly treated. If captured during an escape, we were beaten and subjected to spells in the punishment block, followed by charges in the Diplock courts. Hugh Coney was shot dead by the British army during an escape attempt in November 1974.

Successful efforts to escape over or through the wire were aided by the fog which frequently enveloped Long Kesh in winter. Some of these escapes were unplanned. It was just a matter of being in the right place at the right time, but it helped, of course, to have wire-cutters or other equipment.

A team of us in Cage 6 – Marshall Mooney, Tommy Toland, Marty O'Rawe and myself, all from the Murph – gathered up all the necessary tools, including camouflaged clothing, bolt cutters and hacksaws. We studied weather reports and spent months sitting up for hours waiting for the fog to fall. It didn't. After a while we got bored with this standing by and, to pass the time, we used to escape from the hut – as a dummy run – and sneak around the cage. Marshall Mooney became particularly adept at this, but despite his ingenuity it was obvious that we were getting nowhere fast.

Fog or no fog, we decided to make a bid on Christmas Eve of 1973 during the midnight mass. By now we had established the blind spots on the wire, and we had perfected a method of getting to them. Christmas Eve eventually arrived, and when the rest of the inmates were locked up, we four lay outside Cage 6, in a gap between the internee and sentenced ends of the Kesh, and watched the camp slowly settle down for the night. It was ten o'clock. It was also a very bright night and we were surrounded by miles of razor wire rolled in long tunnels and with watch-towers overlooking it all. Progress was slow; we crawled along inch by inch. By midnight a slight fog fell. Security was immediately tightened. We could hear orders being shouted all around us, and extra patrols were put out on the catwalk, which ran within feet of us to our right. Inside Cage 6, to our left, a patrol was put in the cage. Unfortunately, the fog was too light to assist us. The extra patrols meant we couldn't move. We decided to sit tight until the security was lifted.

'What's that over there?' I heard one screw ask.

'Only an old football,' replied his fellow screw.

I realised it was Marshall Mooney's head they had spotted, but fortunately they continued on their patrolling rounds and we continued to sit tight.

However, they returned after a while, and one of them was convinced he could see something other than a football. The game was up.

'Ho, ho, ho, Merry Christmas to you all!' shouted Marshall Mooney suddenly as he emerged from the razor wire. Then he moved along the wire, trying to draw attention away from Tommy Toland, Marty O'Rawe and me.

Searchlights cut through the darkness and the light fog; sirens sounded. Pandemonium broke out in the camp as shouting screws and soldiers ran around all over the place, guard dogs snarling and barking.

Screws were shouting at Marshall to go to the other side of the wire, but when he produced his wire cutters and started to cut his way through they shouted at him to stop. Still trying to draw attention away from us, he walked on along the wire, but there was just too much light and too much attention focused on us, so I decided to try another ruse in the hope that the others might still be missed by the screws.

I stood up and walked away from the others. Marshall, who copped on immediately to what I was at, shouted out 'Hello!' as if he were greatly surprised to see me. We rushed into each other's arms, greeting each other like long-lost pals, ignoring the screws, the dogs and the chaos which surrounded us. But the barking and shouting rose to a new crescendo. The diversion didn't work, and the screws threatened to set the dogs on us if we didn't go back the way we had come.

The screws and soldiers were pretty fired up as they bustled us up to the punishment block, and Marshall and I took bad beatings. I was wearing a pair of glasses, which I had tied on, and a very senior official pulled my glasses down and when he realised they weren't coming off he gouged my face so that the flesh was pulled away in a deep and ugly wound.

Meanwhile Tommy Toland had hit on the trick of shouting at Marty O'Rawe in a British accent and marching him up to the punishment cells, all the time shouting insults at him. This succeeded in confusing the Brits, and so Marty and Tommy escaped being beaten.

In the punishment block all of us were stripped naked and put in separate cells, and the dogs were set loose in the corridor outside. We feared that at any moment soldiers and warders would descend on us, and so we kept our spirits up by shouting jokes back and forth to each other.

Marshall and Toddler in particular gave the British soldiers a hard time.

'Hi, Brit, my name's Tommy Toland,' Marshall shouted, 'and I'm going to knock your bollocks in.'

'What rank are you?' Toddler asked the soldier.

'Corporal,' came the reply.

'Corporal? Corporal! My mate's a general. His name's Marshall Mooney and he could take you.'

Despite their provocations, or maybe because of them, the night passed without incident, though at one stage a couple of British army officers came to have a look at us.

The next day, Christmas Day, an army doctor was sent in to see me as part of the routine of checking that we were still alive.

'Can you give me some cream for my face?' I asked him.

'What's wrong with your face?' he replied, looking straight at the ugly wound on the side of my nose and across my cheek.

'Happy Christmas!' I said, and away he went.

The next day, St Stephen's Day, I had a visit with Colette and Gearóid. That was a funny old Christmas.

In July 1974, in another attempt to escape, I went on a visit wearing two sets of clothes, a wig and a false beard. A friend of mine on the outside, Big Harry, had noticed a guy who he said was the image of me. This man was to be sent to visit Ivor, and when he arrived in the visiting box we were to change clothes; he was to don my false beard and wig and, hey presto, he was to go into the Kesh and I was to walk out. So at the appointed time I went on a visit and, when the screws weren't looking, I slipped into Ding-Dong's visiting box where he and his visitor were waiting. To my amazement my double was inches shorter than I was. I cursed Big Harry. Ivor and I looked at each other. Then on impulse I decided to go ahead. I took off my wig and beard and my outer layer of clothing to reveal clothes like the visitor's; he put on my outer clothes. I left the visiting box without being detected and approached the outer gate, but a screw copped me.

In evidence at my subsequent trial on a charge of attempting to escape, the screw said, 'I knew there was something wrong. When this man went in, I was looking down at him. When he came out, I was looking up at him.'

Infuriated by the rebels in Cage 6, the authorities placed extra sentry boxes around us and mounted extra patrols. We soon found that, understandably, fewer people were choosing to be in our half-hut. We were getting raided all the time, forced into the search position, spreadeagled out on the wire, then thrown back in the hut; and then an hour later the patrol might come back and go through the same thing again. The rate of attrition was severe, but it was a good way to do time, better than sitting there day in, day out, just waiting and wondering when you'd ever get out.

Sometimes the Brits would sneak in on a raid, and sometimes they'd come in roaring like lunatics, battering at the ends of all the beds and trying to terrorise and intimidate us. We were quite capable of being just as crazy, and at times there were stand-up fights or standoffs between us and the raiding parties. This became so intense that there came a time when we had to decide to only engage in passive resistance, because some of the older people and some of those less able for physical confrontation were coming under acute pressure. I was delighted.

Some of my fellow-internees and prisoners were great characters. There were naturally humorous people like Dominic O'Neill, who went once to a new screw and gave him a ten bob note – we weren't supposed to have any money, of course – and asked him to go down and get him an *Irish News* and a bap. The young screw came back an hour later saying he couldn't find the shop! That kind of business kept us going and kept our spirits up.

A man from South Armagh was interned just as his cow was about to calf, and he used to go to the welfare officer to get news about the cow. As he was coming past our cage, one of our Belfast guys would shout over, 'How's she coming?' and so on, and our agricultural comrade would take him seriously and give a running report on the cow's progress.

One of the older internees was my friend from Leitrim, John Joe McGirl, who had been arrested as he arrived in Belfast to speak at an Easter Sunday commemoration. The RUC thought he was Seamus Twomey. A real veteran of the struggle, he had previously been imprisoned in Arbour Hill in Dublin and in the Curragh, where he and my Uncle Dominic, among others, had been very severely beaten. He was put into our cage, which was almost entirely populated by wild young fellas much less than half his age, but he had great tolerance and a natural affinity with younger people, which stood him in good stead.

Our Paddy was in our hut, and our family association with the camp is such that ever since it opened at least one of us has been imprisoned there. My father, my Uncle Liam Hannaway and a couple of my cousins were amongst the first to be interned, in August 1971, in Belfast prison, being transferred the following month to the Kesh. Liam was for some time OC of the camp and was highly respected. My brother Dominic was only six years old then, but he has since done several years in the Kesh, as have our Sean and our Liam. The women of our families, like Colette and my mother, and many other wives, mothers, sisters, sisters-in-law, sweethearts and aunts, have spent twenty years and more visiting prisons.

Our Paddy moved out of our hut, along with a number of

233

others, because of Harvey, the hut ghost, who was alleged to have been a British airman who was killed in a plane crash during the Second World War when Long Kesh had been an airfield. Harvey visited us every night; or something did. In reality the phenomenon was a mixture of wind-up, auto-suggestion and who knows what, as a result of which most of us couldn't get to sleep. At least that's what I hope it was; but who knows?

Prisoners were organised in cages with their own command structure. In the course of the previous three years, the command structure had found its own level, and thus I rarely had anything to do with screws at all. The atmosphere was quite relaxed much of the time, except when tension rose for specific reasons, but by and large, except for special incidents, the screws went about their business and the internees got on with theirs.

Bigotry expressed itself in small ways. At Christmas, for example, we received hundreds of Christmas cards, and the screws scrawled 'Fuck the Pope' and the like on the religious ones, especially those with pictures of the Virgin Mary. Some of the British screws were quite bewildered by the whole situation of internment. One day when one gave me an order, I just told him to catch himself on. I said, 'We're political prisoners: you remember that.' We argued for a minute or so until another screw intervened, and that ended our little altercation. A few weeks later the same guy came to me and said, 'I'm going back. I didn't realise that it was anything like this, and you're right, you are political prisoners.' And he did resign and returned to England.

One day shortly after my arrival in Long Kesh, some of the boys came and told me that a screw wanted me at the gate and that they thought Colette had had a wee boy. I wouldn't go out, because I had no need to, once I knew. I was delighted at the thought that I now had a son, Gearóid, and that Colette had come through it OK. Colette was in hospital, so my mother came up on my next visit, though she must have found me in a completely distracted mood. I was concerned only that Colette would arrive up with all speed with our new child. I wanted all the news I could get about the two of them. When Colette did get up, immediately after her release from hospital, I was ten feet tall coming back off that visit and after holding Gearóid for the first time.

A cruel cat-and-mouse situation existed in relation to families. If a man had four or five children and his wife was ill, he would naturally be consumed by awful anxieties. At one time no physical contact was permitted on visits, and people just sat on either side of a desk. There were many protests about this and about the searching of relatives, and by dint of internees pushing the issue, conditions were relaxed and the screws were pushed back from the actual visiting boxes. Our Gearóid came with Colette on visits every week, right from birth. In a way it was easier for those with young children; those with teenage children had a much more difficult time, and it was difficult for the children themselves. In many families it was the breadwinner who was interned, and his removal could have all sorts of consequences for families. At the same time, many women who were married to internees became liberated through the experience, tough though it was; they were forced back on their own resilience and strength, which they found to be considerable. I have always had a sense that in Ireland there is a matriarchal background which on occasion and under certain influences comes to the fore. Women had to cope with generating and managing the family income, bringing children through all of the trauma of growing up, and dealing with the often harsh realities of the wider world, such as British army harassment or raids, as well as taking up leadership positions in campaigns around the issue of the prisoners and sometimes in wider campaigns about community resistance and so on.

During the Ulster Workers' Council strike in May 1974, life in Long Kesh was particularly Stalag-like. In the previous October a power-sharing executive for the north had been formed, with Brian Faulkner, former prime minister and the man who introduced internment, as its chief executive, and Gerry Fitt of the SDLP as his deputy. In December, London, Dublin and Belfast had, in the Sunningdale agreement, decided upon the establishment of a Council of Ireland. On the one hand, the

British sold the agreement to Dublin and the SDLP as constituting a major step towards a united Ireland and as providing for a degree of control over the RUC. On the other hand, they sold it to the unionists as guaranteeing Dublin's recognition of the constitutional status of the statelet in the north and providing for increased suppression of the IRA in the south. Meanwhile, the Council of Ireland would be entirely toothless.

The majority of unionist politicians who were resolutely opposed to power-sharing and rejected any notion of a Council of Ireland, mobilised with the loyalist paramilitaries to bring down the power-sharing executive. In May the Ulster Workers' Council declared a 'constitutional stoppage' against the Sunningdale agreement. UDA roadblocks, with the collusion of the British army and the RUC, prevented people from getting to work; workers entering or leaving factories were attacked. On 16 May former Minister for Home Affairs William Craig warned that 'there will be further actions taken against the Irish Republic'. The following day three no-warning rush-hour car-bombs exploded in Dublin and Monaghan, killing thirty-three people. Within the north the UWC demonstrated the economic power of loyalism by almost completely cutting off the supply of both electricity and petrol, while the UDA controlled the streets. Four days later the British government finally decided to use its troops to end the stoppage, but the British army refused. On 28 May the executive and the Sunningdale agreement collapsed.

Throughout the UWC 'strike', nationalists felt the power of loyalism very directly, in the absence of fuel, food and other essentials. They had also witnessed streets outside the nationalist enclaves being taken over by club-wielding paramilitaries who chatted easily with British troops and the RUC. The widespread fear, adequately supported by past experience, was that attacks on nationalist areas would be next on the loyalist agenda. In Long Kesh, too, we were aware of the danger of attack, and because of the dangerous climate we cancelled visits and food parcels, surviving only on prison grub re-cooked in fires which we lit in the yard, stripping wood from our huts for fuel.

The principal sources of conflict with the prison authorities were the visits and the food. Camp food arrived in large containers on the back of a lorry, and at the gate to each cage the containers were taken down and placed on a trolley; POWs trundled the trolley across the yard, loading the containers on to a hot-plate in the hut designated as a canteen. The actual contents of these containers was usually disgusting; if it were especially revolting, it would be refused by our camp or cage staff. In the internment cages we were allowed to receive food parcels from outside, but in the sentenced cages access to food parcels was restricted, and so people there had to eat the prison grub on a fairly regular basis. Other uses were, however, found for some of these culinary delights, and we discovered that the cakes, which were rock-hard, could be used in volleys to keep British army raids at bay on occasion.

At the beginning of September 1974, having tried unsuccessfully through representations and delegations to get an improvement in the food, we protested by dumping the food over the wire. The authorities responded by stopping our food parcels, and we were reduced to half a pint of milk and three rounds of bread a day. In protest also against the lack of clean sheets, we draped our bedclothes on the cage wire. The camp OCs had presented a list of complaints to the governor: food, laundry, living conditions, lack of educational facilities and the treatment of remand prisoners. When there was no response on any of the issues, we started protests.

Tension increased in the second week of October, and there were rumours of large numbers of British troops gathering around the visiting area. On a previous occasion when troops had handed out particularly heavy beatings during a raid, our camp OC had promised to burn the camp down if they tried it again. Now we debated amongst ourselves whether we could combine burning the camp down with a mass escape, and it was while I was at a meeting in our cage about this that things blew up in the sentenced end, in Cage 13.

Standing outside and looking towards the sentenced end, we could see a single plume of black smoke rising into the sky.

'Burn it all!' shouted the OC of the internees through the wire to our cage OC.

Everything was set alight. I was one of three men delegated to check that no one had been left behind when we moved off from our burning cage to an assembly point at Cage 4. All the huts were ablaze, and through the flames, smoke and confusion I could hear Kris Kristofferson singing 'Bobby Magee', his voice getting slower and more distorted as the heat reached the record player and the LP our friend Kathleen had sent me.

It was late evening, and the light was fading rapidly. Soon the screws were shining searchlights down on us and firing rubber bullets and CR gas. This gas was quite different from CS gas, and it seemed to me that it induced a sense of what it must be like to drown, as it smothered windpipe and lungs. We milled around in some confusion before we were formed up, a couple of hundred of us who had not managed to link up with the people in the sentenced end of the camp, and order was restored in our ranks. We met with little interference from the screws, though rubber bullets were fired at the squads which were sent out to burn places outside the cages. For two hours, however, they continued to pump CR gas into the camp.

For our part we just watched the camp burn. The night sky was blazing. A burning watchtower toppled over, collapsing in a fireworks display of sparks. Explosions could be heard from all parts of the camp as gas containers blew up. Rubber bullets and gas grenades were fired in at us, while helicopters with search-lights circled over our heads, occasionally dropping gas bombs. As I strolled around in the fire, smoke and general ruin of the place, I came across incongruous sights: a fellow internee with a blanket over him, under which he had a mess-tin of sausages; he reached in, pulled one out and handed it to me. Meeting Dickie Glenholmes, another comrade, I said I'd love a smoke, and a few minutes later he returned with a Hamlet cigar. I encountered my old friend John Joe McGirl and asked him if he was all right.

'If you're all right, I'm all right,' he said. His jaw had been broken by a rubber bullet.

As dawn approached we huddled together in the centre of what remained of Cage Four, our faces grey with soot and grime, and contemplated the grey, smouldering debris of the camp, the grey wire around us and the grey sky above.

Then the British army came in, squealing and whooping. We met them with studied silence. Soon they stood silently too as they faced us outside our cage. When an officer ordered us all through a megaphone to get to our feet, we remained silently sitting. Our OC broke the stand-off by advancing and negotiating with the officer for the wounded to be taken away, while the rest of our men would be paraded by our own staff for identification by the screws. As we moved away, the British army filled the centre of the cage and demanded that I and another man be brought forward. The tension rose, and some of our strongest and fittest internees gathered around the two of us, but a compromise was reached and a single screw was brought by one of the camp staff to where we stood. The tension relaxed when it became clear that the Brits only wanted to check that we had not escaped.

The atmosphere became charged again soon enough when we were all ordered against the wire for a body-search. No one moved until one of our staff defused the situation by stepping forward and instructing us to go to the wire. There we were searched and identified, then walked back to our cages.

The sounds of rubber bullets and gas grenades could still be heard from the sentenced end of the camp, but after a while this eased off. Later the internees who had broken through to the sentenced end returned in a long crocodile procession between rows of heavily-armed Brits; bloodied but unbowed, they were all grinning broadly.

They had fought a pitched battle up at the football pitch at the sentenced end. Our lads had captured a Brit and had come under air attack, scores of gas grenades being thrown at them from a helicopter. Many had been injured, some seriously, and many received dog bites, rubber-bullet wounds and bruised and broken limbs. When the Brits had finally, by force of arms, subdued them, they had been put on the wire for as long as five hours. Now the fight was over and, lying where we had stood, we slept at last.

We lived rough for weeks. It was a remarkable time of great unity among all the prisoners. Then Long Kesh began slowly to emerge out of the ashes. After the burning of the camp, we were rehoused in Cage 6.

In the aftermath of the fire, there was a lot of talk about releases and about the possibility of internment's ending. Then out of the blue a number of us were taken from the embers of the camp, with no proper clothes, to Hillsborough Court. I was sewing a pair of jeans when I was taken out. I merely stuck the needle in the denim and went on my way. I continued sewing in the cell at Hillsborough and, given the state my clothes were in, I was intent on finishing the job in the court, but we were all cuffed. To show their disregard for the courts, some republicans read books or papers, so as well as fulfilling my tailoring needs I was making a statement of sorts to the court. I asked the screw to take the cuffs off me and when he refused, I said to the magistrate that this was a severe infringement of our rights, and so on. He said, 'Well, this is a security matter.' Ten minutes later I said that I wanted to remove my coat, and he said, 'Yes, of course you may remove your coat.' They took the cuffs off; I took off my coat, and refused to let them put the cuffs back on. There was little they could do so I finished sewing my jeans. The magistrate ignored me, but that didn't matter. It was the kind of small, silly victory that helped keep up one's fighting spirit.

Several of us who had been involved in escapes and who had been caught, including Ivor Bell, who had since been recaptured, Tommy Toland, myself and a handful of others, were filmed for a television news programme as we entered the court. When it was broadcast Robert Kee named both me and Ivor Bell as having taken part in discussions with Whitelaw in London and asserted that there was no question of our being involved in any further discussions. This seemed strange to me because I had no sense of having any public profile. On the contrary I had a sense of being anonymous and of valuing my anonymity, and I was disconcerted when my name appeared in the newspapers because I was doing nothing, as I saw it, to deserve this attention.

Years earlier the UDA had held a press conference to publicise their access to British and RUC intelligence files; two or three hooded men sat behind a table which was spread with scores of photographs, and to my surprise my mug shot was in among all the other unfortunates. I had felt slightly removed from the sinister threat of it all at the time, as if that wasn't really me. Once when I was on the run I went into a shop to buy some cigarettes and there amongst all the newspapers laid out on the counter I saw myself looking out at the world from the front page of the *Daily Mirror*. I was mortified. Whatever part I had to play in the struggle, it didn't include a public role; that, I presumed, was for others. The *Daily Mirror* story was rubbish and was my first encounter with that type of tabloid journalism, light years away from Bud Bossence's honourable profession, which writes about people they have never bothered to interview or about subjects they have not researched. As I heard of Robert Kee's news item I was surprised and sorry that I was considered in any way to be newsworthy.

So I found myself with a sentence of eighteen months (later I was to get a further three years for the other escape) and a new bed in Cage 11. Things were different in the sentenced cage. There were a lot of people here whom we didn't know, and they'd been in for a long time. The atmosphere was quiet, subdued, quite monastic, totally different from the internment cages. Shortly after we moved, the last of the internees were released.

Prison, especially long-term imprisonment, affects everyone differently. It can be a mind-bending experience, sucking the very marrow from the spirit. The actual structure of Long Kesh was particularly difficult. While the communal nature of the place had huge advantages in terms of solidarity and company, at the same time privacy was impossible. I rarely was able to be on my own. It was the same for everyone else. And such was the character of the place that walking alone invited bantering and ridicule. At times in conversation about these matters, some prisoners voiced a preference for the cellular accommodation which they had had in Belfast's Crumlin Road prison while on remand.

'At least you can bang up (lock up) in your own cell when you want your head showered.'

Belfast prison, everyone agreed, was a hole. As Cleeky Clarke once said, 'The Crum's so bad it would put you off going to jail.'

Imprisonment was particularly difficult for families. Separation brought its own problems for all involved, and the reality or the prospect of long-term imprisonment was a daunting one. Relationships broke up with subsequent heartbreak. When family or friends died outside, there was no way for the prisoner to grieve inside.

For all these reasons prison was to be avoided like the plague. I would not recommend it to anyone, even though I was one of the lucky ones, in that my imprisonment was for a relatively short period. But I was conscious of the hardship I was inflicting upon my wife and child. It was an even heavier trip for long-termers and their families, and I am constantly humbled by the resilience of the families of prisoners and amazed at how they continue to engage actively in struggle.

In Cage 11 I was delighted to be reunited with Brendan Hughes, who had been recaptured, Marshall Mooney and Toddler. We were allocated beds in the middle hut. I was put in close to the Dark and later we shared a cubicle when these were built. For the first few weeks we readjusted to the new regime, enjoying encounters at the wire with old friends from the Murph and elsewhere, including Tony and Alex who had almost shared my honeymoon with me.

Soon, however, it became clear that there was some tension in Cage 11. As far as I could see, there was really no good cause for this: both sides of the argument were sound, and it appeared to be mostly a problem of communication, or the lack of it, within the cage itself, as well perhaps as a symptom of the general mood throughout the camp, which was run by the prisoners' staff in a regimented way. I had only been a short time in the cage when I was lobbied to take charge of it. I resisted. As a sentenced prisoner I had my own agenda, which had to do with reading, writing and studying, and nothing to do with public service within the cage. The lobbying continued from both factions now; reluctantly and conditionally – which included re-forming a representative and united cage staff – I got dragged into taking on a position of authority.

Bobby Sands was one of the prisoners in Cage 11 at this time. Bobby was in the Gaeltacht hut, a hut set aside by the POWs in most cages for Irish speakers and students of the Irish language. These had developed years before under the influence of Proinsias MacAirt. Bobby learnt his Irish from Cyril McCurtain, who had come all the way from County Limerick to be with us in the Lazy K.

Bobby was a relatively self-contained young man, at that time not long turned twenty. He was a keen and competitive sportsman and a good Gaelic footballer and soccer player who enjoyed his games very much. He had a mane of long hair, but that wasn't unusual at the time: so had I and many others. Bobby wasn't very big, but he was wiry and solidly built. His family had been driven out of their home in Rathcoole in North Belfast by loyalists in 1972, and Bobby, who was apprenticed as a coach builder, had lost his job as a consequence. When the Sands family moved to Twinbrook, Bobby joined the IRA at the age of eighteen. A month later he was charged with possession of a weapon found in a house and sentenced to three years in Long Kesh.

I got to know him better when we started to develop political lectures and other collective efforts in the cage, and he became very interested and involved in these. However, the fact that we were in different huts meant that we didn't share in any social events, which usually involved illicit alcohol and thus occurred after lock-up when the screws left us to our own devices. Although I never drank the stuff, poteen-making was brought to a fine art in Long Kesh, and I witnessed amazing sights as a result of its effects on other people. After some earlier shenanigans, the camp staff had decreed that it was only to be made for special occasions, like St Patrick's Day or Christmas.

However, Bobby, who did his best to play guitar, was present at one event which involved the whole cage in a memorable Christmas Eve concert. We all brought a pile of tables into the large hut to make a stage at the end, across which improvised curtains were hung to create very successfully the effect of a theatre. We also installed chairs for the audience and a bar, at which a group of comrades served beer, cider and poteen they had brewed up for the occasion. In the course of the concert Bobby Sands and Martin McAllister got up on stage and played some lovely sets, providing the traditional music content to the concert. The finale and highlight of the night, which we often reminisced about afterwards, consisted of a bunch of prisoners suitably bewigged and costumed miming Freddy Mercury's *A Night At the Opera*, for which Igor, our cage handyman, had concocted a version of dried ice out of crushed table tennis balls, which at the appropriate moment in 'Galileo Galileo' he released. The intention was to envelop the stage in an atmosphere of suitably theatrical mist. In the event, while Igor got the visuals right, he did not allow for the toxic nature of his product. Or the smell. It was ghastly, choking everyone and bringing our concert to a fittingly farcical end.

Brendan (Bik) McFarlane from Ardoyne, like Bobby a keen musician, graduated to Cage 11 during this time, along with Skeet Hamilton, a great character. At around the same time, Gerry Kelly from the Whiterock and Hugh Feeney were transferred back to Ireland, along with Dolours and Marion Price, after 205 days of force-feeding in a prison in Britain. All these men brought their own colour into our lives, and our cage soon gained a reputation of being slightly different from the rest. This, of course, may be a matter which would be disputed by prisoners who were in the other cages.

In the period following the republican split of 1969, the Goulding faction had continued to engage in armed actions. While these were not of the same intensity as the IRA campaign, the tensions within the Goulding ranks came to the surface when they called a cessation in May 1972. Two years later Seamus Costello and others formed the Irish Republican Socialist Party (IRSP) and later an armed group as well; they outlined a policy position which echoed the opposition to the Goulding/MacGiolla policies which had underpinned the 1969 split. Costello was an extremely competent leader and a formidable personality. However, the public acrimony between him and his former comrades degenerated quickly into feuding. Seamus Costello was killed in October 1977, and the IRSP lost its only figure of national standing and ability. Liam McMillen remained loyal to the Goulding leadership, but in April 1975 he, too, was shot dead. Only recently married at the time, he was buying nails in a Falls Road hardware shop when he was killed. For all the bitterness which followed the 1969 split, I was very sorry to hear the news of his death and I thought the circumstances were particularly poignant. Billy McMillen and I had parted on good personal terms despite our differences of opinion, but I didn't see him again after 1969, apart from an isolated meeting or two. I have no notion of how, if he had lived, he would stand now, given all the twists and turns, splits and schisms which have taken place within the faction with which he stayed after the 1969 split. But I was saddened by his death.

There is always a great solidarity between republican prisoners in Ireland and others imprisoned abroad, especially in Britain. Of particular concern for us in Long Kesh was the hunger strike of Frank Stagg. In June 1974 Michael Gaughan, a republican prisoner from Ballina, County Mayo, had died on hunger strike while being force-fed in a jail in Britain. We didn't want the same thing to happen to Frank Stagg. We started a letter-writing and lobbying campaign, and as his condition worsened, prisoners in our cage established a fund to finance putting advertisements in the *Irish News*, in most cases cancelling parcels and handicraft supplies to raise the cash. When Frank died in February 1976, a great anger filled Long Kesh.

In general, though, this was a relatively stable period for me, and I built up a fairly good, structured programme of reading and educational work in the cage. For myself, I concentrated on reading, on my writing, and learning Irish. I also wanted to develop collective political discussion and education, and as a project we took *Éire Nua*, the Sinn Féin programme. First we educated ourselves as to its content, then we critically reviewed the programme and identified what we thought was wrong with it. We came up with the notion of having extra tiers of community councils to add to the governmental structures, and we also discussed the role of the activist in all of this. We considered questions such as communication with the base of our support, the role of newspapers, bulletins, co-ops, tenants' associations and women's organisations, as means of empowering people. One of these projects later resulted in Tom Hartley, a Sinn Féin activist in Belfast, being charged with treason when we sent submissions out of the cage to Sinn Féin about people's councils. In 1976, when the Brits were trawling around for charges they could use against republicans, they discovered one submission which had gone to Tom and they decided that arguing for people's councils was a treasonable offence.

Cage 11 was made up of all sorts of people, some of them quite innocent and uninvolved, others who were innocent but had been politically active. Some simply wanted to get their time done, mostly by doing handicrafts; but many of these came along occasionally for a debate on a topic they were interested in. Then there was a core of people who were political animals, who were keen to kick issues around. They became the catalyst for an intensive process of debate, dialogue and education, and we succeeded in getting a large turn-out for a number of projects, in which we explored new ways of examining issues. These assumed a special importance for those who were going back out again soon and who were interested in the struggle and in examining its needs and demands and conduct, particularly in terms of what role they would have for themselves outside. As he came towards release in April 1976, Bobby Sands focused in more and more on me. We talked more about the struggle and things outside while

246

walking around the cage together with some of his close friends or in one-to-one conversations in the study hut, a portacabin separate from the huts and relatively private. Bobby was obviously one of the people who were committed to going back to the struggle, but even in his case I was very careful about how I answered some of the questions he put to me about the situation outside. What Bobby, or anyone else, did on their release was a matter for them. What role they played, if they went back to the struggle, was equally their own business and the prerogative of those in the leadership outside.

In mid-1975 Danny Morrison, editor of the Belfast-based weekly Sinn Féin newspaper, *Republican News*, had asked me to contribute some pieces. When I started to write, I began to develop a focused view of things outside, and to write quite critically. At the same time I was very conscious of the fact that I was imprisoned and not aware of all that was happening outside. I was also very wedded to the principle that a leadership needed support, especially that of prisoners and others in position of influence. That was why I was so careful in my conversations with fellow prisoners, including Bobby Sands and others like him, whom I considered to be very sound. With old friends like the Dark, I was more open, but it was only when I started to write that I began to be more openly critical. Even then I was always very guarded in my criticism; indeed, sometimes my criticisms were so subtle that they weren't even picked up on.

In my first 'Brownie' article, which appeared on 16 August 1975, I adopted a lighthearted tone, but also addressed the very serious question of sectarian killings.

'Taigues and orangies, Prods and micks. But it goes deeper than name-calling, as you know better than I do, and only the British reap the benefits. "Let you and him fight," sez one wily Sassenach. "While yez are at it I'll be left alone to impose solutions, to build new profits on the backs of old scores. Let you and him fight and me and the privileged few will see things through." '

In general I tended not to address immediately current events.

This was partly because of the practical constraints involved in getting articles written and then getting them out of the camp, but principally because what I wanted to address were more underlying questions regarding the nature and relevance of our political beliefs and practice.

Early on in the series of articles, I wrote about the importance of the Irish language in building freedom, and I embarked on discussions of what I called 'Active Abstentionism' and 'Active Republicanism'. I suggested that we as republicans should be engaged in building the elements of alternative administration – alternative, that is, to the sectarian, colonial British administration. I harked back to my experience in the late '6os.

'I remember those young people breaking up corporation meetings, I remember them squatting families, I recall them painting road signs, mending safety rails, repairing old people's homes ... I remember them (much to the chagrin of the leadership) doing more aggressive things and defending as well as they could with the few weapons begrudged to them, areas that were under siege from loyalist and state institutionalised sectarian violence.' (*Republican News*, 11 October 1975)

In writing of 'The National Alternative', I argued the need to build structures, including street committees, establishing people's taxis in place of the bus service, people's militias in place of the RUC (*Republican News*, 3 April 1976). In arguing for 'Active Republicanism' I wrote that: 'We fight for the people who find it hard to make ends meet, whether they be small farmers being pushed off the land by big ranchers or factory workers being sold out by their trade union leaderships. They are our fight and our fight must be based among them.'

Reflecting the reading and educational discussions that were taking place in Cage 11, I wrote about and quoted extensively from the political writings of Lalor, Mellowes and other republican authors, and I argued the need for a thirty-two-county struggle. On one occasion, after the death of Danny 'the Dosser' Lennon, a friend who had recently been released from Cage 11, and the Maguire children, in an incident which led to the formation of the 'Peace People', a newspaper article seemed too short to express what I wanted to write about. I penned a longer piece which was published as a sixteen-page pamphlet entitled *Peace in Ireland*. Again I referred to my home base.

'Ballymurphy has always wanted peace. Violence existed there long before the IRA became active and, indeed, the IRA is a symptom of that violence, not the cause of it.'

I did not confine myself in my 'Brownie' articles to discussing political issues. I also used them to try to paint what I hoped was an entertaining portrait of life in Long Kesh, and it was this element of my writings that I later developed into a book, *Cage Eleven*.

During my time in Cage 11, there were a number of escape bids, but to no avail. Security had been tightened considerably since the fire. There were also a number of encounters with the screws and some potentially dangerous confrontations which fortunately we defused before the situations got out of hand. To a large extent this aggravation was caused by stories of ill-treatment of prisoners up in the newly built H Blocks. In 1976 the British government removed political, or 'special category', status for prisoners sentenced from March of that year. So while we continued in the cages to enjoy this status, other republicans were denied it. As this policy of criminalisation was enforced and the numbers of protesting prisoners increased, conditions between us and the prison regime took a nose-dive.

As part of its counter-insurgency campaign, the British government had for some time been trying to implement a policy of criminalising the republican struggle. It appeared to me inside Long Kesh that the protracted truce which the IRA started in December 1974, and the confusion which arose as this continued in tandem with these British strategies, was to the benefit of the British and not to the advantage of the anti-imperialist struggle.

Not that I was against the truce – that was a matter for those in the leadership of the IRA – but everyone needed to be clear about where the struggle was going. For me it was becoming clearer that the main problem was that the struggle had been limited to armed struggle. Once this stopped, the struggle stopped.

I asked for and received a visit with leadership people. Maire Drumm and her husband Jimmy visited me, and I told them of my concerns. Later I wrote a lengthy paper and had it smuggled outside to the leadership.

For all these reasons, 1976 was a difficult year. Some of the prisoners looked to me for guidance on events outside. I gave them the leadership line, while privately and with the utmost discretion, I conveyed our concerns to the leadership.

One night in late October 1976, as I was finishing one of my articles, there was a newsflash on the television. I was lying on my bed in my cubicle writing and I couldn't see the TV, but I heard the sounds of hushing from other prisoners as the programme was interrupted and seconds later came the announcement that Maire Drumm had been shot dead in the Mater hospital. I was deeply shocked. Maire, a grandmother, had been receiving treatment for an eye complaint. She was a particular and undeserving target for British propaganda. A victim of loyalist assassins, she had not a sectarian bone in her body. News of Maire's death and its circumstances, and the ghoulish way in which sections of the media dealt with it, were deeply resented by republicans.

In *Republican News* on 19 February 1977, I cast my mind back over what I had tried to do in my 'Brownie' pieces:

'We tried to suggest attitudes to such things as sectarianism, active republicanism, the plight of prisoners in England, and the strategy employed by both the British and Free State governments. We also suggested attitudes towards the recent truce and the "Peace" campaign.'

By now I was thinking of my own release, and I found that I was good and ready to draw a line under my experience in Long Kesh concentration camp. In *Republican News* I bade farewell to my home of recent years:

'So jail is a place where you're watched over, inspected, spied on, directed, legislated, locked up, caged in, regimented, preached at, controlled, assessed, registered, handcuffed, prevented, stripped naked, extorted, pressured, robbed, beaten up, shot, censored, commanded, photographed, all by creatures that have neither the right nor wisdom nor virtue to do so.

'And the killer about it all is that outside is no better. It's all the same difference. Just a wee bit more subtle and a wee bit less blatant.'

My release came in the spring of 1977. I gave the Dark a hug, embraced my other friends, and with my meagre belongings wrapped in a brown paper bag, I stepped out of Long Kesh and into the arms of Colette and our four and a half-year-old son.

Ten

When I came out of the gate of Long Kesh into the car park, Colette was there before me, holding on to a very excited young boy, our Gearóid. I was very moved that we were united now for the first time outside a prison visiting box. More than anything I wanted to be able to spend some time with my family, though I knew also that I had no doubts about going back to the struggle.

We drove into West Belfast to a get-together at my parents' house in the Whiterock Road with all my brothers and sisters. I had brought with me presents of crosses and harps that the lads had given me. From there we called to see Colette's parents. My intention was to go on to the house in Ughtyneill in County Meath where Colette and I had spent a short break years before. The owner and our contact there had been in touch with Colette before my release, and she and I were looking forward to returning to that idyllic spot. Politics, however, were once more to intervene. Another old friend was also at my mother's. He wanted me to go to Dublin so that I could meet with Seamus Twomey, who was on the run, to discuss the political situation.

So instead of going to County Meath that evening, we set off for Dublin, where we were brought to stay with two women, a mother and daughter, who were to become good friends of our family. The following morning I left Colette and Gearóid and walked across Dublin to see Seamus. He and I spent most of the day together, and it was nightfall before I returned. The next day I took Gearóid shopping to get him clothes for the country. He and I left Colette with our new friends and we went off together downtown on a grand tour of Clery's, Arnott's and other Dublin stores. Quite unused to this business, the Wellington boots, jacket and other clothes I bought for Gearóid were a model of colour mismatching.

We had a splendid time in Meath, walking around in the countryside. For our arrival the place had been wonderfully well stocked up with food, and the three of us were left on our own to enjoy each other's company. It was a house sitting on its own at a crossroads with a river at the end of the back garden and a small shop opposite. Every day of our two weeks there I spent time out walking in the fields with Gearóid, and he had no problem at all adjusting to my being out; there wasn't even a transition period, and I appreciated that this was due to a very large degree to Colette. When we returned to Belfast, it was as if the family unit had never been sundered.

However, I had no intention of going home on a regular basis. Colette had by this time rationalised the situation over the house in Harrogate Street. She probably hoped that when I got out I would be going home and, whatever my political involvement, that there would be some semblance of normality in our life together. I knew that to be an activist meant to live an underground existence, and I immediately went on the run again. This obviously caused great difficulty for the three of us, but Colette was strongly committed and she accepted it. I was with her and Gearóid on a daily basis, but I rarely slept at home and I tried to vary my times of visiting and take precautionary measures.

In the run-up to the truce of 1974–75, republican activity had been narrowed to solely military operations. When these had ceased, then the struggle itself had effectively ceased. I and some of my associates set about reviewing the situation, and sought to initiate a process of regrouping the organisation. I had been elected to the Ard Chomhairle (National Committee) of Sinn Féin a couple of times before but had been unable to take up the position. On my release, however, I was able to.

The public mood at the time of my release in the spring of 1977 was strongly antagonistic towards republicans. In part this had to do with the advent of the 'Peace People'. Danny Lennon, an IRA volunteer, had been shot dead at the wheel of his car by British soldiers in a street where people were walking on the pavements. The soldiers had continued firing as the car, out of control, ploughed into the Maguire family, who were at the side of the road. Mrs Maguire was seriously injured and three of her children, the oldest of whom was eight years and the youngest only six weeks, were killed, whether by British army bullets or by the car was never made clear since the results of the autopsy were suppressed.

The tragedy of the deaths of the children and of Danny Lennon had been compounded by the cynical manipulation of the incident, as newspaper headlines shouted their message that an IRA car had killed three children. The 'Peace People', set up in the aftermath of the Maguire children's deaths, had immediately received enormous international publicity, and for some months their marches were supported by large numbers of people. In nationalist areas sympathy for the Maguires and, indeed, for the Lennons lay behind this support, but it evaporated very quickly. Only four days after the deaths of the Maguire children, a twelve-year-old girl was shot and killed by British soldiers in South Armagh; the 'Peace People' offered no criticism. Two months later a fourteen-year-old boy was shot dead by British soldiers in West Belfast; again, the 'Peace People' were silent. As soon as they tried to examine what peace was and how it could be attained, the leadership of the 'Peace People' began to collapse, and in the end it brought into question the credibility of both its own leaders and others who had associated themselves with it.

Nevertheless the 'Peace People' possessed a certain significance on account of the extent to which they coincided with a new approach being pursued with a large measure of success by the

254

British government. British strategy between the fall of Stormont and the end of 1975 had consisted principally of a war of political suppression, with the British army playing the leading role. But by 1975 a strategy had begun to be implemented which sought, in broad terms, to deny the political nature of the struggle while also refining the forms of suppression. New emphasis was placed on the RUC, which had always been more of an army than a police force; its intelligence capabilities were built up, with special emphasis on the use of informers, surveillance and detention for questioning. In advancing this strategy of 'Ulsterisation', 'normal-isation' and 'criminalisation', the British government used the lengthy bilateral truce of 1974–75, and were unwittingly assisted by republicans, whose self-destructive feuding spread dismay and contempt amongst many of their supporters.

In October 1975 the IRA had started a feud with the 'Officials' of such dimensions that they terrified the people of the very areas they were supposed to be defending. After they had accidentally killed a six-year-old girl, a hundred women courageously marched in Short Strand, calling for an end to the feud. Yet it continued, until the chairman of the Falls Taximen's Association (FTA) was killed in November by the 'Officials' and taxi drivers successfully demanded that the feuding be stopped. It was an episode which inflicted substantial damage on the republican struggle.

I was very critical of what had happened. It wasn't that feuds were previously unknown. They arose from the very existence of rival armed republican groups. In republican West Belfast, both armed groups were asserting themselves to be the IRA and were putting out propaganda about each other. Indeed, the aggrava-tions arising from the split caused particular difficulties in our family with my sister Margaret and her fiancé Mickey McCorry. In Belfast the antagonisms which had surrounded the 1969 split did not dissipate; rather, they solidified. During any eruption of bad feeling anyone attached to either side of the dispute was at risk, as were many who had no connection with the particular cause of the trouble, and on at least one occasion my father was badly beaten in the course of a feud. The experience of the feuding in 1971 and in 1975 had taught me that, however one viewed the issues in a feud, the republican cause could only be the loser. There was no way that one group could wipe out another which was ideologically committed, and to attempt to do so was wrong, tactically, morally or from any perspective.

Now, shortly after my release in 1977, another feud blew up. The loyalists planted a bomb in Beechmount Avenue (it may have been British intelligence, but the loyalists claimed it); it hit the Officials' Easter parade, and everyone there blamed it on the IRA. Colette and I and Gearóid were now spending a lot of our time in a house belonging to our friend Kathleen. Her husband Eamonn, who had made me so nervous with his rubbish bin escapades years before, had been tragically killed in a car crash in July 1973. She had recently remarried, to another friend of ours, and we had remained close friends. Colette and I were with them after the Easter parade when we got word of the explosion and subsequent scuffles when people at the two separate republican parades clashed with each other. To me this was craziness, and Kathleen and I moved immediately to see if we could get someone to calm things down. It was easy to establish that there was no republican involvement in the bomb attack, but by now there was a report of shootings. I tried to get a priest to go to the 'Officials'; two of them refused me, but after a while I found one, Father Alex Reid, who had played a part in other mediation efforts, and who was willing to get involved. He arranged a meeting at which I explained to a member of the Officials that I had no authority in the situation; I was acting as an individual. He agreed that he would try and get the fighting stopped from his side. However, even as we moved about, talking to our respective comrades, a number of people were shot. Nevertheless, I succeeded in getting a commitment from IRA personnel, though they were clearly wounded and angered by events.

I went to a very tense second meeting between leaders from both sides. I had now secured the involvement of a second priest, and so both Father Alex Reid and Father Des Wilson were present as guarantors and facilitators of any peace agreement we might conclude. As the meeting began we received news that a man from New Barnsley who was a supporter of the Officials had been shot dead. The atmosphere was difficult, to say the least. Then, as the meeting drew to a close, we received word that my very good friend, Tommy Toland, who had been with Colette and me only a few days before, had been shot dead in Ballymurphy. In all, four people had been killed and eighteen had been injured.

Father Alex spoke in the atmosphere taut with tension: 'I think we should say a few prayers to the Holy Ghost.'

'I think,' someone else said, 'that we need much more than the Holy Ghost to sort this out.'

But as a result of the determined efforts of several people, not only did we sort out the feud, but the two priests also established an arbitration and mediation procedure which we hoped would stand us in good stead in the future. Thankfully, despite everything, the problems of feuding passed, a regrettable product of their time and a symptom of political immaturity.

Republican feuding contributed significantly to feelings of alienation on the part of the nationalist people, who had long provided the essential support for the IRA. It also coincided and dovetailed with a sustained British propaganda campaign to portray IRA members as 'common criminals'.

Father Alex Reid and Father Des Wilson not only helped to resolve feuds, they also played leading roles in various efforts to end the conflict. They were two of only a very small number of clergy who engaged in such work, and in many ways the inability or unwillingness of any of the churches to develop a coherent strategy for justice and peace has been one of the great failures of our time. Father Des, a radical community priest, and Father Reid, a Redemptorist priest based at Clonard, were both dissatisfied with the absence of any real strategy by the church establishments or the wider political establishment. Their main objective in 1976 and 1977 was to establish dialogue between republicans and other parties to the conflict, against the background of the failure of the Sunningdale Agreement and the breakdown of the IRA truce. They devoted considerable time and effort to lobbying the various groups, and found that Sinn Féin's attitude, in contrast to the position of our opponents, was to favour inclusive dialogue. In fact, this has been the republican position for as long as I can remember.

They had also become acquainted with two prominent loyalists whom they met through the good offices of a prominent Catholic Belfast businessman. These loyalists, one of whom was John McKeague, editor of *Loyalist News* and a founder and past chairman of the Shankill Defence Association, were flirting with the notion of independence for the six counties. McKeague had been associated with Ian Paisley in the late '60s and later with the loyalist paramilitary group, the Red Hand Commando, and he had been jailed for armed robbery; to many people he was known for his publication of a *Loyalist Song Book*, which included many songs expressing rabid sectarian hatred. After a time the two priests persuaded their unlikely converts to agree to enter into dialogue, at least on an indirect basis, under church auspices. To broaden the church dimension of the initiative, a Church of Ireland minister from East Belfast agreed to be part of the group. Ruairí Ó Bradaigh and Dáithí Ó Conaill had already given their support to these endeavours, as had Billy McKee and Proinsias MacAirt.

So in the spring of 1977, despite personal and political risks, John McKeague and his colleague travelled to Dundalk. There they and members of the republican leadership agreed, during a lengthy and friendly lunch, that they would seek the help of Sean MacBride and Desmond Boal. Sean MacBride was a prominent Dublin barrister and winner of the Nobel Peace Prize who had been a leading republican in the 1920s and '30s, and who had at various times served as Minister for External Affairs in the Dublin government (1948–51), as General Secretary of the International Commission of Jurists (1963–70) and as United Nations Commissioner for Namibia. Desmond Boal was also a barrister, and he had been a Stormont MP for Belfast, Shankill (1960–72); the first chairman of the Democratic Unionist Party, he had been a close associate of Ian Paisley, but had broken with him in 1974.

It was agreed at Ruairí Ó Bradaigh's suggestion that these two would be asked to develop dialogue in a public way. They met at Easter, around the same time as the feuding broke out in Belfast, and Sean MacBride agreed to work on a joint statement which he and Des Boal hoped to submit for consideration by both republicans and loyalists. However, the loyalists refused to consider this unless the IRA ceased all operations for a month. By now loyalist responsibility for the bomb at the Easter parade at Beechmount had emerged, and against this background the initiative foundered. In an effort to improve the situation, I went a number of times to meet with Sean MacBride at his home, Roebuck House. Here in the great drawing room, resplendent with memorabilia of Maud Gonne and Major John MacBride and other heroes of the Irish revolutionary tradition in which the MacBride family was steeped, we endeavoured to make progress.

Sean MacBride and Desmond Boal met a few times during this period, once in Paris, once in County Down, and once in Dublin on the night of Fianna Fáil's landslide election victory in June 1977, but mostly they met in Roebuck House. It was there that Sean and I met with Desmond Boal for a very frank and constructive exchange of views. Despite our best efforts, however, we made little progress. Some time later John McKeague and I met in South Belfast. Father Wilson, who was to host our discussion, drove me to the meeting place in his clapped-out old minicar, which chugged its way slowly through the staunchly loyalist Sandy Row; blissfully unaware of my nervousness, he chatted cheerfully throughout our thankfully uneventful voyage through these, for me, uncharted waters.

My meeting with John McKeague was a friendly and informal one. By now many loyalists were dissatisfied with the British and unionist establishments. They felt as if they were being used by Ian Paisley and others. Their exploration of the notion of independence for the six counties was in many ways an indication of the conditional nature of their loyalty to the English crown.

John McKeague and I met a few more times, and even though these discussions failed to come to formal conclusions I consider them to have been very useful. Over the years I and other Sinn Féin representatives have had many discussions with many people, some of them from very unlikely quarters. While these failed in most cases to come to formal conclusions, the exchanges helped to break down barriers. Dialogue is always helpful, and honest discussion never killed anyone.

In the meantime the British were busy with their own strategy. In March 1976 they had abolished political status for prisoners charged with offences related to the war, which had been won by Billy McKee's hunger strike on the eve of the 1972 truce. Now they mounted an energetic campaign of psychological warfare, or 'psy-ops'. Press releases, speeches and statements from the administration referred consistently to republican leaders as 'godfathers'. While stories of corruption and gangsterism within republicanism were invented and judiciously placed in the media, a strategy based on promoting the 'primacy of the RUC' was implemented.

I was arrested in Andersonstown by the RUC and held for a short period in Castlereagh. By now I had some experience of interrogations. The RUC took away all my clothes and gave me ridiculously oversized dungarees and white plimsolls in exchange. I refused to wear them. I demanded my own clothes or different clothing. They refused. I demanded to see my solicitor. Again they said no. When they took me from my cell to the interrogation room I went naked. They returned me quickly to my cell. When my own doctor arrived to see me as requested by Colette, I wrapped a blanket around myself. Within hours of his visit my clothes were returned to me. A few minutes later I was released.

Relying now on the courts rather than internment to dispose of republicans, the British government opened interrogation centres at Castlereagh and Gough barracks in 1977. Through the systematic application of torture techniques, these supplied the statements required to secure convictions in the courts. Despite the availability of well-documented evidence of torture and ill-treatment, people continued to be brutalised in large numbers and locked away. Faced with evidence of the wholesale ill-treatment of suspects, the RUC chief, Kenneth Newman, claimed in June 1977 that republican prisoners were deliberately injuring themselves in order to discredit the police. In June 1978 an Amnesty International report expressed disquiet: 'Maltreatment of suspected terrorists by the RUC has taken place with sufficient frequency to warrant establishment of a public inquiry to investigate it.' Britain's Independent Broadcasting Authority banned a programme on the Amnesty report. However, in March 1979, ITN did broadcast an interview with Dr Robert Irwin, who had been attending Castlereagh for three years and in that time had treated many detainees for punctured ear-drums and broken bones. He knew of at least 150 people who had been injured by the RUC while in custody. A week later the government's Bennett Report was published and largely supported Amnesty's findings, but wrote about the situation in exceptionally restrained language. Other doctors now came out to confirm that they, too, had treated many detainees who had been beaten up in interrogation. British counter-insurgency was on an offensive; the leash was off the RUC.

Such was the success of the British administration's methods that 86% of all defendants appearing before Diplock courts between January and April 1979 had made confessions; 56% of prosecutions in relation to these relied solely on confessions, while another 30% relied primarily on confessions.

British strategy sought further to isolate the republican resistance through the development of 'counter-insurgency architecture', whereby the RUC and British army were closely involved in local authority planning, and especially in planning the redevelopment of nationalist areas, aiming to confine nationalists within ghettos with a limited number of access and exit points. Powers of arrest and detention were used extensively as a means of intimidation and for intelligence gathering and screening. In one period of ten months, 3,868 people were arrested under the Emergency Provisions Act and the Prevention of Terrorism Act and detained for more than four hours; of these, only 11% were charged. Special new RUC units received training from the British army's SAS in techniques that equipped them to carry out a 'shoot-to-kill' policy against republicans.

From the low point induced by the truce, its consequences and feuds, we desperately needed to rebuild a sense of political direction which would govern all our activities and which would offer us a strategic overview. Meanwhile, I was given specific responsibility within Sinn Féin for publications, such as *An Phoblacht* and *Republican News*, and before too long we launched *Saoirse*, a theoretical journal, and *Iris*, an international information magazine.

It seemed anomalous that we had two newspapers, each with a different focus and a different style, based north and south of the border. A Belfast republican and contemporary of mine, Danny Morrison, had with a few others taken *Republican News* from being a fairly conservative bulletin to constituting quite a vibrant weekly newspaper. As part of a broad review within Sinn Féin, Danny produced a discussion paper about the newspaper and its role, which was circulated throughout the organisation and it was decided, amongst other things, to merge the two newspapers. At the same time we were trying to generate a cohesiveness in our politics and our organisation and were arguing strongly for an all-Ireland approach to the struggle.

A number of Dublin republicans who had come out of jail had begun to play a significant role in community work in their areas and were especially active with concerned residents against drugs in Dublin. There had always been individual republicans – John Joe McGirl was an outstanding example – who had built bases in their own areas and who were involved in social, economic and political work locally, but now a number were also working quite consistently in the capital, one of whom stood in an election and received a reasonable vote.

At the level of the Ard Chomhairle people such as Ruairí Ó Bradaigh, Dáithí Ó Conaill and myself were working to develop our politics. Ruairí and Dáithí were very close; both had been active together during the 1950s, when Ruairí had been elected as an abstentionist TD, and in 1958 they had escaped together from the Curragh camp. Ruairí occupied a particularly difficult role as president of Sinn Féin because the republican struggle was at the time entirely dominated by the IRA. Abstentionism and the lack of an electoral strategy (except in terms of local government elections in the Twenty-six Counties) had their effect, but more tellingly Sinn Féin was in many ways a victim of the aversion to politics which marked republicanism at this time. Politics and politicians were widely blamed for the calamity of 1969.

While Ruairí was himself quite liberal in his political outlook on social and economic matters, the main propaganda focus was on the political effects of British rule, and the main focus of work was, understandably enough, on the north. In this context Sinn Féin was eclipsed by the IRA, and there was little appetite for political work of the more conventional kind. Sinn Féin's political programme based itself upon the defence of the nationalist people in the north. While there were some innovative ideas on social, economic and cultural issues and good proposals on alternative all-Ireland governmental structures, these were propagated only in a limited way through publicity outlets. Of course, republican ideology also opposed any participation in the partitionist parliament in Dublin. Apart from the theoretical basis of the position, in practice it meant that Sinn Féin was abandoning this ground to the other parties. As to my own views, I would not at that time have even thought of trying to find the answers to all the questions which arose from this situation; and anyway events in the north were dominating politics on the whole island. However, the failure to consolidate politically the support flowing towards Sinn Féin, or even to establish a more durable way of quantifying support than the holding of demonstrations, left crucial room for the political establishment in the south to manoeuvre. Frightened by the pace of events, they increasingly sought refuge in censorship, revisionism and coercion.

Within Sinn Féin a younger, northern element, of which I was

263

one, began to play a greater role in seeking development and change in political strategy. We raised criticisms and advanced ideas which we thought and hoped would be taken on board by the leadership. We brought into question their handling of the truce and we were disturbed when we couldn't find minutes for the meetings with the British or other records. There was little tension as we thrashed out issues, either about the issues themselves or about personalities. Politically, however, we encountered resistance to the direction we were pursuing, particularly when we argued for the development of an electoral strategy. Ruairí Ó Bradaigh was quite logically concerned that if we became involved in electoralism we would have to get rid of abstentionism, an important constitutional issue within the party. I didn't understand that then, but he did, and so he resisted the electoral approach. At the same time, the leadership, while resisting some of our criticisms and proposals, were relieved to see some of us younger activists out of jail and taking a serious interest in questions of political direction for the movement.

We wanted to put down a marker regarding republican strategy, and an opportunity came with the Bodenstown speech of 1977, on which Danny Morrison and I collaborated. The involvement of Jimmy Drumm in delivering the speech was important, too, because he had a long track record in the movement. It was a speech which tried to review the situation, to clarify republican attitudes to some issues, and which sought to indicate new directions for republican strategy.

'The isolation of socialist republicans around the armed struggle is dangerous and has produced a reformist notion that "Ulster" is the issue, without the mobilisation of the working class in the Twenty-six Counties . . . The British government is *not* withdrawing from the Six Counties and the substantial pull-out of business and the closing of factories in 1975 and 1976 was due to world recession, though mistakenly attributed at the time [as] symptoms of withdrawal . . . Indeed the British government is committed to stabilising the Six Counties and is pouring in vast sums of money . . . to assure loyalists and secure from loyalists

264

support for a long haul against the IRA ... We find that a successful war of liberation cannot be fought exclusively on the backs of the oppressed in the Six Counties, nor around the physical presence of the British army. Hatred and resentment of the army cannot sustain the war.'

We were not attempting to mount a challenge to the leadership; on the contrary, we were trying to regroup and move forward on the basis of reaching a consensus, not by getting rid of people or creating a new leadership. We had not yet developed an integrated or strategic overview, but our entire struggle was at a crucial juncture, a defining moment, and we were convinced that the struggle needed to sort itself out and to go on. We wanted to go back to our radical republican roots, as we saw it, and we wanted to popularise the base of the struggle. For its part there was a need also for the IRA to fight in a more cohesive way and in a manner which encouraged the development and building of popular struggle on a thirty-two-county basis.

As we entered 1978 I felt that our work on regrouping was going well and I was pleased that it seemed to be passing largely unnoticed by the British. But then disaster occurred. On 17 February, twelve people were killed and twenty-three were injured when IRA fire-bombs exploded, creating a fire-storm at the La Mon Hotel near Comber, about ten miles from Belfast. In an intensive series of fire-bombings of commercial targets in twenty different towns two months earlier, the IRA had given adequate warnings, but in this case only a nine-minute warning was given which, as the IRA statement later put it, 'proved totally inadequate given the disastrous consequences. We accept condemnation and criticism from only two sources: from the relatives and friends of those who were accidentally killed, and from our supporters who have rightly and severely criticised us.'

Deeply shocked by the news, I lingered with Colette and Gearóid in the house at Harrogate Street instead of going to another house as I had intended. I hadn't slept at home in the nights before, and I was just leaving home that fateful night when I heard the news reports. I had no knowledge of its being the responsibility of the IRA, but my gut instinct told me that it was. Shocked by the death toll I despondently sat up to get the late news reports. I was depressed by the carnage and deeply affected by the deaths and injuries. I could also feel two years of work going down the drain. By the time the last news came in, it was too late to leave.

The British army and the RUC hit the house the next morning and I was taken to Castlereagh; later I learned that about twenty other republicans had also been arrested. They may have had no intention of charging me when first they arrested me, but one of the peelers said to me several days into my interrogation: 'We're going to have to charge you because there's been such a kick-up about you being arrested.'

The interrogations were run of the mill, but continued for seven days. Although I was obviously not pleased to be in Castlereagh, I had enough experience by this time to realise that, unlike my first session in Palace barracks, I didn't need a crutch to sustain me through questioning. I just sat there and said nothing. It was now a matter of political commitment, of believing in my cause and rejecting theirs.

One of my questioners described himself as a born-again Christian. He spoke to me at great length about the need to embrace God. Another one was much less Christian. He ranted and raved a lot, and one day while firing questions at me he suddenly produced a sheaf of photographs and thrust them into my face. I could see photographs of burnt bodies, horrific incinerated remains.

'This is what your friends did, you bastard!' he screamed.

This was the only time La Mon was mentioned during my interrogation. During the course of another day, they tried to trick me into signing a statement by insisting that Colette had been charged with something or other. I was subjected to no brutality during this interrogation, which was quite different from previous occasions, when I had been beaten or attempts had been made to frighten or intimidate me or to coerce or bribe me. Now by virtue of the seven-day detention period, they had refined

266

interrogation to a psychological operation during which an actual relationship was built between the interrogator and the interroga-tee. After long periods, perhaps even days of isolation with no interrogations, it was good to hear a human voice, and so one would actually be glad to see the questioner if only to pass the time. And all along, the temptation, the instinct was to talk. About anything: about football, books, films. The secret, of course, was to stay silent. Whatever you say, say nothing.

On my fifth or sixth day, the pattern of interrogations changed. Two new detectives came in armed with a sheaf of typed pages. The senior one explained that he was going to ask me a series of questions and that he was going to note my answers and invite me to initial the notes when he had finished. He then read a list of prepared questions from the pages before him. I knew then that I was going to be charged, but I had no notion what the charge would be about. This became no clearer as he intoned his questions. They were all about Sinn Féin activities, and to each of them I replied: 'I am answering no questions until I can consult my solicitor,' or words to that effect. When he was finished, I was taken back to my cell.

On 25 February I was charged that from my release in March 1977 I had been a member of the IRA. They hadn't a shred of evidence against me, but they used the time they held me on remand to try to gather any evidence they could. The night I was charged in Townhall Street, I had a brief, emotional visit with Colette. She brought me sandwiches, and as I ate them later in a dirty little cell beside a noisy boiler which rumbled all night in the basement, I felt sorry for all the trouble I had brought her. The next morning I was charged in court and ferried from there to Belfast prison.

When the policy of 'special category' or political status had ended in March 1976, Kieran Nugent, the first person to be sentenced for a 'scheduled offence', had been first to go 'on the blanket', to refuse, on 14 September 1976, to wear prison clothing. 'If they want me to wear a convict's uniform,' he had said, 'they'll have to nail it to my back.'

The republican attitude was well captured in Francie Brolly's song:

> I'll wear no convict's uniform
> Nor meekly serve my time
> That England might
> Brand Ireland's fight
> 800 years of crime.

As I entered Crumlin Road prison I was nervous that I was going to be stuck in with loyalists, but the screw just said, 'So you're going in with the Provos', and that was it. Despite the official ending of political status, and despite the picture that was being presented outside, the republican command structure existed in the prison, with its own elected leadership which dealt with the prison regime.

I was feeling quite chastened by the fact that I was back in jail, that I had been careless enough to get caught in the house, and I was fully aware that the La Mon bombing constituted a major tragedy. It didn't make me feel any happier to find that I was stuck in with two young fellow prisoners who insisted on playing pop music on the radio until all hours. Frequently they also joined the scores of other prisoners who stood at the windows swapping the most obscene verbal abuse with the loyalists.

Belfast prison was a madhouse. This was my first time in a remand prison, and I found that everyone on remand lived in a state of great uncertainty. You had yet to be sentenced, and despite everything there was a chance that you might be released. Failing that, you might get a relatively light sentence. On the other hand, there was also a greater chance that you would not be released, and that the sentence might be very long indeed. So it was that many remand prisoners became great experts in legal matters, or what passes for these in the north of Ireland.

The Crum was an old prison, overcrowded and unable to cope in any positive way with its inmates. There were constant protest actions over conditions, and as part of a protracted campaign for segregation, loyalists and republicans had agreed to exercise separately on alternate days. As only one hour's exercise was permitted – and sometimes even this was withheld – it meant we were on almost total lock-up in our cells, apart from that brief exercise period and other short excursions into the wing for slopping out, washing and collecting our meals.

I read voraciously everything I could get my hands on, sometimes three books a day. There was nothing else to do. Often we were refused toilet facilities, and this was always the case when the screws withdrew down the wing into the circle for the night. Those who had not managed to clear their bowels could use the chamber pot and leave their cellmates with a nightmare. Most chose to shit into a plastic bag, which was then flung from the cell window into the yard below. Some mornings the place was littered with these 'mystery parcels'.

In spite of occasional clashes with the loyalists, the period I spent there was generally uneventful, though many of the screws were quite aggressive, some of them markedly hostile. At Easter we smuggled in a tricolour for our Easter parade and afterwards we split the flag into its three sections and hid it. Coming off the yard that day, we got an especially vigorous and aggressive search, and when I protested to one screw who was manhandling me, I was taken to the deputy governor. Here for the first time I saw the prison service in all its pettiness. I was flanked by screws who responded to commands shouted in sergeant-major fashion by a senior officer, and our little trio, with me in the middle and the senior officer taking up the rear, was supposed to pirouette into the governor's office, wheel around and come to attention in front of his desk. I was to give my number, stand to attention, speak only when spoken to, and then I and my minders were to march out again. However, I ignored the screws' orders and, amid all their bellowing and marching and snapping to attention, I was sentenced to loss of remission for making 'false allegations' to an officer.

The only thing I liked about the Crum was that the grub was far superior to that at the Kesh, especially the custard and the porridge, and I refused to believe stories that the more extreme screws spat into these.

Visiting conditions were primitive. Though visits were more frequent than in the Kesh, the jail could not cope with the numbers, and the conditions were archaic. Colette visited me faithfully. By now Gearóid was at school – my old school, St Finian's – and he wasn't up on every visit, but he was there at least once a week. Prisoners also received legal visits – sometimes not for months, then as trials came close perhaps every day.

We were taken to Belfast court via a tunnel which ran below the Crumlin Road from the jail into the courthouse. It was along this that Jim Bryson had made one of his escapes, and when I made my first journey along it, I thought of him. I also thought of escape myself, but not in the same concentrated way as I had during my other periods inside. For one thing, after only a very short stay in the Crum, I was moved up to the H-Blocks, the new prison which had been built next to Long Kesh.

Paddy John McGrory was fairly confident that the charge against me would not hold up, but he was too experienced a lawyer to assume anything. We both knew that the case against me was only now being cobbled together, after I had been charged. P.J. told me that the attorney general in London was in direct charge of the case. While trying to establish the nature of the evidence that was being sought, P.J. also tried to ensure that my time on remand would not be a lengthy one. It was not unusual for some republicans to be held for as long as two years while awaiting trial, only to have the charges dropped at the last minute: internment by remand. So P.J. made a number of regular applications for bail for me. This had the effect of ensuring that the prosecution, which opposed bail, had at least to give some justification for holding me. In my first bail application, the prosecution opposed bail on the grounds that I was a member of the IRA. P.J. made his submission with his usual skill, and after it had been rejected I asked the judge to consider if it was not a contradiction to refuse me bail on the basis of an allegation which was actually the charge against me and in support of which the prosecution could not even provide enough evidence to go to trial. I had taken the rejection of my bail application in good humour, and the judge dealt with my intervention in the same spirit, asking the prosecution to process the case speedily. Shortly afterwards I was given a date for my preliminary hearing and moved to a remand wing in the H–Blocks to await that development.

This was a different form of imprisonment from that I had experienced before. Here prisoners were held in small numbers in special control units. The circle was provided by the crossbar of the H. Joined to this were the four control units, two on each of the uprights. I felt frankly apprehensive: not only was I concerned about the regime, a harsh one aimed at breaking the prisoners, but I was also aware that although I would not be on a wing where the 'blanket' protest was in full swing, there was a 'no wash' protest going on. I need not have worried, for I was put into a cell on my own, which I quite enjoyed after the overcrowding of the Crum.

I was struck by the spirit of the prisoners. In my other jail experiences, we had been cushioned by our numbers and by the prisoners' own command structure from dealing directly with the screws; it had been possible for prisoners in the cages to serve long terms with little or no contact with the administration. Here in our individual cells, in the Blocks, it was different. If you wanted to resist a search, you had to face the screws on your own. But the screws couldn't run the prison without the prisoners, and the prisoners were completely defiant. I listened in amused admiration as they shouted their defiance at particularly notorious prison officers. Most of those on my wing were younger than I was and were strongly assertive.

At night–time on most wings throughout the Blocks there would be a sing-song, a quiz, a storytelling session, or occasionally we would just swap banter. I would lie back on my bed listening to the better singers competing for our applause. We had good singers: we had Elvis impersonators, Mick Jagger sing–alikes, Bobby Vees and Johnny Cashes; and, of course, we had rebel songs.

One memorable night on the anniversary of internment there was a great session on our wing which went on until the early hours of the morning. At about four o'clock, near the time of the original internment swoops, the entire jail was aroused by the clamour from republican cells as the lads re-created the sound of the binlids by banging the pipes. The screws came rushing on to the wings in riot gear, adding to the noise by battering on their shields and on the cell doors, and screaming at us to desist. After a few minutes of frenzy and mutual abuse all fell silent for a moment. No one really knew what was going to happen next. I could hear the screws moving up and down outside my cell.

'The next fucker who makes a sound is for the boards,' an English voice commanded.

'Give us a song!' someone shouted.

'Fuck up, you Fenian bastard!'

'Give us the fucking "One Road"!'

Heavy footsteps could be heard rushing towards the source of the voice. Suddenly the lights went on.

'All prisoners stand by your beds!' came the command. The screws started a head-count. I was perched on the side of my bed, feeling the tension in the air as I listened to them and wondering whether all hell was about to break loose. The Judas hole in the cell door flickered open, then shut again.

After a while the screws left the wing, their footsteps, more slowly than before, moving on and the sound dying away into the distance.

I imagined I could hear a collective sigh of held breath being released as an eerie silence settled over the wing.

Suddenly a voice rose in song from one of the cells near me.

> 'We're on the one road, sharing the one load,
> We're on the road to God knows where . . .'

The first voice was joined by another from a cell further down the wing.

> 'We're on the one road, it may be the wrong road . . .'

Then another and another.

'But we're together now, who cares . . .'

And soon we were all singing.

> 'Northmen, southmen, comrades all,
> Dublin, Belfast, Cork and Donegal.
> We're on the one road swinging along,
> Singing a soldier's song.'

By now everyone was in full voice, but as the chorus ended the first singer took up a verse on his own.

> 'Night is darkest just before the dawn,
> From dissensions Ireland is reborn.
> Soon we'll all, united Irish men,
> Make our land a nation once again.'

And then we were all back in for the chorus again. By the time we had the song finished our appetites had been whetted and our concert continued until some time after the light of dawn had entered our cells.

I was treated as a special security prisoner, which meant that I was taken on my own when I had to go somewhere in the jail, normally for visits, and this was a bonus for me. Not only did Colette and I usually have an entire visiting block to ourselves – the one I had attempted to escape from – but it also meant that I got to see some of the blanket men when nobody else was seeing them. They were like characters from Solzhenitsyn's Gulag, shuffling along in big boots without laces, wearing, for their visits, ill-fitting jackets and trousers. Most of the trousers had their backsides slit open, and all of the blanket men had long, unwashed hair and unkempt beards. All of them were in great form, and some of them I knew. In particular there was a crowd from Cage 11, including Bobby Sands, who had been rearrested in November 1976, but there were also people like Pat McGeown, Gerry Kelly and Larry Marley, who had been caught trying to escape. Also there were Brendan Hughes, Cleeky Clarke, his brother Seamus, Gerard Burns and Teddy Crane. They had intervened when Joe Barnes was assaulted by screws coming back to the cage from a visit; for their trouble they received additional sentences and were moved to the Blocks.

This group formed part of a core of older, jail-wise prisoners. Whereas at first the bulk of the prisoners in the Blocks had been people with little jail experience, these older prisoners provided an element of stability. During my short sojourn in the Blocks, I had a regular weekly soirée with some comrades from the blanket Blocks and I was able to keep them supplied with cigarettes and polo mints, much sought-after commodities. I also sent detailed reports outside about their conditions.

The 'no-wash' protest had started when wash-up and cleaning facilities had been withdrawn throughout the Blocks, and later – after my time – it escalated when slop-out and toilet facilities were also withdrawn. For now it was only a matter of not washing yourself or cleaning out the cells, and as I was a new arrival my cell was clean enough anyway.

Some months later when I was moved back to the Crum for trial, the image of the blanket men stayed with me. Soon I might be joining them, but if I got off – and P.J. had yet to be supplied with any evidence – I was resolved to do something about their plight.

Back in Belfast prison Tom Hartley and other Sinn Féin comrades awaited me. Tom was in on his treason charge. As part of their crackdown on Sinn Féin, the Brits had raided our offices; they had also smashed up the *Republican News* office and raided the printers of the paper. The owner of the printing company, whose connection with the paper was solely commercial, was arrested and charged along with others, including a French journalist, probably the first foreign national to be charged with IRA membership. All of these had a special interest in my case and whatever precedent it might set.

The trial was a fiasco – from the attorney general's point of view. The 'evidence' against me quoted my 'Brownie' articles;

they used posters from the Sinn Féin centre; they used the fact that I had been in Cage 11, and they even used a speech I had given at the recent Sinn Féin Ard Fheis. Jeremy Paxman, a well-known BBC broadcaster and newsman, was brought along to court to give evidence that I had actually given this speech, in which I had used words like 'war zone' and 'billet'. The charges were dismissed. P.J.'s submission that I had no case to answer won the day and set an important legal precedent, and my da, Colette and I walked down the Crumlin Road pursued by a posse of journalists. That morning in the washroom in C wing, Tom Hartley and I had joined in giving a spontaneous rendering of 'The Creggan White Hare'. Now, unlike the hare, I was free again, and I wondered what lay ahead.

After seven months in jail on remand, I was pleased to be able to return to the struggle and delighted to be able to return to my family, though, as before, I saw less of them than I would have wished. Two things were uppermost in my mind: the plight of the prisoners and the need to develop the political capability of our struggle. In November 1978 I was elected one of the two vice-presidents of Sinn Féin.

In the previous year, Roy Mason, Britain's Northern Ireland secretary, had claimed that normalisation was going ahead full steam and that he was 'squeezing the IRA like toothpaste', yet in August of that year he had had to deploy 32,336 soldiers, RUC and Ulster Defence Regiment to enable Queen Elizabeth to visit two staunchly loyalist towns, while 800 nationalists were rounded up and imprisoned for the occasion. One member of the armed state forces was deployed for every fifteen Catholics.

Mason had increased RUC numbers and armed them with M1 carbines in addition to their revolvers and Sterling sub-machine guns. He had also increased the numbers of the RUC Reserve and UDR and promised more SAS action, and in November 1977 Major General Timothy 'Bull' Creasey was appointed GOC Northern Ireland. Creasey had commanded British forces in Oman fighting in support of the feudal sultan and was closely associated with the SAS, which now became very active. The

British army and RUC onslaught was directed against Sinn Féin as well as the IRA.

Late in 1978 the minority Labour government of Jim Callaghan did a deal with the unionists to stay in power, allocating five new MPs to the representation of the north in the Westminster parliament. This opportunist move bought Labour little time, for exactly four months later they were defeated, and by early May 1979 Margaret Thatcher had formed a new, Conservative government.

The IRA had regrouped and were causing the British renewed concern. Sinn Féin had a lot to do to catch up. Brigadier Glover of the British army produced a telling report which appreciated the falseness of Mason's claims and recognised that the element of British strategy which required the military suppression of the resistance could not be implemented. In May 1979 Humphrey Atkins, the newly appointed Northern Ireland secretary, admitted in his inaugural speech to the House of Commons: 'The first months of this year have shown a marked increase in the level of terrorism (*sic*) and have demonstrated that we are up against a very professional enemy.'

Popular support for the republican struggle had been mobilised anew, and in August 1979 an IRA party appeared at a 10,000-strong internment anniversary rally in Belfast and was warmly applauded. Later that same month, on 27 August 1979, eighteen soldiers, most of whom were attached to the Parachute regiment, were killed by the IRA.

Attitudes had changed in the ten years since British troops had taken up their positions in the streets of Belfast and Derry, and most nationalists now felt an overwhelming hostility towards the troops and the British establishment. Many people who had protested in 1969 for nothing more than to be allowed to live their lives in conditions of relative freedom and equality had experienced such an intensity of political and military oppression in the intervening years that they contemplated many IRA operations with grim satisfaction. Perhaps the key to these feelings lay back in those first days when the troops had moved in but had chosen not to intervene when loyalists had burnt down Bombay Street. But the blade of enmity had been sharpened by the killing of Danny O'Hagan, by the rape of the Falls, by Bloody Sunday, by internment, by brutal house raids, by the torture at Castlereagh, by the killings in Ballymurphy and Springhill, by the construction of military forts on the sites of schools and playing fields, and by the thousands of incidents of violence inflicted upon ordinary nationalists by British forces.

Now the contrast between British and Irish nationalist perceptions could not have been more marked. Many British people regarded the war in Ireland as mindless terrorism or as the 'bloody Irish' fighting as usual. Media censorship and bias encouraged such views. Many even saw it as a religious war. Few stopped to consider what business their troops or their government had in our country. Yet that was precisely the first thing most nationalists thought of. Republicans had a historical and political view. We wanted the reconquest of Ireland by the Irish people. We knew that ordinary people in Britain were not our enemy, but we wanted no truck with British rule in Ireland. In our view that was the cause of the war and the source of the divisions between our people. We wanted British rule ended.

In 1980 the British sought to gain new ground in the battle against the IRA by investing heavily in the activities of military intelligence, which were now co-ordinated by intelligence supremo Maurice Oldfield. Three hundred million pounds was invested in closed circuit TV surveillance of the nationalist community, all installations connected to computers linking all RUC vehicles, posts and personnel. Special units of the RUC trained as death squads at a time which saw the assassinations by loyalists, with RUC or British intelligence assistance, of political activists such as John Turnly of the Irish Independence Party, Miriam Daly, Noel Little and Ronnie Bunting of the IRSP, and the attempted assassination of Bernadette (Devlin) McAliskey.

On the political front I used the keynote occasion in the republican year of the 1979 Bodenstown commemoration to address the need to build a political alternative.

'[T]he Republic declared in 1916 . . . cannot be fully re-established solely by military means, for while obstructions and obstacles may be cleared militarily and gains made may be protected militarily, the re-establishment of the Republic needs more than a military alternative to the establishment . . . Our movement needs constructive and thoughtful self-criticism. We also require strong links with those oppressed by economic and social pressures . . . [O]ur most glaring weakness to date lies in our failure to develop revolutionary politics and to build a strong political alternative to so-called constitutional politics.'

I returned to the theme of political development in an article called 'Scenario for a Socialist Republic' in April 1980:

'It is possible and indeed probable given present conditions that the IRA will eventually secure a withdrawal. However, . . . given the IRA's present reliance on its military "strength" and because of the real lack of a comparable political movement, it is most likely that the British will succeed in withdrawing in circumstances and conditions most suitable to their own long-term interests and to imperialist interests in general.

'A British withdrawal can be secured more quickly and in more favourable conditions if it is achieved not only because of the IRA military threat, but also because resistance to British rule has been channelled and built into an alternative political movement.'

To my surprise this article caused some controversy in Sinn Féin leadership circles.

In retrospect the biggest weakness of Sinn Féin in the north was our failure to build either alliances with the SDLP or a party political electoral alternative. The formation of the Irish Independence Party in October 1977 by Frank McManus and Fergus McAteer had shown that Sinn Féin was surrendering political ground not only to the SDLP but also to a new party to the left of the SDLP. Later electoral campaigns by Bernadette McAliskey and local electoral successes on the part of People's Democracy and the Irish Republican Socialist Party saw us surrendering further ground. Of course, any attempt by us to build an electoral alternative would have been dogged by problems regarding the

278

question of abstentionism, but clearly our failure to develop either one of these political options constituted a critical weakness on our part. The situation was even worse in the south.

Sinn Féin was a protest movement; its illegal, conspiratorial background (even though we were by now unbanned) meant that we were temperamentally and organisationally disinclined to co-operate or combine in action with elements outside the movement itself. Armed struggle had dominated the movement to the extent of being considered almost the only form of struggle. What I was arguing was that we must build a political practice, and that it must be open and public rather than conspiratorial.

Changes were occurring in the SDLP, which in November 1978 finally came out in favour of a British withdrawal. In 1979 Gerry Fitt, who was the SDLP's only elected representative, resigned not only from the leadership but from the party itself. The development of a campaign in relation to the prisoners in the H-Blocks and Armagh women's prison, which Gerry Fitt opposed, had led to him being increasingly questioned and opposed by people in his constituency who might not have minded his attacking the IRA but who resented his position on the prisons issue. Sinn Féin had been opposing the SDLP hammer and tongs, but when someone in the SDLP said something which I thought was actually quite good, I welcomed it. On the day Gerry Fitt resigned, my instinct told me he was about to. When I jumped in with a statement, he alleged that my intervention was evidence of his claim that the SDLP was becoming more nationalist. John Hume succeeded Fitt as leader of the SDLP and in the European elections of that year was elected as an MEP.

We had decided to boycott the elections ourselves, and when Bernadette McAliskey stood on the prisons issue in June 1979 we did not support her; she nevertheless received a very substantial vote. We were still involved in a learning process, lacking cohesion, taking an ad hoc approach. In 1980 Jim Gibney argued at our Ard Fheis that we should contest local government elections in the Six Counties, but his proposal was defeated. In

279

the next local elections in May 1981, however, candidates supporting the H-Block/Armagh campaign won about thirty seats. In a real sense these should have been Sinn Féin seats.

In the Six Counties, political ground had been surrendered by Sinn Féin to the SDLP, the IIP, the IRSP, independents such as Bernadette, and PD. In the Twenty-six Counties, we had surrendered political ground to 'Official' Sinn Féin, which in 1977 changed its name to Sinn Féin the Workers' Party (in 1982 dropping Sinn Féin from its name), and which continually garnered votes from southern electors, even though their political position was now almost indistinguishable from unionism.

In June 1977, Fianna Fáil under Jack Lynch had returned to power in Dublin with a twenty-seat majority, displacing a coalition Fine Gael/Labour government which had set new standards in collaboration with the British armed forces and in police-state methods against republicans. Foremost amongst those who had pressed the anti-nationalist agenda of that government had been Conor Cruise O'Brien, an enthusiast for censorship who had been remarkably successful in generating a McCarthyite atmosphere, which derived further force from the activities of a special Garda unit dubbed, for obvious reasons, 'the Heavy Gang'. No Sinn Féin spokesperson had been interviewed on RTE, the state broadcasting network, since 1976 and, increasingly, nationalist opinion was ignored by the broadcasters. This censorship ethos extended even to songs, drama and poetry, which had long been part of the rich vein of Irish culture.

Conor Cruise O'Brien's hostility to the democratic demands of nationalists in the north was intimately connected with his denial of the colonial nature of Britain's presence in Ireland. Irish republicans, however, saw ourselves as part of an international movement in favour of the self-determination of peoples and against colonialism. The Irish nationalist movement had played a leading role in the international development of the struggle to overthrow colonialism. Throughout its history, republicanism had been significantly influenced by progressive movements in other countries, ever since the United Irishmen had been inspired by the American War of Independence and the French Revolution. In India and Africa, the Irish revolutionary tradition had been one of the strongest influences in the anti-colonial movements.

Internationalism had remained an important element in modern republicanism, in terms of both the development of political ideas and the tactics of guerrilla war. It was an influence which worked both ways. Republicans learned from struggles in other countries, while most guerrilla and independence movements studied the IRA and saw it as an important example of how to develop a people's war.

Irish republicans had a natural, instinctive and deep affinity with the oppressed black majority in South Africa and with the ANC. A free federation of free peoples was what we sought and was the only conception of internationalism I felt was worth struggling for.

During my time on remand I had been forcibly struck by what our prisoners in Armagh and in the H-Blocks were suffering, and impressed with their fortitude in carrying out their own form of struggle in the most difficult of circumstances. Their campaign had been going on since 1976, and had escalated, and I was concerned by the lack of any sign of movement from the British. Our own agitation in support of the prisoners was clearly inadequate. Relatives' Action Committees had been formed from April 1976, but for all their trojan work they were not getting the political support from us which the issue demanded.

Before being jailed on remand I had believed, a victim of our own bad propaganda work, that the prisoners had started what was called the 'dirty' protest as part of an escalation of the blanket protest, whereas in fact the prisoners had been forced into a no-wash protest because their toilet facilities had been withdrawn from them. To me it was a very important point. There was certainly a difference in such an unsavoury protest between whether you do it voluntarily or whether you're forced into it. Prison warders had subjected the 'blanket men' to constant harassment and had attacked prisoners as they went to and from the latrines, kicking over chamber pots in cells and throwing the contents of pots on to beds. The prisoners had thus been forced to respond by escalating the 'blanket' protest to a 'no-wash' stage, in which they refused to shave, wash or empty chamber pots. Conditions had rapidly become appalling. In Armagh women's prison, the attempt to force through the criminalisation policy followed a similar course.

Cardinal Tomás Ó Fiaich visited the H-Blocks in August 1978 and gave the following description:

'One could hardly allow an animal to remain in such conditions, let alone a human being. The nearest approach to it that I have ever seen was the spectacle of hundreds of homeless people living in the sewer pipes of the slums of Calcutta. The stench and the filth in some of the cells with the remains of rotten food and human excreta scattered around the walls was almost unbearable.

'The authorities refuse to admit that these prisoners are in a different category from the ordinary, yet everything about their trials and family background indicates that they are different. They were sentenced by special courts without juries. The vast majority were convicted on allegedly voluntary confessions obtained in circumstances which are now placed under grave suspicion by the recent report of Amnesty International. Many are very youthful and come from families which had never been in trouble with the law, though they lived in areas which suffered discrimination in housing and jobs. How can one explain the jump in the prison population of Northern Ireland from 500 to 3,000 unless a new type of prisoner has emerged? The problem of these prisoners is one of the great obstacles to peace in our community. As long as it continues it will be a potent cause of resentment in the prisoners themselves, breeding frustration among their relatives and friends and leading to bitterness between the prisoners and prison staff. It is only sowing the seeds of future conflict.'

When I had been released I had come out with a very clear view of the prison issue and I had gone straight to Ruairí Ó Bradaigh, just before the 1978 Ard Fheis, and briefed him, as a result of which he revised his presidential address to update the prison issue. We formed a small committee to take care of the prison protests and we re-grouped the POW department which then became the vehicle for a better understanding and, in time, more pro-active work around the prisoner issue. We held a special POW conference in Dublin in 1979, at which a sizeable number of activists discussed these matters.

Jim Gibney had for some time liaised with the Relatives' Action Committee for Sinn Féin, and now we tried to build on that. I attended some RAC meetings and we were talking about trying to get some sort of mass action going, involving people outside of Sinn Féin. Then we took our eye off the ball very badly. A conference was called in Coalisland, at which one of our people insisted that anyone involved in campaigning for the prisoners should accept the legitimacy of the armed struggle. It was perhaps an instinctive response – certainly the traditional response – in the context of the British criminalisation policy, but I knew it was a mistake the moment I heard about it.

We were working out approaches to a wide range of issues, politically trying to make advances. We had looked positively at electoralism, and we had recognised the importance of the prison issue. We had incipient plans for our own initiatives, but we weren't sophisticated enough to take advantage of the opportunity represented by the Coalisland conference, which other people, including grass-root republicans, had pulled together to discuss the building of a broad anti-unionist front. However, by October 1979, we had our act together, and at a conference in the Green Briar Hotel in Andersonstown, organised by the Relatives' Action Committee, the organisations which set up the H-Block/Armagh Committee included Sinn Féin, the Irish Republican Socialist Party (IRSP), People's Democracy (PD), the Trade Union Campaign Against Repression (TUCAR) and Women Against Imperialism (WAI). There were even representatives present from the 'Peace People'.

We now worked with the prisoners around five demands, which expressed in a way which was devoid of jargon the substance of what they wanted. We sought to make it easier for the British to move, while also appearing reasonable to a broader range of people than those who were already committed in support of the political prisoners and against the prison regime.

After ten years of struggle large numbers of republicans were in prison, and the prisoners had become a prime focus of the republican struggle. Apart from the politics of the situation, all of us had friends or family inside. Over half of those charged in the special Diplock courts were under twenty-one, and those who were activists had taken up a specifically political fight to defend their streets from the attacks of loyalists, in and out of uniform, and of the British army. Many of them had progressed from building barricades and throwing stones at Saracens to involvement in the IRA's campaign to achieve the political objective of British withdrawal. The British contention that republican prisoners were not political prisoners defied logic; but it was a powerful weapon of political rhetoric, backed by all the armed and legal forces of the state, and it aimed at achieving the suppression of the republican struggle while also distorting the international perception of the British-Irish conflict. It was inevitable that republicans would confront this British strategy head-on, to defeat the policy of 'criminalisation' and to insist upon the political character of our struggle.

Eleven

The hunger strikes which culminated with the deaths of Bobby Sands and nine other republicans came at a time when my own political priority was to develop Sinn Féin's political capacity and capability in a planned way, which could include a new electoral strategy. I resisted the hunger strike option when it was advanced by the prisoners because I was convinced that it would divert attention and energy from the tasks of political development; it would also undoubtedly prove an extremely draining experience for republicans; and it might very well result in a substantial, deeply demoralising defeat.

As things turned out, the effects of the hunger strikes were contradictory.

Attention *was* diverted from the planned efforts to build an electoral intervention; yet we found ourselves achieving, more by accident than by calculation, a series of resounding electoral victories. Physically, emotionally and spiritually, the hunger strikes were intensely draining; yet we derived immense new energy, commitment and direction from the extraordinary period during which our ten comrades slowly and painfully sacrificed their lives.

I have been shaped by many influences and many intense experiences. There have been occasions which have been turning points for me as an individual, and there have been times which have been turning points not only for me but for an entire people. When with the advantage of distance the history is written of Ireland in the years in which I have lived, I know that an Everest amongst the mountains of traumatic events which the Irish people have experienced will be the republican hunger strikes of 1980–81.

I knew Bobby Sands quite well from our time together in Cage 11. He had been released from the Kesh in April 1976; he was married and had a son, yet he resumed activity with the IRA. He had also been involved in Sinn Féin, helping to set up a local branch and, as a local community activist, writing articles and editing a local community newspaper called *Liberty*; all the while he continued playing and singing at concerts. However, he had been jailed again when he and three others were stopped in a car in which there was a gun. For six days he had been subjected to the Castlereagh treatment but had not signed a confession. For joint possession with the three others of a single revolver, he had been sentenced to fourteen years.

When he was sentenced he joined the protesting prisoners 'on the blanket' in the Blocks, refusing to wear prison uniform. It was not an unknown means of struggle; indeed, my father had been on the blanket for a time when he had been in prison, but no prison protest had gone on as long and involved as many people, including the women in Armagh prison. Most of the prisoners were obstinate, stubborn, determined young fighters, who hadn't been in prison before and who refused to co-operate in the Blocks, but there was also a seasoning of old hands like Bobby, who had been through the system and who knew their way about the place. By now the protest was five years old.

Bitterness between prisoners and screws was extreme, compared to the situation when I had been an internee. The screws were implementing a criminalisation regime, which included the violence and indignity of forced washing. The IRA meanwhile were carrying out a policy on the outside of shooting members of prison staffs. Bobby was pretty hard on the screws, and the depth of his hostility to them was later reflected in his writings.

Although he had written a few scraps of songs before, he only started writing seriously when he became PRO in the Blocks and was encouraged by Danny Morrison, editor of *Republican News*. Bobby's poetry, which was written on tiny scraps of paper in the most difficult of circumstances, without access to reference materials, is the work of a very creative mind, and there is no doubt that he had great ability. He also wrote pieces which were valuable contributions to political debate.

'It must be said that an armed people are by no means a sure guarantee to liberation. Our guns may kill our enemies but unless we direct them with the politics of a revolutionary people they will eventually kill ourselves. Guns don't win wars; guns and bombs may kill a man but they cannot lead a man . . . nor will they ever coerce an unyielding man to yield.'

His fellow prisoners loved to hear him as he told, in instalments and in his own version, the story of Leon Uris's novel, *Trinity*, shouting it out through the cell door so that all those along the corridor could hear it. Bobby was also one of the leaders of the Gaelicisation of the Blocks and one of the best of the Irish language teachers in the prison.

The crisis in the prisons, which had been building gradually since 1976, intensified in early 1980. Male guards wrecked the cells of republican prisoners at Armagh jail and beat up several of the women, who responded by embarking on a 'no-wash' protest. In March the British government extended the denial of political status to those prisoners who had been sentenced before 1 March 1976. In Sinn Féin we had promised to intensify our efforts on the outside, but hard as the H-Block/Armagh Committee worked, there was no sign of movement on the issue from the British government. The prisoners felt that little progress was being made either by our campaign of protests or by the IRA's campaign of shooting prison warders.

On 27 October seven H-Block prisoners, including Brendan Hughes, started a hunger strike; Bobby Sands took over as OC. From then until the end of the strike at Christmas, I was in daily contact with Bobby. During this intensely traumatic period, he and I got to know each other thoroughly. In late November three women prisoners in Armagh joined the H-Block men on hunger strike and, in December, thirty more H-Block prisoners went on hunger strike. One of the seven, Sean McKenna, weakened rapidly: on the verge of lapsing into a coma, he was losing his sight. Even as the hunger strike began, the British government, despite its public posturing about not talking to 'terrorists', opened up contact with republicans, reactivating a channel of communication which had been used during the protracted bilateral truce of 1974–75. Through this contact in the Foreign Office, it was suggested that a compromise could be reached; a document setting out details of a settlement would be presented to the prisoners if they came off hunger strike. Sean McKenna was too ill to take part in their deliberations as his fellow hunger strikers considered their options, but on the fifty-third day of the strike, 18 December, they called off the protest. Later that day, the British presented a document to the prisoners, but what they announced to the world's media was a story of surrender, omitting mention of any compromise package.

I had a funny experience of the confused ending to this first hunger strike. Knowing that the British had put out a statement claiming surrender by the prisoners, I returned home in a depressed state to find a note from Colette telling me that she and a friend of ours had gone out to celebrate, under the mistaken impression that the strike had been successfully resolved. All over Belfast, and beyond, republicans were relieved and delighted. Later the two of them came in stocious drunk, and I had to put both of them to bed. I was miserable and sober, knowing the truth; they were happy in their ignorance.

That Christmas, as usual, Colette, Gearóid and I visited my ma and Colette's mother. We were relieved that Brendan and his friends were off the hunger strike, yet there was a feeling of despondency in the air. Colette visited the Dark in the Block. It was clear that the issues which had caused the hunger strike still needed to be resolved.

Bobby Sands, as OC in the Kesh, went through hoops between Christmas and March 1981, trying to make the settlement work, to deal with the prison regime, to get the British to work their own document. All this he did under duress, because on the outside we in Sinn Féin were so opposed to a second hunger strike, even though he and others wanted to embark on one long before March. Twenty prisoners, in a dry run, came off the protest, and their relatives brought clothes to Long Kesh, but the prison authorities refused to distribute the clothes to the men. Within the terms of their own document, the British government could have arranged a step-by-step implementation of the prisoners' demands, but instead they obstructed any form of movement within the prisons.

The prisoners were now determined to embark on another hunger strike, knowing that they faced the prospect of death, yet feeling that the spectacle of their deaths would be politically productive for the cause to which they were committed. But a second hunger strike would be quite different from the first. They would be engaging in a fight with the British government which went beyond the issue of prison conditions, and this had enormous implications for the entire republican struggle. In Sinn Féin we resisted it very, very strenuously, not just because of the problems it would mean for the people on hunger strike, but also because of the problems it would create for the struggle if there were a second defeat.

Hunger strike was unlike any other form of struggle. IRA volunteers did not go out to get killed, even though they risked their lives. But hunger strikers embarked on a process which was intended, if need be, to result in their deaths. I had had my own brief experience of hunger strike in 1972 and I knew how difficult that was. I also knew that others were more resolute than I. Republicans Michael Gaughan in 1974 and Frank Stagg in 1976 had died on hunger strike in prisons in England; Dolours and Marian Price, who had been subjected to force-feeding, had endured 205 days on hunger strike. Considering the calibre and character of the people proposing to go on hunger strike now, I could have no doubt but that they were resolute. At the same time, there could be no guarantee that they would go through with it to the end, that they would resist the voices of doubt that might arise in their own heads, the concern of friends and family, and the pressures of the prison regime and the British government.

Our opposition in Sinn Féin to the prison protest had to do partly with the inherent problems of hunger strike as a tactic and partly with the fact that close personal relationships existed between the prisoners themselves and between prisoners and republicans on the outside; we all knew that if they embarked on a second hunger strike we would be entering a period of intense anguish. Beyond that there was the question of the relationship between the prisoners and the nationalist community. With so many republicans in prison, especially as a result of the 'conveyor belt' system from Castlereagh to Diplock courts, no nationalist community was untouched by the experience of imprisonment. In areas such as Ballymurphy, several houses in many streets had sons or daughters in prison. And so whatever anguish we shared as republicans on the outside with our comrades on hunger strike would be an anguish shared also with almost the entire nationalist population of the Six Counties.

Principally, however, we opposed the second hunger strike because we did not believe that it would succeed in moving the British government. As well as that, we were just beginning our attempts to remedy the political underdevelopment of our struggle and, in particular, we were working out our strategy in relation to elections. We were well aware that a hunger strike such as was proposed would demand our exclusive attention. I spelled out my opposition directly and personally in no uncertain terms.

'Bobby,' I wrote, 'we are tactically, strategically, physically and morally opposed to a hunger strike.'

However, by the time we had gone through all the arguments in our smuggled correspondence, I knew that Bobby Sands was going to die. He was a twenty-seven-year-old veteran of struggle, twice imprisoned, and he knew what he was at. In the House of Commons, the British Secretary of State for Northern Ireland,

Humphrey Atkins, declared that there would be no concession of political status. Behind the scenes contact was re-established between us and the civil servant in the Foreign Office.

My role now was to chair Sinn Féin's hunger strike committee, and so as well as dealing, along with Martin McGuinness, with communications with the British government, I participated in a unique intensity of relationships which developed during this extraordinary period, mostly through the medium of 'comms', messages written on cigarette papers and smuggled in and out of the Blocks. A couple of years older than any of the hunger strikers who died, who ranged in age between twenty-three and thirty, I was painfully aware that these were young men, most of whose lives should lie ahead of them, yet who were preparing to sacrifice themselves.

Apart from Bobby, the person I knew best was Bik McFarlane. He had been involved in the first hunger strike and, when Bobby went on hunger strike, he became the OC. He came from Ardoyne and knew my aunt Kathleen and my cousins there. I had met him in Cage 11 and had asked him to become our PRO. A rounded character who was remarkably open, including in his emotions, he had studied in a seminary. He was a good musician, and did the arrangements of some of Bobby's songs. Throughout the agonising course of the hunger strike, it was principally with Bik I communicated, often receiving from him several comms in one day.

Bobby Sands started his hunger strike on 1 March 1981, the fifth anniversary of the phasing out of political status. That day a large demonstration marched down the Falls Road in support of the five demands of the prisoners:

1. The right to wear their own clothing at all times.
2. Exemption from all forms of penal labour.
3. Free association with each other at all hours.
4. The right to organise their own recreational and educational programmes.
5. Full restoration of remission.

There was a huge crowd from Ballymurphy there that day. One placard read 'Divismore Park Supports the Five Demands'.

Francis Hughes joined Bobby on hunger strike on 15 March, Ray McCreesh and Patsy O'Hara a week later. They were pitching themselves, with the only weapons at their command – their lives – against the imperial power.

Then came a development which was entirely unexpected and could not have been predicted, yet which transformed the prisoners' campaign. Frank Maguire, independent MP for the constituency of Fermanagh/South Tyrone, died suddenly, and a by-election was called to fill the seat.

We had been discussing developing an electoral strategy, but almost by definition we had no experience of electoral contests. While we thought and talked about having a prisoner go forward, it was only following the intervention of Bernadette Devlin McAliskey in the constituency that Jim Gibney raised the possibility that Bobby Sands should stand in the election. Bernadette was aware of the talk of a prisoner's standing and when she announced that she would be a candidate she said that she would stand down if there were an H-Block candidate. Bobby only had a chance of being elected if he were unopposed by any other candidate on the nationalist side; the electoral demographics meant that a split vote would almost certainly result in a unionist's being elected. Noel Maguire, Frank's brother, had been nominated and was expected to take the seat, but the SDLP also put forward a candidate. Jim Gibney and I journeyed down to Lisnaskea to talk to the Maguire family, and they, too, agreed that if a prisoner stood they would support that candidate. The local Sinn Féin organisation in Fermanagh and South Tyrone had to be convinced that a prisoner could win the seat, and Ruairí Ó Bradaigh, Dáithí Ó Conaill, myself and others tackled this head-on. When a few days later we nominated Bobby Sands, the SDLP withdrew their candidate rather than split the vote. But with fifteen minutes to go before the close of nominations, Noel Maguire had still not withdrawn, and I found myself sitting tensely with colleagues in a car outside the electoral office, ready to withdraw Bobby's name if he were going to have to go up against Noel Maguire, who was in himself a very worthy candidate. We could not afford to have Bobby defeated. The stakes were too high. With only ten minutes to go to the deadline, however, Noel Maguire withdrew his nomination, and the campaign to elect a hunger-striking prisoner was on.

In the event Bernadette and the Maguires proved noble and energetic supporters of the campaign to elect Bobby Sands. We Sinn Féin activists had no idea of how to run an election campaign, but we had to learn at breakneck speed or face humiliation. In this we were also helped by a Kerry republican, well known in sporting circles, Joe Keohane. Owen Carron from Fermanagh was Bobby's election agent.

That campaign was an education for us. We galvanised our people in Fermanagh and Tyrone, and they responded with great commitment. I was rarely at home during that time, spending almost the entire campaign in the constituency. I met scores of great people and, in the midst of all the activity, I enjoyed the wonderful beauty of those two counties. We learned about presiding officers, personation officers, how to campaign. It was exhilarating. Sometimes we would come into a little town with the Catholics corralled away up at the top as usual, the loyalists living along the main street in the business end of the town. We would have the tricolour flying, the music blaring – and the nationalists up on the top of the hill would come out to us as though we were the relief cavalry.

I stayed overnight in Enniskillen on the eve of the poll, then crossed the border to Clones the next day to report to Ruairí Ó Bradaigh, who was barred from entering the north. I was convinced we were going to win. As I drove away afterwards to meet with Colette, I heard the news on the car radio: Bobby Sands had won the election. I was ecstatic.

Bobby Sands topped the poll with 30,492 votes. The British government and opposition, followed enthusiastically by the media, had constantly maintained that republicans – and especially the hunger strikers – represented nobody and enjoyed no support; that republicans were criminal 'godfathers' operating by intimidation; that they were isolated fanatics. Now that lie had been exposed. The British propaganda campaign had been refuted and the election victory resounded internationally. I pondered with a certain wry satisfaction the comparison between my first electoral experience, folding leaflets for Liam McMillen in 1964 and suffering lost deposits, and the tremendous impact of Bobby's election.

There was a feeling amongst some of our members and supporters that surely the British government must yield sufficiently to bring about an end to the hunger strike. I did not share that optimism. We had been challenged for years to submit ourselves to the ballot box, and now we had done so, demonstrating massive popular support in the election. Yet the British government, as we had feared from the outset, showed no willingness to make concessions. We began to receive a stream of messages from the Dublin government to the effect that the British government were about to concede the five demands. However, as soon as we asked for anything in writing, all agreement collapsed. Dublin placed great emphasis on the International Red Cross, but there was no real substance to that intervention. Margaret Thatcher maintained her inflexible approach and, despite all the earnest assurances of their envoys, the Dublin government did nothing to shift her from it.

The most remarkable feature of the hunger strikes, apart from the courage and tenacity of the hunger strikers themselves, was the way in which we built relationships between people outside and inside the Blocks – relationships which were extraordinary, unique, and which resisted enormous pressures. We were physically separate, having only the most tenuous of contact with each other. During the year of the hunger strikes, apart from one meeting in the prison hospital, I never talked to any of the hunger strikers. Pressure was put on the prisoners, and on the hunger strikers specifically; pressure was put on us and on the bond which developed in the course of the hunger strike; pressure was put on our lines of communication by the tactics of the British negotiators; and pressure was put on the families of the hunger strikers.

We established a very solid support structure for dealing with the families of our prisoners. Jimmy Drumm used to go and visit the families, and we made sure they were informed of everything that was happening. We tried to facilitate them, get them up and down to the Kesh and to meetings. There was a very good liaison with them, but in the final analysis, although we gave the families what help was within our power, it was up to the prisoner to work out the consequences of the hunger strike with his family; it wasn't up to us.

Bobby Sands died at 1.17 am on Tuesday, 5 May, the sixty-sixth day of his hunger strike, in the company of his parents, his sister Marcella and his brother Sean.

I was in a house in Oakman Street in the Beechmount area when I heard the bin-lids announce his death. I left the house by the back door and crossed the yard into the entry. It was deserted. The tom-tom beat of the bin-lids echoed everywhere, and when I emerged unseen from the back entry it was to streets brimming with people, mostly women, banging bin-lids, crying, intense with anger.

In Harrogate Street, Colette was already out with the neighbours and others, on protest. She asked me if I was all right. I told her yes and walked to the Sinn Féin centre on the Falls Road. By now British army and RUC patrols, out in full force, were being attacked by young people. Outside our office there was bedlam. Inside, Danny Morrison and I and the rest of us applied ourselves to telling the world that our friend was dead.

Jim Gibney had been the last of us to see Bobby, but we had all known that he was very ill, and we knew that if the Brits didn't give, Bobby was going. When Jim came out of the prison, he said that Bobby was very, very weak, although he had known that Jim was there and he had been quite conscious of what was happening.

Bik wrote a comm to me at 2.15 am:

'Comrade *mór*, I just heard the news – I'm shattered – just can't believe it. This is a terrible feeling I have. I don't even know what to say. Comrade, I'm sorry, but I just can't say anything else. May God in his infinite mercy grant eternal rest to his soul. Jesus Christ protect and guide us all.

God bless.

xoxo Bik xoxo'

Grief at the death of Bobby Sands extended far beyond his family and friends into a community which had experienced his struggle as their own. At the wake house in Bobby's parents' home, our Paddy, who hadn't even known Bobby Sands, kissed him and started to cry. Danny Morrison broke down very badly; Jim Gibney broke down . . . it was an enormously emotional occasion. At the requiem mass, which was held in St Luke's, only a few hundred yards from the Sands home, the priest talked about Bobby's 'illness'; I was disgusted at this avoidance of the truth.

But what I remember most about Bobby's funeral is the wailing lamentation of the pipes as the piper played the air of the song, 'I'll wear no convict's uniform'.

I was moved, too, by the death of a man and his son delivering milk in North Belfast. They were killed on the morning Bobby Sands died. A crowd had tried to hijack the milk lorry, but the man had driven through; somebody threw a brick at the vehicle, which crashed, and the man and his son were killed. I was conscious, too, that a number of other civilians had been killed in the course of the hunger strike.

The funeral procession set out at 2.00 pm on its four-mile journey from St Luke's in Twinbrook to Milltown cemetery. A hundred thousand people lined the route in silence in the rain. In Andersonstown there was a temporary halt, during which the coffin was placed on trestles; IRA volunteers shot three rifle volleys over the coffin, reversed rifles, and observed a one-minute silence, disappearing then into the crowd. On the arrival of the coffin at the gates of Milltown cemetery, there was a spontaneous outburst of prayer from the crowd. A guard of honour accompanied the coffin to the graveside. The 'Last Post' was played, and Owen Carron delivered an oration.

Bobby's father, brother and eight-year-old son Gerard each threw a spadeful of earth. Gerard had to be helped with the heavy spade. The folded tricolour, his gloves and beret were presented to Bobby's mother by the honour guard.

The death on hunger strike of Bobby Sands had a greater international impact than any other event in Ireland in my lifetime, although for me at the time it was something which had much more to do with my feelings about comrades and friends.

In the USA there were marches in New York, Boston, Chicago and San Francisco. The state of Rhode Island declared a day of mourning. The New York state legislature passed a resolution of sympathy condemning the British government. The New Jersey state legislature passed a resolution honouring Bobby's 'courage and commitment'. The Longshoremen's Union blacked all British ships on the day of the funeral. Ted Kennedy and other senators sent a letter to the British prime minister protesting at her 'inflexible posture which must lead inevitably to more senseless violence and death'. The *New York Daily News* said: 'He was a rare one, a young man who thought enough of the place where he lived to want to die for it.' The *New York Times* remarked that 'Despite proximity and a common language the British have persistently misjudged the depth of Irish nationalism.'

From Poland Lech Walesa sent sympathy on behalf of the Solidarity movement. The Portuguese parliament observed a minute's silence. In France protests took place, thousands marching behind a huge portrait of Bobby Sands; a street in Le Mans was named Bobby Sands Street. *Le Monde* wrote: 'His memory and recognition of the meaning of his sacrifice are heavy with an emotion that several times this century has aroused the passions of the world against Britain.' There were protests, too, in Switzerland, West Germany, Belgium, Holland, Greece and Italy, where the president of the Italian senate expressed condolences to the Sands family and 5,000 students marched in Milan, burning the Union Jack.

There were demonstrations in Australia and in Norway, where

demonstrators in Oslo threw a balloon filled with tomato sauce at the Queen of England, who was on a visit. The Indian parliament in New Delhi observed a minute's silence. The *Hindustan Times* observed that Thatcher had 'allowed a member of the House of Commons, a colleague in fact, to die of starvation. Never had such an incident occurred in a civilised country.'

In Ireland the Dublin government did not declare a day of mourning, but many stayed away from work, some businesses closed, and there were silent marches. The *Irish Press* wrote: 'Belfast narrowed his options as a boy, gunmen chased him from his home and from his job . . . In jail Britain narrowed his options to two: live as a criminal or die for an ideal. His choice will be long remembered.'

That period is now very much a blur for me and for many republicans who were involved in it. It remains a very evocative, emotional memory for many people. I cannot yet think with any intensity of the death of Bobby Sands and the circumstances of his passing without crying. It was a time of overwhelming public grief and of identification with Bobby Sands and the other hunger strikers and their families. There are several songs which are sung about the hunger strikes and one particular song names them in turn. Wherever it is sung there is spontaneous applause for each of the names.

Francie Hughes died on 12 May after fifty-nine days on hunger strike. From a small farm in Tamlaghtduff near Bellaghy in rural County Derry, Frank had become a legendary IRA man, his photograph in police barracks all over the north. In 1971 as a fifteen-year-old, just like my brothers in Divismore Park, he had seen one of his older brothers, with whom he was sharing a bedroom, taken from the house in the early hours of the morning and interned. Francie and some of his friends had spent a memorable few nights with Colette and Gearóid and me years before up in Donegal when we were on holidays and he was stranded.

On 19 May, the IRA killed five British soldiers with a land mine in South Armagh.

Patsy O'Hara and Ray McCreesh both died on 21 May, both after sixty-one days on hunger strike. Raymond McCreesh I didn't know. I knew Patsy O'Hara's brother Sean 'Scatter' O'Hara, but I didn't know Patsy himself. I got to know both families and I was honoured and humbled by their friendship. Through the haze of the years and the emotion of the time, I can still hear the music of the pipes again at Raymond McCreesh's funeral, at which an old piper from that area played 'Úr Chill an Chreagáin'.

On 23 May, local elections took place in the Six Counties. Sinn Féin did not participate, but two Irish Republican Socialist Party and two People's Democracy members stood, campaigned in support of the prisoners, and were elected to Belfast city council, in the process unceremoniously dumping Gerry Fitt from the seat he had occupied for twenty-three years. Fitt had publicly called on Thatcher not to concede the five demands; now the Conservative Party's favourite Irishman, his political life in Ireland was over. In 1983 Margaret Thatcher rewarded him with a life peerage.

When the Dublin government called a general election for 11 June, the National H-Block/Armagh Committee put up nine republican prisoners – four of them hunger strikers – as candidates. The media dismissed the prisoners' campaign as insignificant and ignored it. However, despite the fact that our campaign offered nothing at a time of severe economic difficulty for many voters, but asked simply for support for the five demands of the prisoners in the Six Counties, and despite the fact that the National H-Block/Armagh Committee had no base of constituency workers, two prisoner candidates – Paddy Agnew and Kieran Doherty – were elected; a third, Joe McDonnell, came within 300 votes of being elected, and the nine together ran up a very respectable tally of votes. It was a triumphant expression of popular support for the prisoners.

The new Dublin government ignored the message of the elections and refused to take any effective steps to help resolve the hunger strike protest. British intransigence was criticised, but no measure was taken which might have caused Margaret Thatcher to modify her stance.

In late June the British parliament passed the 'Sands Bill', a new law to prevent convicted felons from standing for Westminster elections. They had long demanded that republicans should submit to the ballot box, but when we had done so and had been spectacularly successful, their response was to refuse to recognise the MP and the voters he represented, and to change the rules to prevent a similar candidate's being elected again.

Our response was to stand Bobby's election agent, Owen Carron, for the new by-election in Fermanagh/South Tyrone, and our campaign workers pitched in again with a will.

Now Joe McDonnell was the most seriously ill of the hunger strikers. The oldest of them at 30, he came from Lenadoon in Belfast and had been arrested with Bobby Sands. I had known him when he had been interned with us. Joe was a very happy-go-lucky guy and a most unlikely hunger striker. I didn't recall having any political discussions with him, but I did remember his sense of fun. On the day he started his hunger strike, he sent me out a King Edward cigar from his prison cell.

The representatives of the British government with whom we on the hunger strike committee were in contact used to leave it until someone was at a very weak point on hunger strike before entering into negotiations. They also dealt with us only at times when it was impossible for us to communicate with our comrades in the prison. There was no mistaking their constant efforts to fragment us, to explore weaknesses in our position and to divide us. On our side the negotiating procedure was necessarily cumbersome; since we were negotiating on behalf of the prisoners, we had to constantly get back to them. The Brits exploited this by entering into negotiations at ten or eleven o'clock at night, knowing that we were likely to be tired and that if we did bring discussions to some point of decision we would have to wait until prison visiting times to pass information in and out. I, therefore, started cat-napping during the day in order to be relatively fresh for negotiations at night.

The hunger strike campaign was all-consuming, and not only for me and others like me who were centrally involved. Republican Ireland was fully mobilising behind the protest. My mother with other women from the upper Springfield took part in daily demonstrations. Colette and her friends were similarly involved. Everyone was engaged. If I saw my father at all at this time, it was at funerals and demonstrations. We also started to do all-night shifts in the Sinn Féin office. There was little time to go home.

Very early one morning I and another member of our committee were in telephone discussion with the British from a living-room in a house in Andersonstown when, all of a sudden, they cut the conversation, which we thought was quite strange. Then, later, when we turned on the first news broadcast of the morning, we heard that Joe McDonnell was dead. Obviously they had cut the conversation when they got the word. They had misjudged the timing of their negotiations, and Joe had died much earlier than they had anticipated.

Joe McDonnell died on 8 July after 61 days on hunger strike.

I arrived late at his funeral on 10 July, having been at the funeral of John Dempsey, a sixteen-year-old member of Fianna Éireann, the republican youth movement, who had been shot by the British army.

I followed the slow, sad procession to the chapel on a bright warm summer morning. After mass, the girl piper heralded our passing as we made our way, once again, to Milltown. John's three sisters – Angela, Diana and Martina – with his brother Stephen, aged from nine to eighteen years old, accompanied their dead brother's remains, while green-clad young boys in Fianna uniform flanked his tricolour-draped coffin.

Turf Lodge was a socially deprived area, one of the newer Belfast ghettos, a jerrybuilt housing estate at the foot of the Black Mountain, where we used to play as boys just above the Murph, and where I first heard the corncrake many years before. There was one main road – Monagh Road – into the area. At the upper end this was flanked by a huge new British army fortress. Until recently the lower end had been flanked by the equally repressive, though smaller, Fort Monagh. John Dempsey had lived in one of the grey houses which sprawled on either side of Monagh Road.

We walked down from the heights of Turf Lodge, past the spot where John had been murdered, and by the British army barracks, through the open gates of the cemetery, to the republican plot, where two open graves – one for Joe McDonnell – awaited our arrival.

John had left school at Easter. He had played hurling and football for Gort na Móna and soccer for Corpus Christi, and like his father and his many uncles he had been a keep-fit enthusiast with an interest in body-building.

At the wake he had looked only twelve years old, his body laid in an open coffin flanked by a guard of honour. At his age I was still at St Mary's.

Hardened by many funerals, by too many sudden deaths, I had yet been riveted to the spot, unable to grasp the logic, the divine wisdom, the insanity, which had tightened a British soldier's trigger finger and produced yet another corpse.

'He's so young,' exclaimed those who had called to pay their respects. 'Jesus, he's only a child.'

He had joined Na Fianna Éireann in October 1980 and, like many young people from Turf Lodge, was subjected to regular harassment by British soldiers. Now these young people gathered, with veteran republicans and family friends at John's open grave, where a priest recited prayers and a recently released blanket man said the rosary in Irish. Dáithí Ó Buidh gave the oration in Irish and English, and wreaths were laid before we left for Lenadoon and the funeral of Joe McDonnell.

John Dempsey's funeral, a smaller and in many ways a sadder ceremony than Joe's, was a stark reminder that for the first time in contemporary Irish history the struggle had crossed the generation gap. When Joe McDonnell had first been interned in 1972, John Dempsey was a mere seven years old. Yet they were to die in the service of a common cause and against the same enemy and be buried in the same republican plot, within hours of each other.

As Jimmy Dempsey said of his son, 'John has joined the elite. He died for the freedom of his country.'

These words from a heart-broken father were tribute enough to his eldest son. The mourners, mere spectators to the family's grief, walked slowly from the republican plot and noticed, almost unconsciously, John's friends and contemporaries, earnest beyond their years, striding purposefully by us.

An old woman shuffling her way homewards informed all who passed of the murder by British troops that morning of another youngster, fifteen-year-old Daniel Barrett from Ardoyne.

The older mourners, shocked by the news, talked quietly among ourselves as we walked towards Lenadoon. The young people, unmoved by the news – not openly anyway, for they had known, and had grown to expect, nothing less from British troops – strode purposefully on . . .

Later that day, Joe McDonnell's funeral was attacked by the RUC and the British army on the Andersonstown Road. They were trying to arrest the IRA firing party. In seconds a quiet, sombre and dignified tribute to the dead hunger striker became a terrifying mêlée. First we heard the short, sharp whack of live rounds, then the dull thud of plastic bullets. Then bedlam!

Martin McGuinness and I fought our way from the front of the funeral towards the centre of the storm. We battled against the tide of men, women and children who were scattering towards us. The air was filled with plastic bullets; in St Agnes Drive beside the chapel they flew like birds from the slits in the RUC and British army vehicles parked up the hill. Everything was noise. Screams, bangs, thuds. The whirr of helicopters.

Somebody told me that our Paddy had been shot. Somebody else told me that he was in a Saracen which sat behind the Land Rovers. A crowd dashed in that direction. The Saracen started to reverse away. An elderly man lay on the deserted road behind it, blocking its path. The Saracen's engine revved. The elderly man didn't move. It was my Uncle Paddy. The Saracen moved forward now, towards the approaching crowd. We scattered before it. Some people punched its sides in despair.

Martin and I made our way back. We tried to calm the crowd. Now the RUC vehicles moved slowly towards us, trying to herd the mourners up the road. The plastic bullets continued their frightening flights into the packed ranks of people. We regrouped the funeral procession, defying the approaching Land Rovers and the plastic bullets, moving people away and down the road towards Milltown cemetery. Minutes later a civilian ambulance came screaming towards us. The funeral separated to let it pass.

Shortly afterwards someone came up to tell me that our Paddy had been in the ambulance, not in the Saracen. He had been shot in the back and seriously wounded. I went down along the funeral looking for his wife Anne Marie, for Colette, for my ma and da to tell them. Someone got a car to bring them to the Royal Hospital.

The rest of us continued to Milltown and buried Joe McDonnell. John Joe McGirl gave the oration; Eamon McCrory chaired the proceedings.

A week later I visited our Paddy in Musgrave Park military hospital, where he was under armed guard. He was badly shot up. I recalled that the last occasion on which I had visited him in hospital was that time after we had all got our BCG injections when my da and I had had to walk all the way from the Murph to Crawfordsburn. Paddy told me that he had been lying in a garden slipping in and out of consciousness during the fracas with the Saracen. The Brits had been kicking and punching him. He could see our Uncle Paddy. The Brit who had shot him was saying, 'Die, you bastard!' and as his head had filled with red darkness our Paddy remembered saying over and over again: 'No, I'm not going to die. I'm not going to die . . .'

Martin Hurson died on 13 July after forty-six days on hunger strike. I never knew him but I knew that he came from a farming family in County Tyrone, where he had played football for the local Galbally GAA club. I had campaigned for him in the general election south of the border the previous month when over 4,500 people had given him their first preference vote in the Longford/ Westmeath constituency.

I am told that members of the British cabinet met every day to discuss the hunger strike and that the only other time there had been such a focus on Ireland was during the treaty negotiations in 1921. We were at the same time, with the approval of Thatcher, dealing with British government officials through a line of communication which was mostly by phone through a third party. I never got any particular sense of her character during this period, although of course she was a hate figure for nationalists and republicans, but I do think that I understand what happened when her meeting with Cardinal Ó Fiaich turned into a shouting match. He went to her with a sense of who he was as an Irish man, with a sense of history, of nationhood, which I think that other representatives going to see British ministers didn't possess. When she began to lecture him, he responded strongly.

Margaret Thatcher presented a public face as the Iron Lady who was 'not for turning', yet she was no stranger to expediency. During our contact in the course of the hunger strike, her government representatives approached us in advance of a world leaders' conference in Canada at which she was due to speak on 21 July. 'The Prime Minister,' they said, 'would like to announce at the conference that the hunger strike has ended.' They outlined the support we had and the support we didn't have, and then went on to tell us: 'This is what the Prime Minister is prepared to say.' They fed us a draft of the speech that Thatcher was going to deliver in Toronto, and there was no doubt that they were prepared to take amendments to her text from us if it had been possible to come to some sort of resolution at that time.

The international campaign of support for the five demands was, apart from in the USA and Britain and some of the solidarity groups, entirely spontaneous, because Sinn Féin was simply too small and didn't have a developed international perspective. The Dublin government, which did have the consular and diplomatic services, refused to use them. Instead of going to the British with an Irish position, Charlie Haughey came to us with an Irish version of the British position. When Mr Haughey tried to involve the European Human Rights Commission, he earned a stinging rebuke from Bobby Sands himself: 'Because Mr

Haughey has the means to end the H-Block/Armagh crisis and has consistently refused to do so, I view his prompting of my family as cynical and cold-blooded manipulation of people clearly vulnerable to this type of pressure. The Commissioners' intervention has been diversionary and has served to aid the British attempts to confuse the issue.'

In July a group of families was brought together by Father Faul at Toomebridge, at a meeting attended by Bernadette McAliskey. At Father Faul's request I met them later that night for what proved to be a very difficult discussion. Father Faul had almost persuaded some of the families that I could order an end to the hunger strike. Of course, he knew that this was not true. For me to undermine the hunger strikers would have been disastrous. When I explained this to the families, they accepted my explanation. The next day I reflected on our conversation and I then contacted Cardinal Ó Fiaich to arrange a visit to Long Kesh to talk to the hunger strikers.

On Wednesday, 29 July, I went to Long Kesh in the company of Owen Carron, now a candidate in the new election for Bobby's seat, and Seamus Ruddy of the IRSP. It took us an hour to pass through the various security checks from the main gate of Long Kesh to the prison hospital, as the screws, sullenly resentful of our presence, quizzed our escort and driver.

I had mixed feelings going into the prison, where I had been a reluctant resident myself. I knew both Kieran Doherty and Pat McGeown, two of the hunger strikers, and Bik, of course, and had written to or read notes from most of the others. Apart from a slight feeling of déjà vu, the prison, with its permanent prisoners, the screws and armed British soldiers, didn't disturb me, though in its grey hostility Long Kesh was a forbidding and intimidating place. My apprehension was about the physical state of the hunger strikers, and I feared that our arrival might falsely raise their hopes.

Brendan (Bik) McFarlane, Tom McElwee, Laurence McKeown, Matt Devlin, Pat McGeown, Paddy Quinn and Mickey Devine were assembled in the canteen of the prison hospital when we arrived. Paddy Quinn was in a wheelchair and sat with the others around two tables which had been pushed together in the centre of the room. Brendan, Pat McGeown and Matt had been taken from their cells to the prison hospital while the others, dressed in prison-issue pyjamas and dressing gowns, had been brought from their cells in the prison hospital itself. Kevin Lynch and Kieran Doherty were too ill to attend, but Bik indicated that he would make arrangements for us to see them later.

They all looked rough, prison-pale skin stretched across young skull-like faces, legs and arms indescribably thin, eyes with that penetrating look which I had often noticed among fellow prisoners in the past, and which Bobby Sands had described as 'that awful stare, of the pierced or glazed eyes, the tell-tale sign of the rigours of torture'. Someone else wrote that our eyes are the windows to our souls. The eyes of the blanket men, the hunger strikers, were the unshuttered, unveiled, curtainless windows through which one could see reflections of the intense cruelties they had endured.

As they smiled across the table at us, all my fears and apprehension vanished. Big Tom (McElwee) offered me a jug of spring water.

'*Ar mhaith leat deoch uisce?*' ('Would you like a drink of water?')

'*Ba mhaith,*' *arsa mise*. ('I would,' said I.)

'*Lean ar aghaidh, tá a lán uisce san áit seo,*' *arsa sé*. ('Go ahead, there's a lot of water in this place,' he said.)

There were a number of small white jugs of spring water, and two or three blue plastic mugs of ordinary tap water, on the table. The lads sat, as pensively as wine tasters, as I took a delicate swig from one of the white jugs.

'*Cad a shíleann tú faoi sin?*' ('What do you think of that?')

I took a longer slug. 'Hold on,' Big Tom admonished. 'It costs the British government a lot of money for that stuff.'

The screw at the large peephole at the end of the canteen peered in at the outburst of laughter which followed Tom's slagging. His appearance was greeted with bantering, in both Irish and English, among the boys. Otherwise the screws were ignored and spoken to, politely, only when necessary.

We were left alone again and began to discuss the hunger strike, the campaign outside, the British government's position and the hunger strikers' personal attitudes to events.

We outlined the situation to them. The lads were fully aware of all developments, but we persisted in detailing in a factual and harsh manner everything which had happened over the past few weeks. They sat quietly, smoking or sipping water, listening intently to what we had to say.

Occasionally Paddy Quinn, who was sitting beside me, used the spittoon which he held on his lap. Paddy, heavily bearded, was by far the worst looking of the hunger strikers.

As I talked, or listened to Owen Carron or Seamus Ruddy or Bik talking, I couldn't stop my eyes straying below the tables where the scrawny legs of the hunger strikers were stretched. We smoked in relays, in the absence of matches keeping our cigarettes alight by ensuring that somebody was always smoking, thus avoiding having to ask the screw for a light.

When we had finished our lengthy piece, a discussion involving everyone commenced. All the lads were crystal clear in their attitudes. There was no basis for a settlement. The British government were still persisting in their refusal to move meaningfully on work, association, or segregation. Yes, they knew they could come off the hunger strike at any time. Yes, they knew the movement would have no difficulties in explaining the end of the hunger strike. If there was an alternative to the strike, they wouldn't be on it. Five years of protest was too much. A reasonable and common-sense approach by the British would end, permanently, all the prison protests.

No, they were not motivated by a personal loyalty to Bobby, Raymond, Francie, Patsy, Martin or Joe. They knew the score; they didn't want to die, but they needed a settlement of the issues which caused the hunger strike before they would end their fasts. No, they were not driven by a personal loyalty to each other. Regardless of what the others chose to do, each was personally committed to the five demands and to the hunger strike. They were not under any duress.

Apologetically at first, because I knew all those things myself, I told the lads that I felt duty-bound to satisfy the clergymen and all those who were pressurising their families. I painted the darkest and blackest picture possible: between ten and twenty prisoners dead, nationalist Ireland demoralised, and no advance from the British government.

'You could all be dead,' I said. 'Everyone left in this room when we leave will be dead.'

'*Sin é*,' said somebody. ('That's it.') 'They won't break us. If we don't get the five demands, then the rest of the boys and the women will.'

'We're right,' declared another. 'The British government is wrong and if they think they can break us they're wrong twice. *Lean ar aghaidh*.' ('Keep going.')

By this time I was starting to feel absurd, but I persisted in probing them harshly, questioning them all, outlining the republican attitude to the hunger strike, explaining that we could go out and announce it had ended or that any one of them had finished it; but the lads, individually and collectively, remained unmoved.

By this time I had emptied two jugs of Tom McElwee's spring water, much to the amusement of Lorny McKeown and Matt Devlin.

'We're not letting you in again,' said Tom, as he went to get a refill.

'What about Danny Morrison?' somebody asked. 'We heard he was sick.'

'Working his ticket,' I replied.

'And your brother? How's he?'

Our gathering was starting to dissolve into a bantering session. Tom McElwee was trying on my glasses. Somebody was seriously and genuinely concerned that Bik had missed his tea. We were inundated with queries about the struggle outside, about their

309

families, about fellow prisoners, about the women in Armagh, the lads in the Crum.

Paddy Quinn informed us that his sight had gone since the meeting started. I spoke to him privately.

'*Ná bac,*' *arsa sé.* '*Lean ar aghaidh.*' ('Don't bother,' he said. 'Keep going.')

Bik arranged for us to go and see Kieran Doherty. I told the lads that I wouldn't tell Doc of their position.

'He knows it anyway,' someone said.

'We saw him last night.'

'I know,' said I.

Doc was propped up on one elbow; his eyes, unseeing, scanned the cell as he heard us entering.

'*Mise atá ann,*' ('It's me') said Brendan McFarlane.

'*Ahh Bik, cad é mar atá tú?*' *arsa Doc.* ('Ahh Bik, how are you?' Doc said.)

'*Nílim romh dhona, agus tú féin?*' ('I'm not too bad, and yourself?')

'*Tá mé go hiontach; tá daoine eile anseo? Cé . . . ?*' ('I'm great; are there other people here? Who . . . ?')

'*Tá Gerry Adams, Owen Carron agus Seamus Ruddy anseo. Teastaíonn uatha caint leat.*' ('Gerry Adams, Owen Carron and Seamus Ruddy are here. They want to speak to you.')

'*Gerry A', fáilte.*' ('Gerry A', welcome.') He greeted us all, his eyes following our voices. We crowded around the bed, the cell much too small for four visitors. I sat on the side of the bed. Doc, whom I hadn't seen in years, looked massive in his gauntness, as his eyes, fierce in their quiet defiance, scanned my face.

I spoke to him quietly and slowly, somewhat awed by the man's dignity and resolve and by the enormity of our mission.

He responded to my probing with patience.

'You know the score yourself,' he said. 'I've a week in me yet. How is Kevin (Lynch) holding out?'

'You'll both be dead soon. I can go out now, Doc, and announce that it's over.'

He paused momentarily, and reflected, then: 'We haven't got

our five demands and that's the only way I'm coming off. Too much suffered for too long, too many good men dead. Thatcher can't break us. *Lean ar aghaidh*. I'm not a criminal.'

I continued with my probing. Doc responded.

'For too long our people have been broken. The Free Staters, the church, the SDLP. We won't be broken. We'll get our five demands. If I'm dead . . . well, the others will have them. I don't want to die, but that's up to the Brits. They think they can break us. Well they can't.' He grinned self-consciously. '*Tiocfaidh ár lá*.' ('Our day will come.')

'How are you all keeping? I'm glad you came in. I can only see blurred shapes. I'm glad to be with friends. *Cá bhfuil Bik?* (Where is Bik?) Bik, stay staunch. How's the boys doing?'

We talked quietly for a few minutes. Owen got another ribbing about the election. We got up to go. I told Doc to get the screw to give us a shout if he wanted anything.

We shook hands, an old internee's hand-shake, firm and strong.

'Thanks for coming in, I'm glad we had that wee yarn. Tell everyone, all the lads, I was asking for them and . . .' He continued to grip my hand.

'Don't worry, we'll get our five demands. We'll break Thatcher. *Lean ar aghaidh*.'

Outside Doc's cell, the screw led us in to speak to Kieran's father, Alfie, and brother, Michael, who had just arrived to relieve Kieran's mother.

We spoke for about five minutes. I felt an immense solidarity with the Doherty family, broken-hearted, like all the families, as they watched Kieran die. Yet because they understood their son, they were prepared to accept his wishes and were completely committed to the five demands for which he was fasting.

Talking to Alfie, his eyes brimming with unshed tears, in the quiet cells in the H-Blocks of Long Kesh, I felt a raw hatred for the injustice which created this crisis. Alfie, concerned for us, had a quiet word with Bik McFarlane and left to sit with Kieran.

We went in to speak to Kevin Lynch's family. The prison

chaplains were with Kevin, and the screws had advised Bik that Kevin should not be disturbed. We spent a few minutes with Kevin's father and older brother. Kevin was totally determined to continue his fast, unless the five demands were conceded.

Kevin's father, distraught at his son's imminent death, told us of his anguish in the face of British intransigence. 'To rear a son and see him die like this . . .'

We left, unable to speak with Kevin. I paused at the open cell door: a priest knelt at Kevin's bedside, Kevin lay stretched on the prison bed. The screw closed the door on us.

Back to the canteen, Paddy Quinn, by now restricted to his cell, was absent. The lads asked us about Kevin and Doc's condition. Someone heard on the radio that the press were outside. One of the lads suggested that the hunger strikers write an agreed statement signed by them all.

'Send it out yourselves tomorrow. They'll think we solicited it from you,' I advised.

'They're not still at that?' said one of the lads in disgust. 'They must think we can't write.'

I scribbled out an account of our visit and read it to the boys. They suggested that we put in two paragraphs calling upon the Catholic hierarchy, SDLP and Dublin government to publicly pressurise the British government.

'And tell them to get off our families' backs.'

'Thank our supporters and all the prisoners' families.'

They dictated two paragraphs to me on these issues, then, satisfied at the final draft, we spent the last few minutes talking. Matt Devlin and Owen Carron; Seamus, Paddy, and Mickey Devine; myself and Brendan McFarlane. Then a few words with Pat McGeown, Tom and Lorny.

'Before we leave, have any of you any questions? You might never see us again.' I looked around at the thin, half-starved, defiant young men.

'Have we got any heavy gear yet?' one of them asked.

'Get us our five demands,' somebody else said.

'*Beidh an bua againn. Brisfimíd Maggie Thatcher.*' ('We'll win. We'll break Maggie Thatcher.')

We all shook hands. 'Mind yourselves, and tell our families we're sound.'

'*Beannacht Dé ort,*' arsa Bik, '*agus bí cúramach.*' (God bless you,' said Bik, 'and be careful.')

'*Tiocfaidh ár lá,*' ('Our day will come,') they shouted as we departed.

We left through the same gates we had entered by, past watch-towers, Brit soldiers, RUC men and screws.

We went out the last gate to where the press were gathered. The huge double gates of Long Kesh slammed shut behind us. I never saw Kevin Lynch or Kieran Doherty, Tom McElwee or Mickey Devine alive again.

Kevin Lynch died on 1 August after seventy-one days on hunger strike. A member of the Irish National Liberation Army (INLA), the military wing of the Irish Republican Socialist Party (IRSP), I never knew him, but I came to know his parents. The INLA, because of their nature, and because of their size, didn't have a good support network. In the case of Kevin Lynch a representative of the INLA had just gone to the family and told them: 'Kevin's going on hunger strike.' Of course, they bridled at that because they hadn't heard this from him. The upshot was that Kevin's people sought to liaise with us in Sinn Féin, and we ended up keeping them informed. His family came from Dungiven in County Derry; their son had gone on hunger strike and was dying; it was terribly hard for them to take. Later, from being in despair about their son, they came to be very proud of him.

Kieran Doherty, who had been elected by the people of Cavan/Monaghan to the Dublin parliament, died on 2 August after seventy-three days on hunger strike.

Tom McElwee died on 8 August after sixty-five days on hunger strike.

Mickey Devine died on 20 August after sixty-six days on hunger strike.

On the same day, Owen Carron was elected as MP for Fermanagh/South Tyrone, exceeding Bobby Sands's vote by 800.

On 3 October, over a month later, the six remaining hunger strikers ended their protest. In the meantime, some of the hunger strikers had taken individual decisions to end their hunger strikes. Ten men had sacrificed their lives and massive popular support for their stand had been shown in demonstrations, funerals and elections.

The hunger strikes ended when Catholic clergy intervened with relatives of hunger strikers to encourage them to bring about an end to the fasts by requesting medical help. Even without their intervention, it was inevitable that some hunger strikers would eventually pull back in the face of death, and that some families would move to take their sons or husbands off the hunger strike. The prisoners had explored, to what I thought were quite extraordinary lengths, the possibility of being able to prevent their families from doing so. Some of them even explored whether they could legally prevent anyone from taking them off hunger strike by signing some kind of a will or testament. But when some ended their fasts and it was clear that this was the beginning of the end, I had no regrets whatsoever about their decisions. My regrets I reserved for those who had died; my anger I reserved for the British government, which could quite easily have reached an honourable compromise in the face of the ultimate in selfless dedication to a cause.

On 6 October, my thirty-third birthday, the British government announced that all prisoners would be allowed to wear their own clothes. Adjustments to the prison regime began to be made along the lines of the five demands. The prisoners had insisted upon their identity as prisoners in a war of national liberation, and they had been recognised as such throughout the world. Britain had been exposed as an intransigent force clinging to its last remnant of colonial control. The political and moral standing of Irish republicanism had never been higher.

The deaths of the hunger strikers and the H–Block/Armagh

campaign had built up a process of republicanisation which was at first gradual and uncertain, but which gained in strength as rivulets flowing into streams flowed into the flood waters of a broad river of resistance. Republicans who had dropped out of the movement having done their time in prison responded to the suffering of the hunger strikers and came back to the movement, bringing with them valuable experience and maturity. There was a feeling and a reality in nationalist communities that the hunger strike had done away with the role of spectator; the atmosphere resembled that of the insurrectionary period between August '69 and the fall of Stormont. Armed struggle, which had for some years in the '70s been almost the only form of struggle being waged, only needed a small number of people to engage in it. But during the hunger strike, people played active roles which could be as limited or as important as billposting, writing letters, taking part in numerous forms of protest, or joining electoral campaigns both north and south of the border. Everyone could play their part.

Identification with the IRA increased very significantly. Although they eased back on operations during the hunger strike, at the funerals of hunger strikers, crowds of tens of thousands of mourners applauded when IRA colour parties appeared. There were some strange consequences: after the hunger strike IRA volunteers came out on the streets of West Belfast to engage in armed action, only to have to withdraw because people were crowding around, applauding and patting them on the back.

In 1976 the British government had tried to criminalise the republican prisoners. They had resisted criminalisation through the blanket and 'no-wash' protests, and ultimately through the hunger strikes. In 1981 the republican prisoners criminalised the British government.

In the months after the hunger strike, we all tried to recover from the emotion and the intensity of that period. All of us grieved. It was a time for reflection, even as we intensified our publicity and propaganda efforts; as we reviewed the standing of Sinn Féin and the mood of our support base; as we learned the lessons of mass mobilisation and popular actions, of electoralism and broad front work.

That Christmas, Colette and I called as usual with Gearóid to see our parents. As snow fell on St Stephen's Day I went for a walk through the Murph, and I thought on the year that had passed. Strolling through the old familiar streets, I thought of the children of these houses, of their excitement at the snow and at their presents of new bikes or prams and other toys which Santa had brought them, and I thought of my own childhood and of my happy times here. Everywhere I walked marked some childish escapade and later teenage adventures as well. There had, after all, been a life before 1969. But I also passed the homes of friends who had died. I paused at places where some had been gunned down.

It was a long time and a long journey from Divis Street in 1964, from the security of Abercorn Street North before that and the innocent fun of childhood in Divismore Park. Those days were gone. Even 11 Divismore Park itself was gone. Jerry-built structures are no match for British army vehicles. Number 11 was finally demolished by the Housing Executive a couple of years ago.

Many of my childhood friends had died. Too many. For every section of our people there was so much pain. We wanted equality and justice. We wanted freedom. We demanded peace. For all the people of our island.

A thin marzipan layer of snow lay on the Black and Divis Mountains. I could see the black flags for the hunger strikers still hanging from telegraph poles and lamp posts on the Whiterock Road. But the writing on the cemetery wall gave hope for the future. Now things would never be the same again. The graffiti captured the new mood: *Tiocfaidh ár lá* – Our day will come.

Epilogue

The extraordinary sacrifices of the hunger strikers impressed themselves on nationalist consciousness in a way and to an extent which the establishments in both Britain and Ireland underestimated. In the wake of the H–Block and Armagh prison crises the war escalated sharply in the north and in Britain. Indeed the hunger strikes proved to be a watershed in the long struggle between the British state and the Irish movement for national independence. They and their aftermath marked, I believe, the beginning of the end of British rule in Ireland.

Nationalist Ireland underwent an extraordinary collective experience as the hunger strikers died in the face of obduracy on the part of the British government and unwillingness to act on the part of the Dublin government. After the deaths of these republican political prisoners, nationalists reacted with intense resentment to the attempts by both the British and Irish governments to maintain that it was the IRA which was the cause of every wrong. The ritual condemnations of the IRA rang hollow in the context of the continuing injustices suffered by nationalists in the occupied north-eastern counties.

It was against this backdrop, and with the experience of the elections of prisoners north and south, as well as a substantial influx of a new generation of activists, that Sinn Féin adopted an electoral strategy. In our first electoral outing in the north we received over 10% of the votes cast and five of our candidates were elected, on an abstentionist basis, to an assembly sponsored by the latest British Secretary of State, James Prior. In West Belfast, where I was elected, we topped the poll in a landslide result. British propaganda that the republican struggle was an unrepresentative criminal conspiracy was exposed as a lie.

Our struggle, faced with the armed forces of the imperial power, had limited itself for long periods to an almost exclusively military perspective and had failed to build a political alternative. Now, in the wake of the hunger strikes, it had established a greater political and moral weight than at any time in my lifetime.

I had joined Sinn Féin at a time when it was weak and disorganised after the IRA's abortive border campaign of the 1950s. The republican split in 1970 robbed the republican struggle of many of its more political elements. This created a narrower perspective at leadership level. Those who left to form the 'Officials' moved rapidly away from republicanism. The civil rights campaign continued after the eruption of war between the British army and the IRA, but political mobilisation declined under the pressures of war, while the kind of political agitation I had been engaged in during the late '60s was overtaken by the urgent priority of defence which had arisen from the pogroms.

Following the revitalisation of the mass movement during the hunger strikes, Sinn Féin became more deeply involved in and committed to a wide range of political activity at community level. Our electoral mandate was underpinned when we received over 13% of the vote throughout the north and I was elected MP for West Belfast in 1983. In alliances with communities through-out the constituency we set in train a tightly focused series of campaigns to reverse the worst effects of the discrimination which the people of West Belfast had endured for generations. I was especially gratified at the successes of the housing campaigns which in time culminated in the wholesale demolition of the flats in Turf Lodge, and the slums of Moyard, Divis, Springhill and Unity Flats. Given that we had opposed the building of Divis

Flats in the first instance, the success of the Divis campaign was particularly satisfying. In the Thatcher era, with its emasculation of the trade union movement, its sell-off of public utilities and the demolition of the welfare state, for me these campaigns were the only significant working-class victories of that period. Similar campaigns were reinvigorated or initiated on social, economic and cultural issues. Now large numbers of energetic young activists tackled the new tasks of electoral and community political campaigning.

In 1982 I had sought to open up discussion and public debate about the achievement of peace through dialogue and a democratic settlement. In 1983, after I was elected President of Sinn Féin, I tried to advance this proposition and I made clear that our party was willing to open up discussions with the Dublin government and the SDLP. The following year, I and some of my friends were wounded in a murder attack by loyalists. It later emerged that the gang which gunned us down in Belfast city centre was acting with the knowledge of British military intelligence. Later the same year, an IRA bomb attack in Brighton almost killed Margaret Thatcher, architect of the hunger strike deaths, and her Cabinet.

Our election successes set alarm bells ringing in both London and Dublin. The establishment became seriously concerned that the SDLP could be displaced as the sole representative of nationalists in the north. In 1985, in an attempt to counter the rise of Sinn Féin, the Hillsborough Treaty – the Anglo-Irish Agreement – was signed by the London and Dublin governments against a background of widespread and intense unionist opposition.

In 1986 I argued that the military stalemate between the British and republican forces could only be resolved by a political settlement; there was no military solution. By now Sinn Féin had built a solid political platform, from which we launched a peace strategy. This was soon to become our primary political objective as we engaged in dialogue with a wide range of groups and individuals, including members of Protestant churches, peace and reconciliation groups and political organisations.

The evolution of Sinn Féin strategy since the hunger strikes has been the catalyst for much of the change in the political climate. Republicans have always sought to embrace alternatives to war. Those who engaged in armed struggle never regarded it as the sole form of struggle, and on several occasions the IRA sought to explore moves towards a peace settlement. Those who engaged in armed struggle did so as a last resort, feeling that it was an option which arose from the closing off of alternative means of achieving progress. The conflict had been militarised by the British, but it remained essentially political and demanded a political solution.

In my contacts with religious, political and other groups and individuals I outlined the republican view that if there was to be peace, a democratic solution to the conflict needed to be found. In our view that meant an end to British rule. However, Sinn Féin representatives also emphasised in both private discussions and public speeches the aim of discovering the common ground upon which unionists and nationalists could agree to differ, could live together in some kind of mutual accord. In particular I sought to stress the long-held republican aim of uniting 'the whole people of Ireland, to abolish the memory of past dissensions and to substitute the common name of Irish person in place of the denomination of Protestant, Catholic and Dissenter . . .'

The line of communication between republicans and the British which had been used during the hunger strikes of 1980–81 was re-activated by the British government in 1990, leading to a three-year period of dialogue between us. In early 1993 the British proposed that Sinn Féin and British government delegations should meet for an intensive round of negotiations, after which, they asserted, the IRA would be convinced that armed struggle was no longer necessary. The Sinn Féin leadership conveyed a request to the IRA from the British government for a temporary cessation of IRA operations to facilitate discussions, and the IRA responded in May 1993 by agreeing to a two-week suspension. However, at this point the British government backed off, influenced in part at least by the Tory party's difficulties which led Mr Major to depend at that time on unionist support in the House of Commons.

The most important and productive of the contacts developed in the 1980s and 1990s was between myself and the SDLP leader, John Hume. In April 1993 John Hume and I issued the first of several statements of the results of our more than five years of dialogue. We had reached agreement on a process which we believed could create the conditions for a lasting peace; its success depended upon the responses of the British and Irish governments and the IRA. The leadership of the IRA responded that 'If the political will exists or can be created it could provide the basis for peace.' The Dublin government pledged its support. The British government, however, refused to respond positively.

Following contact with the Irish government of Albert Reynolds, a set of core political principles was agreed on the basis of a proposal to move us all out of conflict and towards a negotiated settlement. This Irish Peace Initiative, which was popularly known as the Hume/Adams proposals, contained a process and a dynamic aimed at brokering a new accord with the British government and finding agreement with the unionists to create the conditions for a lasting peace in Ireland.

It was coolly received by the British government, but our initiative had already sparked off a wide, popular debate in Ireland and Britain, which showed enormous support for a political resolution to the conflict. The subsequent emergence of the Downing Street Declaration between the British and Irish governments in December 1993 was largely in response to the document which John Hume and I had given them earlier in the year. The Downing Street Declaration was a significant step by the two governments. But it did not contain the democratic potential or the dynamic which John Hume and I and the Irish government had signed up to. Notwithstanding this, Sinn Féin tried to come to the declaration in a constructive way.

But following the Downing Street Declaration there was a frustrating period in which the British government stalled the peace process by, in particular, refusing to clarify issues for Sinn

Féin or to recognise our democratic mandate. Eventually, the British Prime Minister and other government spokespersons did clarify aspects of the Declaration, and in May 1994 the British government finally responded to a list of questions from Sinn Féin.

By this time John Hume and I and the Irish Taoiseach Albert Reynolds had advanced our project once again. We had established a consensus on how a lasting peace could be won and by now we had also secured the active support of influential elements of Irish America. The dynamic which this presented and the commitments entered into created the conditions in which the IRA announced its historic 'complete cessation of military operations' from 31 August 1994. After twenty-five years of unbroken and unbowed resistance, the IRA leadership made it clear that its intention was to enhance the search for a negotiated peace settlement.

For many republicans, myself included, the days after the IRA announcement were charged with emotion. As I was speaking to a large crowd which had gathered outside Connolly House on the Andersonstown Road our Paddy reminded me that this was Patrick Mulvenna's anniversary. I could see Patrick's parents in the throng. All that week the families of dead IRA volunteers gathered spontaneously at the republican plot in Milltown cemetery. Colette met Mrs Farrell, the mother of Mairead Farrell, the IRA volunteer who was executed by the SAS with two comrades in Gibraltar. Mrs Farrell, a dignified, graceful woman, told her with tears in her eyes: 'I'm sorry my Mairead wasn't here for this.'

The sense of hope throughout Ireland was palpable. The IRA cessation was an historic, unprecedented initiative by an undefeated army. It was welcomed universally and acknowledged even by the British Prime Minister as 'the best opportunity for peace in 75 years', and there was a great popular expectation that the British government would seize the opportunity which had been presented to it.

However, the British government, and consequently the

unionists, responded in a very negative way to the IRA cessation. In total contradiction to his pre-cessation stance, Mr Major placed obstacle after obstacle along the path towards peace. This strategy aimed to slow down the momentum of the peace process, to undermine it and to replace its broadly democratic agenda with a narrower one which reflected the British government's interests.

While stalling on negotiations, the British strategy on other fronts was equally negative. The summer of 1995 saw the release from prison of British Paratrooper Lee Clegg, who served only two years for the murder of a seventeen-year-old West Belfast girl. Clegg was promoted on his return to the British army. British troop levels remained at their 1994 levels, repressive legislation was renewed, and a number of provocative Orange parades were forced through Catholic areas by the RUC. Conditions for Irish political prisoners in Britain seriously deteriorated.

In these circumstances, the utmost determination was required of all the partners to the Irish peace initiative in pursuit of progress to all-party negotiations. Even in the face of a minimalist approach by London it was still possible to maintain a certain confidence in the peace strategy by dint of alternative initiatives, and John Hume and I applied ourselves to this task.

This required the vigorous pursuit by Dublin of the objectives of the process. The increasing influence of Irish America also stymied the British approach to a degree, but with the collapse of the Dublin government led by Albert Reynolds and the emergence of a new coalition government led by John Bruton, there was a significant realignment of Irish political forces. The momentum of the peace process began increasingly to falter in the face of British and unionist stalling.

Before the IRA cessation, the British government had spoken of a start being made to peace negotiations after a period of three months following an IRA cessation. Over a year later, in November 1995, they had still not moved even to suggest a date when talks might begin. London had built a barrier to progress around a new precondition – the demand for the surrender or 'decommissioning' of IRA weapons. Then, after intense diplomatic activity, with the peace process on the point of collapse and on the eve of an historic visit to Britain and Ireland by the US President Bill Clinton, who had played a consistently even-handed and positive role in support of the peace process, Mr Major and Mr Bruton signed an agreement to establish a twin-track approach. This involved a political track led by the two governments to agree an agenda and procedures for all-party talks and an international body headed up by US Senator George Mitchell to investigate ways to resolve the decommissioning issue.

Although Sinn Féin had serious reservations about the British government's commitment to this twin-track approach, we engaged fully with both tracks. Our engagement included a written and a number of oral submissions to the Mitchell body in line with Sinn Féin's policy for demilitarisation as well as our suggestions for all-party talks. The unionist parties refused to engage with the twin-track approach. Mr Paisley ignored both tracks and the UUP would deal only with the decommissioning track.

On 16 January 1996 the Mitchell report was published. I welcomed it, saying: 'It provides a basis for moving forward so that all matters can be settled to the satisfaction of all sides as part of the process . . . in other words the Mitchell report points to a possible avenue into all-party talks.'

But within hours of its release John Major unilaterally dumped the Mitchell report. He retained the decommissioning precondition, which Mitchell had come down against, and added a new precondition – elections – as proposed by the unionists. No date for the commencement of all-party talks, which had been promised for the end of February, was offered.

When I and other republicans attempted to warn that the British government was stretching the peace process to breaking point, we were castigated by our political opponents. But as hopes of peace negotiations died, after almost eighteen months of the cessation, breakdown became inevitable.

As soon as I heard the rumours circulating within the media of an IRA statement announcing the end of the cessation, I phoned John Hume. I spoke to the Taoiseach's office. I phoned the White House. I remembered that Tánaiste Dick Spring was in Washington. By now there was news of a bomb alert in London. In an effort to warn Mr Spring of the developing situation I phoned the Irish ambassador in the USA. As newsflash followed newsflash, as the television pictures of Canary Wharf were shown, and as word of the casualties, and later the two fatalities emerged, my sense of sadness turned to sorrow as I thought of those who had died and been injured, and of their families. The IRA was clearly responsible for the explosion in London and for its consequences. But the responsibility for the breakdown in the peace process lay with John Major. An unprecedented opportunity for peace foundered on the refusal of the British government and the unionist leaders to enter into honest dialogue and substantive negotiations. Mr Major refused to honour commitments given to Sinn Féin, to John Hume and to the Irish government. There was a year and a half of no war and neither London nor the unionist leaders felt compelled to move beyond their own narrow interests.

Even as the dust settled, the establishment in Dublin and London were returning to their old agenda of isolating Sinn Féin in an effort to pressurise the IRA. I warned that this was sheer folly. Breakdowns in the peace in South Africa and the Middle East encouraged leaders there to redouble their efforts and to intensify the dialogue, not to abandon it.

As the storm of reaction broke around Sinn Féin in the aftermath of these attacks, Mr Major announced a date for talks, but even now the date was hedged with preconditions. All-party talks were to begin on 10 June, but only after a confused and confusing election which was to be held on 30 May. For those parties which received a negotiating mandate, Mr Major declared, the elections would provide a route, 'clear, direct and automatic', into all-party negotiations. Except for Sinn Féin.

Sinn Féin and the SDLP argued vigorously against the elections and against another unionist proposal for a forum, an assembly of all those receiving mandates. Our objections were ignored.

In the election, our party increased our share of the vote in all eighteen constituencies throughout the six counties. We received 15.5% of the overall vote, or 42% of the nationalist vote. The vote for Sinn Féin in West Belfast was the highest for any party in any constituency in the north. In Belfast, my home town and the second largest city in Ireland, Sinn Féin became the largest party and for the first time ever nationalists in Belfast outpolled the unionists.

On 10 June talks, now renamed multi-party talks, were launched at Stormont by the two governments. Sinn Féin's seventeen elected peace negotiators were locked out.

Almost a week later, on 15 June, a large bomb exploded in Manchester. It was almost as if we were back to the beginning again.

But no!

We cannot be deflected from the task of building peace on this island. History has placed a challenge at all our doors. The people of Ireland, from every corner of our country and from throughout the Irish diaspora across the world have expressed their yearning for a lasting peace settlement and a new democracy. Building a new accord which can win the allegiance and agreement of all sections of our people may be a daunting challenge, but it is the challenge facing everyone in political leadership on these islands. If this challenge is to be translated into reality then we must all respond to it with courage and imagination.

It will not be easy. The road ahead will be difficult and dangerous and risky for all of us, but working together I am convinced we can succeed. It is my conviction that we will have a peace settlement in Ireland. This will grow from an inclusive process of negotiation, led by the two governments and involving Sinn Féin alongside the other parties. In my view, the people of Britain also support this objective. They too want a lasting peace.

This will be arrived at when peace strategies and processes are converted into a new beginning for both unionists and nationalists, and when a settlement between the people of Britain and the people of the island of Ireland, based on respect for our mutual independence, is achieved.

I am convinced that if we are resilient, if we dig deep, we can overcome all obstacles.

The Nobel laureate Seamus Heaney put it well: 'Once in a lifetime the longed for tidal wave of justice can rise up and hope and history rhyme.'

Let us ignore the naysayers and the begrudgers.

Let us confound the sceptics and the cynics.

Let us make hope and history rhyme.

Gerry Adams
Belfast, 16 June 1996

Index

Abercorn Street North 3, 23–4
abstentionism 123–4, 129–30,
    248, 279
'active abstentionism' 248
'active republicanism' 248
activists, republican, Bogside
    113
Adams, Anne (sister) 4, 7, 8, 31,
    138
Adams, Anne Marie
    (sister–in–law) 304
Adams, Annie, née Hannaway
    (mother) 3, 19–20
    rearing family 4, 15, 17, 18–19
    children not surviving 31
    and Divismore Park 6, 153–4
    and GA's marriage 174
    to Long Kesh 234
    and hunger strike 301
Adams, Colette (wife) see
    McArdle, Colette
Adams, Davy (uncle) and wife

Sheila 3, 21, 22, 25
Adams, Deirdre (sister) 7, 138
Adams, Dominic (uncle) and
    wife Maggie 22, 42, 67,
    183, 233
Adams, Dominic (brother) 7,
    137
  in Long Kesh 233
Adams, Elizabeth (aunt) 22
Adams, Frances (sister) 7, 226
Adams, Frank (uncle) 3, 21, 22,
    148
Adams, Gearóid (son) 231,
    234–5, 251, 252–3, 270, 316
Adams, Gerry (father) 3, 22, 29
    rearing family 4–5, 14, 16, 19,
    29–30
    gaoled for attempted murder
    23
    worker 31–2, 39
    political interests 32
    home improvements 39–40

329

chairman, Irish Republican
    Felons Association 42
religion 43
and Bogside defence 111, 118
against British Army 136
arrested and beaten 139
blanket strike 286
arrested 152
and GA's marriage 173–4
in Long Kesh 196
released 197
feud victim 255
and hunger–strike 301
Adams, Gerry:
birth 1948 3
childhood homes 4–7
childhood exploits 8–12
Kennedy's Bakery episode
    14–17
at St Finian's De La Salle
    school 20–1, 42
living with Granny Adams
    21–7
stammer 22
youthful reading 23
love of dogs 24–5
rarely in town 28
learns facts of life 29–31
to Dublin 32–3
religious instruction 33, 35
first confession 35–7
cycling 38
television 38–9
St Mary's Grammar School
    39, 43–8
helps father on do–it–yourself
    39–41
political background 42

schools 42–3
Irish language 45
Orange march 46
sexual stirrings 48–9
political interests awakened
    51–6
work at the Ark Bar 56–8
political activist 58–9, 76
fired from the Ark 62
new job at the Duke of York
    62
motorcycle 67
hitch–hiking holiday 66–70
hunting with gun 68–70
first suit 71–2
learns more about politics
    73–98
arrested by RUC 79
press officer Andersonstown
    Republican Club 82–3
first public speech 90
first television appearance 98
given administrative work to
    do 109, 111
post–Bogside, editing The
    Barricade 117
chair, Sinn Féin local group
    120
and the republican movement
    122–3
suspended from local
    leadership 128
work in dairy 133
a target for the British Army
    137–8
story written about the IRA
    168–71
marriage to Colette McArdle

173–6
on the run 176, 182–3, 184–6
arrest as Joe McGuigan 189
interrogation 190–2
to *Maidstone* prison ship
    192–6
hunger–strikes 194–5, 197
to Long Kesh 196–8
release 198
meets British officials 1972
    199–200
arrested 217–18
beating 218–19
reinternment 220–1
back in Long Kesh 222–51
attempts escapes 229–31,
    231–2
public profile 240–1
sentences for escapes 241
study agenda 243, 246
writing articles 247–9
pamphlet *Peace in Ireland* 249
book *Cage Eleven* 249
on the run again 253
work with Sinn Féin 253–84
discussion with the Church
    257–60
arrest 260
responsibility for Sinn Féin
    publications 262
political work 263–5
arrested, to Castlereagh 266
charged as IRA member 267
to Crumlin Road prison
    268–70
in H–block 271–4
trial and release 274–5
elected a vice–president of
    Sinn Féin 275
presses political solution
    277–8
prison campaign 281–4
visit to Long Kesh 306–14
elected to West Belfast 317,
    318
elected president of Sinn Féin
    318
wounded in loyalist attack 319
Irish Peace Initiative 321
Adams, Liam (brother) 7, 8, 10,
    11, 13, 16, 41, 139, 152
in Long Kesh 224, 233
Adams, Margaret, née Begley,
    'Granny Adams' 3, 5, 19,
    21, 43
GA living with 21–7
character 22–3
death 148
Adams, Margaret (aunt) 22, 184
Adams, Margaret (sister)
childhood 3, 7, 8, 15, 17,
    19, 22, 35
and Hannaway family 27
at work 39
politics 132, 255
Adams, Maura (sister) 7, 31
Adams, Paddy (uncle) 22,
    32–3, 43, 303
Adams, Paddy (brother) 4, 7, 8,
    9–10, 12–14, 16, 25, 29–30,
    38, 41
tuberculosis 28–9
bar work 65
seeks shelter 103
fighting 105
arrested 139, 179

in Long Kesh 196, 224, 233
released 197
and Bobby Sands' death 296
injured at MacDonnell funeral
304
Adams, Peter (uncle) 22
Adams, Seán (uncle) 3, 5, 21, 22,
148
Adams, Sean (brother) 7, 16, 31
in Long Kesh 233
Agnew, Paddy, elected to Dáil
299
Alex 175, 176, 242
Amnesty International, report
261, 282
An Phoblacht 262
Andersonstown, troubles 1969
112, 114
Andersonstown Republican
Club 82
Ardoyne 94, 97
riots 1970 139
riots 1971 154
Ardoyne defence committee
94–5
Arigna mines, strike 86–7
Ark Bar, Belfast 56–8, 59
Armagh 154
Armagh women's prison 279,
282, 286
armed struggle 319
nature 172–3
and Sinn Féin 283, 315
Army *see* British Army
Atkins, Humphrey 276, 291
Auld, Archie 163
Auxiliaries organisation 113, 126

B Specials 59, 95, 106, 107
to be demobbed 116, 117, 121
Ballymurphy estate 5–7, 18
life after Bogside 118–19
taken by the Paras 157–61
against the British Army
136–7
Ballymurphy Tenants'
Association 84, 135
Bannon, Jimmy 5
Barnes, Joe 274
Barrett, Daniel, death 303
The Barricade 117
barricades 1969 113, 117–18, 119
Beattie, Desmond, death 150
Beechmount, bomb at Easter
parade 259
Begley, Gerry 21
Begley, Margaret *see* Adams,
Margaret
Behan, Brendan 196
Belfast:
history 51
in 1940s 3–4
republicans, against Dublin
126–7
traffic ban 209
Belfast Telegraph 59, 208–9
Bell, Ivor 201, 204, 228, 240
Bennett Report 260
Black Mountain 12–13, 38
'blanket' protests 271, 273–4,
281–2, 286, 315
'Bloody Friday' 21 July 1972 209
'Bloody Sunday' 30 January
1972 179–81
comparison with Bloody
Friday 209–10

Bo the dog 144
Boal, Desmond 50, 258–9
Bodenstown, and Republicans
    81
Bogside 94, 99–116, 180–1
bomb warnings 209
Bond, Bridget 84
Bossence, Ralph 'Bud' 63–4, 241
Britain, relations with Ireland
    1–2, 4
British, view of Northern
    Ireland 277
British Army
    in Bogside 1969 107, 109, 110
    after Bogside 119, 129, 134
    protecting Orange marches
        135, 137
    against nationalists 134, 135–6
    against rioters 1970 138–9,
        140–1
    attacked by IRA 141
    attacks on Ballymurphy 143–5
    first soldier's death by IRA
        148
    greater activity 1971 150
    dawn raids 1971 151
    size increased 152
    patrols 176–7
    with UDA 201–2, 206–7
    reopens war 207
    Operation Motorman 210–11
    into Long Kesh camp 239
    behaviour 276–7
British Government
    talks with IRA 1972 199–200
    allows own clothes to
        prisoners 314
    contact with republicans 1990
        320
Brolly, Francie 268
Brooke, Basil 53
'Brownie' articles 247, 250–1,
    274
Bryson, Jim (alias Emerson) 184,
    202, 270
    death 225–6
Bunting, Ronnie 277
Burns, Gerard 274
Burns, Paddy 193
Butler, Eddie 160
Butler, Paddy 208

Cahill, Frank 84, 118, 134–5,
    136
Cahill, Joe 125, 166–7
Cahill, Tess 138
Cahill, Tom 133, 149, 194,
    217–18, 220
    in Long Kesh 222
Callaghan, Davie 159, 160
Callaghan, James 98, 109, 116,
    119
    in Northern Ireland 117
    1978 Government 276
Cameron Commission 118
Campaign for Nuclear
    Disarmament (CND) 64
Campaign for Social Justice 39,
    60, 85
Canavan, Tony, hunger strike
    216
Carabine, Desi 7
Carrington, Peter (Lord
    Carrington) 187, 209
Carron, Owen 293, 296, 300,
    306, 308, 310, 311, 312

elected MP 314
Castlereagh Barracks 260
Catholic Church:
offended by people's defence,
Bogside 111
influence on ending of
hunger–strike 314
role in politics 257–8
reform 39
Catholic Ex–Servicemen's
Association 114
Catholics, treatment in Northern
Ireland 44, 60–1, 78
see also pogroms
céilís 80
censorship in Ireland 280
Central Citizens' Defence
Committee (CCDC) 117,
119
Channon, Paul 203–4
Church see Catholic Church
Citizens' Defence Association,
Derry 97, 100
citizens' defence committees 117
civil disobedience campaign 173
civil rights committees 92, 173
Clady River 45
Clancy Brothers 80
Clark, James Chichester– 98,
104, 116, 148
Clarke, Bobby 159
Clarke, Cleeky 242, 274
Clarke, Joe 162
Clarke, Seamus 274
Clinton, Bill 324
Clonard 110, 147
Clonard Monastery 33
Cloonagh House 55–6

Coalisland, riots 102
Coalisland Conference 283
Comber, La Mon Hotel, bombs
at 265, 266, 268
Communist Party 62
Coney, Hugh, death 229
confessions, admissible in court
214, 261, 282
Connolly, James 26, 64, 73
Connolly, Joan, death 159
Coogan, Owen 'Daddy' 218, 220
in Long Kesh 222
Corr, Joseph, death 161
Corry, Patrick, death 97
Costello, Seamus 123, 245
death 245
Council of Ireland 215, 235–6
'counter–insurgency
architecture' 261
courts, juryless 214
CR gas 238
Craig, William 116–17, 201
Vanguard movement 195
Craigavon, Lord 54
Crane, Teddy 274
Creasey, Major General
Timothy 'Bull' 275
criminalisation of political
prisoners 284, 286, 315
Crossen, Gerry, death 188
Crumlin Road Prison 242,
268–70
screws at 269–70
CS gas 99, 107, 135, 137–8,
140–1
Cumann na mBan 27
Curran, Frank 9, 10, 11, 28, 65

Curran, Harry 7, 9, 10, 11, 28, 65
Curran, Major L E 78
Currie, Austin 147
Cusack, Seamus, death 150

DUP (Democratic Unionist Party) 216
Dáil Éireann 1919 74–5
Daily Mirror 241
Daly, Miriam 277
de Valera, Eamon 4, 26, 59
    death 188–9
Declaration of Independence 74
Declaration of Rights 116
Delaney, Dee, death 86
Democratic Unionist Party (DUP) 216
Dempsey, Jimmy 303
Dempsey, John, death 301–3
Derry 90, 180
    orange parades 98, 99
    fighting 1971 154
    Bloody Sunday 30 January 1972 179–81
    Operation Motorman 210–11
Derry March 1969 92
Devine, Mickey 306, 312
    death 313
Devlin, Bernadette (later McAliskey):
    MP 94, 181, 278, 306
    attempted assassination 277
    in election 1979 279
    and Bobby Sands 292–3
Devlin, Matt, hunger–strike 306, 307, 309, 312
Devlin, Paddy 117, 147, 198

Diplock Courts 261
Diplock Report 1972 214
'dirty protests' 281–2, 315
'disorderly behaviour' 142
Divis Flats 88–9, 101
Divis Street 49–50, 102
Divismore Park 8–9
    killing field 160–1
    no.11 6–7, 18, 153–4, 316
Doherty, Alfie 311
Doherty, Eddie, death 160
Doherty, Kieran:
    elected to Dáil 299, 313
    hunger–strike 306, 307, 310
    death 313
Doherty, Michael 311
Dolan, Joe 65
Donegal holiday 66–7
Donoghue's, Dublin 87
Doran, Anthony 83, 124
Dougal, John, death 208
Downing Street Declaration 321
Drain, Seanie 46–7
Drumm, Jimmy 224, 250, 264, 295
Drumm, Maire 141, 150, 215, 250
    death 250
Drumshanbo (Co. Leitrim), summer camp 85–6
Dublin:
    visits by GA 32–3, 42, 67
    loyalist bomb 236
Dublin Arms Trial 128
Dublin Government 320–1
    and Belfast 127–8
    and Derry 100–1
    and hunger–strikes 294

refugee camps 161
and Bobby Sands 298
Dubliners (group) 63, 80
Dudley, Martin 207
Duke of York pub, Belfast 62–3,
90, 96
farewell to 104
Dungiven riots 102
Dynan, Dick 51

Easter Rising 1916 74
commemoration 1966 59
Edentubber, and Republicans 81
Éire Nua programme 216, 246
elections, Sinn Féin success 318,
326
see also General Election; local
government
Elizabeth II:
visit to Northern Ireland 275
and Sands demonstration in
Oslo 298
Emergency Provisions Act 262
European Human Rights
Commission 305
'executive detention' 214

Falls district 5, 23–4
community spirit 27–8
and Bogside troubles 105–7
curfew 1970 140–2
Falls Road riots 50–1
Falls Taximen's Association 255
Farrell, Michael 215
hunger–strike 216
Farrell, Orla 215
Faul, Fr 306
Faulkner, Brian, Prime Minister

150
and internment 155
and Bloody Sunday 182
resignation 187
Chief Executive,
power–sharing 235
Feeney, Hugh 244
Feeney, John 76
Felons Club *see* Irish Republican
Felons Association
Fenian Movement 73
Fermanagh/South Tyrone
constituency, campaign for
Bobby Sands 292–3
Fianna Fáil, election victory
1977 259, 280
Fitt, Gerry 147
Deputy Chief Executive,
power–sharing 235
resignation from SDLP 279
not elected 299
peerage 299
Fitzpatrick, Fr Noel, death 208
'The Five Silent Men' 55
Flags and Emblems Act 54
Flannery, Fr Austin 76
fleadh cheoil 87
force, nature of 172–3
Foreign Office, contact with
republicans 288, 291
Fort Pegasus, McRory Park 211
forts, British Army 1972 210–11
Four Square Laundry 212–13
France, and Bobby Sands 297
Franklin Laundry, supply of
bricks 40–1
Free Presbyterian Church 49
Freeland, General Sir Ian 137,

140
Furey, Ted 63, 87–8

Gaelic Athletic Association 73
gaelic football 32–3
Gaelic League (Conradh na
    Gaeilge) 73
Gárdái 81
    The Heavy Gang 280
Gargan, Margaret 208
Gaughan, Michael, death 245,
    289
Gemini Health Studios 212, 213
General Election, Ireland 1982
    299–300
Gibney, Jim 279–80, 283, 292,
    295, 296
Gibson, Herbo 144
Gillen, Jimmy 7
    death 211–12
Glenholmes, Dickie 238
Glover, Brigadier James 276
Gogarty, Frank 95, 100, 142
Gough Barracks, interrogation
    centre 260
Goulding, Cathal 82, 94, 95,
    121, 127, 129, 130
    faction 140, 141, 149, 244–5
Graham, Mark 225, 227
Greencastle district 4–5
Grill group 76
Grogan, Dominic 8
Guevara, Che 115

H–block/Armagh Committee
    283, 287, 299, 314–15
H–blocks 249, 270, 271, 279,

282–3
screws 271, 272
hunger–strikes 288
Hamilton, Skeet 244
Hannaway family 26–7
Hannaway, Alfie (uncle) 27, 192
Hannaway, Alice, née
    Mulholland 26
Hannaway, Annie see Adams,
    Annie
Hannaway, Ena (aunt) 27, 28
Hannaway, Georgina, née
    Mulholland, 'Granny
    Hannaway' 19, 26–7
Hannaway, Kathleen, Mrs
    Murphy (aunt) 43, 227
Hannaway, Kevin (cousin) 43,
    110, 123, 124–5, 132, 148,
    151–2
    arrested 155, 161–2
    treatment 162–4
    to Crumlin Road and Long
        Kesh 164
    in Long Kesh 196, 223
Hannaway, Liam (uncle) 27,
    147, 148
    and Sinn Féin 120
    prisoner 192
    in Long Kesh 196, 197, 198,
        233
Hannaway, Mary (great–aunt)
    27
Hannaway, Michael 26
Hannaway, Seamus 27
Hannaway, William
    (grandfather) 26, 27
Hargey, Jim 66
Harland & Wolff 60

337

Hartley, Hilda 193
Hartley, Tom 246, 274, 275
Harvey, hut ghost, Long Kesh
    234
Hastings St barracks, Belfast 182
Haughey, Charlie 305
Heath, Edward 187
Heffernan, Brother 48, 55, 56
'hen patrols' 137
Hillsborough Treaty
    (Anglo–Irish Agreement)
    319
Hindustan Times 298
Housing Action Committee,
    West Belfast 83, 84, 97, 100
Housing Trust 93, 97, 143
Hughes, Barney, bakery 111
Hughes, Brendan 'the Dark'
    184, 217–18, 220
    in Long Kesh 222, 225, 242,
    251
    escapes 227–8
    H–block 274
    hunger–strike 287, 288
Hughes, Charlie, death 149, 194
Hughes, Francis hunger–strike
    and death 292, 298
Hume, John 147, 198
    leader SDLP 279
    relations with GA 321
Hume/Adams proposals 321
hunger–strikes 194–5, 197
    Michael Farrell and Tony
    Canavan 216
    Frank Stagg and Michael
    Gaughan 245
    1980–81, ending in ten deaths
    285

called off 288
renewed 289–314
ended 314
watershed 317
Hunt Report 120–1
Hurson, Martin, hunger–strike
    and death 304

Independent Broadcasting
    Authority 261
India, and Bobby Sands 298
Inkerman Street 26, 27
international support for five
    demands 305
International Red Cross 294
internationalism 281
internment 108, 152, 155–62,
    224
    treatment of internees 162–4
    torture 164–6, 224–5
Ireland family 8
Ireland, Denis, poem quoted vii
Ireland: partition 1
Ireland, Republic of, cooperation
    with Ulster 55
Ireland Act 53–4
Iris 262
Irish Government *see* Dublin
    Government
Irish Independence Party 277,
    278
Irish National Liberation Party
    313
Irish News 82–3, 93, 195, 245
Irish Peace Initiative (Hume/
    Adams proposals) 321
Irish people 74
Irish Press, and Bobby Sands 298

Irish Republic, proclamation 74
Irish Republican Army (IRA):
  D Company, membership of
    Adams and Hannaway
    families 27
  in Dublin 81
  activity 1950s 32
  border campaign 1956 53, 77
  strength 1961 77
  armed, in Dublin 1969 102–3
  direct action or not, on
    Bogside 104
  inadequate reaction 108, 113,
    121
  some back–up after Bogside
    118
  growth 118, 120, 150
  in Ardoyne 139
  'Officials' and 'Provos'
    149–50
  after internment 167
  versus armed forces 168
  GA's story about 168–71
  after Bloody Sunday 181–2,
    186–7
  deaths 188–9
  3–day ceasefire 198
  talks with British Government
    1972 199–200
  ceasefire 26 June 1972 200
  back into battle 208–9
  bombs in Belfast 209
  hits at MRF 213
  truce from December 1974
    249–50
  feuds 255–7
  bomb, La Mon Hotel,
    Comber 265, 266, 268
  regrouping by 1979 276
  killing of 18 soldiers 276
  shooting of prison guards 286,
    287
  killing of five British soldiers
    298
  popularity at time of
    hunger–strikes 315
  and Sinn Féin 320
  temporary cessation of
    operations 1993 320
  complete cessation of military
    operations 2, 322
  breakdown of cessation 324–5
Irish Republican Brotherhood
    (IRB) 22, 73
Irish Republican Felons
    Association 42, 51, 80, 123
Irish Republican Socialist Party
    (IRSP) 245, 278, 313
  and prison campaign 283
  elected 299
The Irish Times 62
Irwin, Dr Robert 261
ITN 261

'John', tortured 194
Johnson, Roy 123
Johnson, Sean, death 188

Kathleen 256
Kearney, Mrs 67–8
Keaveney, Jimmy 63, 64, 103–4
Kee, Robert 240, 241
Keenan, Sean 100
Kelly, Gerry 244, 273
Kelly, John 127
Kelly, Luke 80

Kennedy, Senator Edward 297
Kennedy, Paddy 117
Kennedy's Bakery 14–17
Kennedy's Dairy 133
Keohane, Joe 293
Kitson, Brigadier Frank
    Low–Intensity Operations
    212, 214

Lagan, DI Frank 50
Lalor, Fintan 73, 248
Larkin, Jim 26
Lavery, John, death 160
Lavery, Terence 160
Lavery, Paddy, pawnshop 19
law, use by Government and
    military 214
Lemass, Sean 55, 59–60, 78
Lenadoon estate 206, 207, 208
Lennon, Danny 'the Dosser',
    death 248–9, 254
Lewis, Tony, death 188
Liberty 286
Little, Noel 277
Littlejohn brothers, bank raid
    213
local elections 1981 299
Long, Davey 228
Long Kesh 196, 223–4, 237
    boisterousness there 196–7
    GA in 222–51
    escapes and attempts 225,
        227–32, 249
    screws 234
    burned 237–40
loyalists:
    and Bogside 106
    riots, after Hunt Report 121

mobs 1971 161
terrorising Catholics 152–3,
    209, 211
after 1972 talks 201
and MRF 213
against power–sharing 236
Lurgan, fighting 1971 154
Lynch, Jack 104, 107, 280
Lynch, Kevin, hunger–strike
    307, 311–12
    death 313
Lyons, Maura 49

MacAirt, Proinsias 62, 63, 66,
    124, 130, 132–3, 149, 243,
    258
McAleavey, John 46–7
McAliskey, Bernadette *see*
    Devlin, Bernadette
McAllister, Martin 244
McArdle, Colette (wife) 134,
    152, 153, 158, 316
    marriage to GA 173–6
    life after marriage 176, 177–8,
        179, 183, 189, 216–17
    pregnancies 183–4, 217
    visit to GA in prison 192
    meets GA 198–9
    visits Long Kesh 231
    has baby Gearóid 234–5
    meets GA after Long Kesh
        251, 252
    life after Long Kesh 256
    and GA in prison 266, 267
    visits Brendan Hughes 288
    and Bobby Sands' death 295
    and Francie Hughes 298
    and hunger–strike 301

McArdle, Jimmy (father–in–law) 173, 175, 182

McArdle, Leah 175

McArdle, Maggie (mother–in–law) 175

MacArdle, Maire 175

McArdle, Paddy 174, 175

MacAtamney, Joe 21–2

McAteer, Fergus 278

McAteer, Hugh 139

McAuley, Geraldo, death 86, 110

MacBride, Sean 201, 258, 259

McBurney, Billy 80

McCafferty, David, death 208

McCann, Anne, née McKnight 76

McCann, Joe 55, 58, 76, 82, 83, 124
  death 194

McCann, Tom, death 188

McCaughey, Revd Terence 76

McCaughley, Eamonn (brother–in–law) 192

McCloskey family 85

McCorry, Michael 132, 255

McCreesh, Ray, hunger–strike and death 292, 299

McCrory, Eamon 304

McCurtain, Cyril 243

McDonnell, Joe
  election to Dáil 299
  hunger–strike and death 300, 301
  funeral 303–4

McElwee, Tom, hunger–strike 306, 307, 309
  death 313

McFarlane, Brendan 'Bik' 244, 291, 295–6, 306, 307, 308, 310, 312, 313

McFaul, Jimmy 82, 83, 85

McGeown, Pat 273
  hunger–strike 306, 307

Mac Giolla/Goulding group 121

McGirl, John Joe 86–7
  in Long Kesh 233, 238–9, 262, 304

McGregor, Captain James 212

McGrory, Paddy 199, 202

McGrory, Paddy John 270, 274, 275

McGuigan, Francie 83, 124, 163, 198

'McGuigan, Joe' (i.e. GA), arrest 189

McGuigan, Sean 83

McGuinness, Martin 198, 201, 291
  meeting 204, 205
  at Joe McDonnell's funeral 303–4

McGuinness, death 149

McGuinness, Maureen 153

McGurk's Bar, bombed 178

McGurran, Malachy 79–80, 130

McIldowney, Eugene 80

McIlhone, Henry, death 140

McKeague, John 258, 259–60

McKearney, Seamus 5, 6

McKee family 8

McKee, Billy 125, 126, 129, 149, 258
  wounded 140
  hunger–strike 197, 260

McKee, Packy 9, 10, 14, 15

death 211–12
McKenna, Sean, hunger–strike 288
McKeown, Laurence 'Lorney', hunger–strike 306, 309
Mackies foundry 60, 147
McLaughlin, Fr 33
McLoughlin, Barney 145
McManus family 8
McManus, Frank 278
McManus, Terence 36
McMillen, Liam 'Billy' 51, 61, 62, 66, 94, 103, 104, 117, 124, 126–7, 129, 133, 149
internment 108
death 245
McParland, Liam 128, 132
McPeakes, The 80
Mac Stiofain, Sean 124, 129, 198, 200
Provisional Army Council 130–1
meeting 203, 204
Magee, Joe: childhood 7, 13–14, 15, 16, 25, 28, 29, 38, 41, 48
adulthood 65–6, 67–70
leaves Ireland 75
Maguire family, death 248–9, 254–5
Maguire, Dorothy 134
death 184
Maguire, Frank, MP 292
Maguire, Noel 292
Maguire, Sean 80, 87
Maidstone prison ship 192–6, 226
Major, John 321

Marley, Larry 273
Marlowe, Paul 225
The Marquee 72–3
Mason, Roy 275, 276
Maudling, Reginald 181
Meehan, Maura, death 184
Mellowes, author 248
military intelligence 277
Military Reconnaissance Force (MRF) 212–13
Mitchell, Senator George
Mitchell report 324
Molotov cocktails 114–15
Monaghan, loyalist bomb in 236
Le Monde 297
Mooney, Marshall 229–31, 242
Morrison, Danny 247, 262, 264, 287, 295, 296, 309
Mulholland, Liam 78, 156, 224
Mullan, Fr Hugh 153, 158–9
Mullan, William 64
Mulvenna, Patrick, death 226
Murphy, Ciaran, death 227
Murphy, Joseph, death 159–60
Murphy, Canon Padraig 58
Murphy, Sean 35, 55
music:
at Duke of York 63
and Sinn Féin 80, 87–8
rebel songs 271–3

National Democratic Party 77, 147
National Liberation Front 122
nationalism 280–1
and IRA 276–7
Nationalist Party 61, 77
New Barnsley 9, 142–3
New York Daily News 297
New York Times 297

Newman, Kenneth 261
Newry, fighting 1971 154
no–go areas 201
Northern Ireland:
    creation 1–2, 4
    a police state 51, 53–4
Northern Ireland Rights
    Association (NICRA) 83,
    85, 90, 91, 156, 181
    demands 91–2
    meets John Taylor 99–100
Northern Ireland Labour Party
    61, 62
Northern Resistance Movement
    (NRM) 215
Nugent, Kieran 267

Ó Bradaigh, Ruairí 94, 124, 132,
    150, 258, 259, 262–3, 264,
    282–3, 292, 293
O'Brien, Conor Cruise 280
Ó Buidh, Dáithí 302
Ó Conaill, Dáithí 124, 198, 207,
    258, 262–3, 292
    meets British officials
    199–200, 204, 205–6
'Official' Sinn Féin 280
Ó Fiaich, Cardinal Tomás 282,
    305, 306
O'Hagan, Danny, death 145, 277
O'Hanlon, Feargal 199
O'Hara, Patsy, hunger–strike
    and death 292, 299
Oldfield, Maurice 277
O'Neill family 22
O'Neill, Dominic 233
O'Neill, Mickey 128
O'Neill, Terence 55, 77–8
    against Easter Rising

Commemoration 59
    reform programme 92
    fall 94
Operation Demetrius 156
    see also internment
Operation Motorman 1972
    210–11
Orange parades 46–7, 65, 134–5,
    138–9
O'Rawe, Marty 229, 230, 231

Paisley, Revd Ian 49–51, 55, 61,
    147, 201, 258, 259
Paisleyites 142–3
Parachute Regiment 153, 276
    attack on Ballymurphy 157–8
    Bloody Sunday at Derry
    179–81
    violent campaign 1972 211–12
Paxman, Jeremy 275
Paxo explosive 104
'Peace People' 249, 254
    and prison campaign 283
people's councils 246
People's Democracy (PD) 83,
    92, 94, 95, 100, 156, 215,
    278
    and prison campaign 283
    election success 299
petrol bombs 114, 115–16
Pettigrew, Brian 207–8
Philbin, Bishop 59, 88, 119, 138
Phillips, Noel, death 159
pogroms 1, 4, 60, 94, 142
    August 1969 122, 123
political awareness, lack of 121–2
Political Hostages Release
    Committee 216

politics:
    1972–73 214–16
    republican 3, 22–3
    and Sinn Féin 263–4, 285
Porter, Robert 65
Portugal, and Bobby Sands 297
poteen–making in Long Kesh
    243–4
Pound Loney district 58–9
poverty 24
power–sharing executive 235–6
    collapse 236
Prevention of Terrorism Act 262
Price, Dolours and Marion 198,
    244, 289
Prior, James, sponsors elections
    318
prison, misery 242
    see also Long Kesh
prison campaign, by Sinn Féin
    and others 281–4
Protestant Telegraph 61
Protestants 34, 35, 43, 142
Provisionals:
    set up 128, 130–1
    in 1970 139–40
    against riots 146
    in trouble 147–8
    reorganized 148–9
'psy–ops' 260
Public Order Act 54

Queen's University Belfast 28,
    82
Quigley, Jimmy, death 86
Quinn, Frank, death 159
Quinn, Paddy, hunger–strike
    306–7, 308, 310, 312

Radio Free Belfast 117
Red Hand Commando 258
refugees 161
Reid, Fr Alex 256–7
Relatives' Action Committees
    (RAC) 281, 283
Republic, proclamation of 74
republican clubs 216
Republican Club, Belfast 78–9,
    82
Republican Club,
    Andersonstown 82
republican movement:
    leadership crisis 121–3, 126–7
Republican News 133, 247–8,
    250–1, 262, 274
republicanism 73, 280–1
    phases 214–15
    growth with hunger–strike
    315
republicans:
    factions 126–7, 244–5
    social life 80–1
    see also Irish Republican
        Army; Sinn Féin
Reynolds, Albert 321, 322
Rock, Dicky 65
Roman Catholicism *see*
    Catholicism
Royal Scots Regiment 134
Royal Ulster Constabulary
    (RUC):
    and Falls Road riots 50
    violence 61
    arrest of GA 79
    versus activists 90, 91–2, 93
    and Derry March 92
    and Bogside 94, 99–116

more violence 95, 97
and Derry Orange parade 99
first RUC man killed 157
and internment 157
disarmament proposed 121
kept out of nationalist areas
133–4
abandons Springfield Road
barracks 138
in 1972 206
emphasis in 1975 255
arrest of GA 260
ill–treatment of suspects 261
re–armed 275
death squads 277
see also B Specials
Ruddy, Seamus 306, 308, 310,
312

St Patrick's Day parades 54
Sands family 297
Sands, Bobby 243–4, 246–7,
273, 286–7, 288–9, 290–1
hunger–strike 285
puts up for MP 292
wins seat 293, 314
death 285, 295
after death 295–7
international reaction 297–8
rebukes Haughey 305–6
on prisoners face 307
Sands, Marcella and Sean 295
'Sands Bill' 300
Saor Éire 66
Saoirse 262
SAS 262, 275
Scott, Barbara 22
Scullion, John, death 61

sectarianism 75, 90
Shane, dog 183, 225
Shankill Defence Association 94,
97
Shannon, Annie and Mary 175
Sherlock family 83–4
Shevlin, Myles 204, 205
Shorland armoured cars 106
Sinclair, Betty 62
Sinn Féin 74–5, 76–7
slow progress 79–80
office Divis Street 50
GA joins 52
after Bogside 120
not split 130
caretaker executive 132
meetings after the 1972 talks
200–1
illegality, and difficulty of
political activity 215–16
GA works with, on Ard
Chomhairle (National
Council) 254
publications 262
and politics 263–5, 278
GA elected a vice–president
275
failure to make alliances 278–9
nature 279
and politics 279–80
and 'Official' Sinn Féin 280
prison campaign 281–4
against hunger–strikes 289–90
Hunger Strike Committee
291, 300–1
five demands 291–2
election successes 318, 326
deeply into political activity

from 1982 318
peace strategy 320–2
see also Éire Nua; Republican News
Sinn Féin the Workers' Party 280
Sirrocco Works 60
Slant 76
Slattery's, Dublin 87
Smith, Theresa 80
Social Democratic & Labour Party (SDLP) 146–7, 150, 216, 278
changes in 1970s 279
less popular 319
civil disobedience campaign 173
Soper, Revd Donald 49
South Africa, Irish sympathy with 281
Special Branch, RUC 85
special constables 60
Special Powers Act 54, 55
and internment 155, 157, 162
Spence, Gusty 61
Springfield area 119
Springfield Park 132
Springmartin, battles in 152
squatting 89, 93, 97
Stagg, Frank, hunger–strike and death 245, 289
Steele, Frank 199, 204
Steele, Jimmy 124, 125
Stewart, Jimmy and Edwina 63
Stormont, proposed power–sharing assembly 215
Stormont Government 116

suspension 187
Strabane, fighting in 154
Sullivan, Jimmy 103, 104, 108, 109, 111, 119–20, 128–9
Sunningdale agreement 1973 235, 236, 257

Taggart, killing field 160–1
Taggart, Daniel, death 159, 160
The Tatler 120
Taylor, Harry 85, 189, 190
Taylor, John 100
Thant, U 104
Thatcher, Margaret 276, 294, 299, 305, 313
Brighton bomb 318
Toland, Tommy 'Toddler' 226, 229, 231, 240, 242
death 257
Tone, Wolfe 73
quoted 1
Tony 174, 175, 176, 177, 242
torture 164–6, 260–1
Trade Union Campaign Against Repression (TUCAR) 283
truce 1972, breakdown 207
Turf Lodge area 301–2
Turnly, John 277
Tuzo, General Sir Harry 155–6, 212
Twomey, Seamus 126, 178–9, 198, 207, 215
meeting with 203, 204–5
GA meets, after Long Kesh 252–3

UDR, increased 275

Ulster Constitution Defence
    Committee 61
Ulster Defence Association
    (UDA) 195, 201–2, 206–7,
    241
  roadblocks 236
Ulster Protestant Action 61
Ulster Protestant Association
    (UPA) 50
Ulster Protestant Volunteers
    (UPV) 61
Ulster Volunteer Force (UVF)
    61, 156–7
Ulster Workers' Council, strike
    1974 235, 236
unemployment 75
Unemployment Action Group
    83
unionists, not interned 157
United Irishman 79
United Nations, and Bogside
    101, 104
United States of America:
  support for Irish Peace
    Initiative 322
  effect of Bobby Sands' death
    297
Unity Flats, violence 94, 96, 97,
    118

Vallely, Marie 134
Vanguard movement 195, 216

Voluntary Service Overseas 75
Vorster, B.J. 54
voting rights, restrictions 78

Walesa, Lech, and Bobby Sands
    297
Ward, Peter, death 61–2, 156
warnings, for bombs 209
West, Harry 116
West Belfast Civil Rights
    Association 90
Whitelaw, William, Secretary of
    State for Northern Ireland
    187, 198, 207, 209
  talks 203–4, 205
Whiterock Road (no. 183) 197,
    199
Williams, Sgt Clive 212
Williams, Tom, hanging of 23,
    125
Wilson, Fr Des 105, 175, 256–7,
    259
Wilson, Harold 116–17, 178
Wolfe Tone Societies 77, 78
women, and the troubles 235
  see also Armagh women's
    prison
Women Against Imperialism
    (WAI) 283
Woodfield, Philip 199, 204
The Workers' Party 280
World War II, and Belfast 4